JAPAN
REAL ESTATE
INVESTMENT

JAPAN

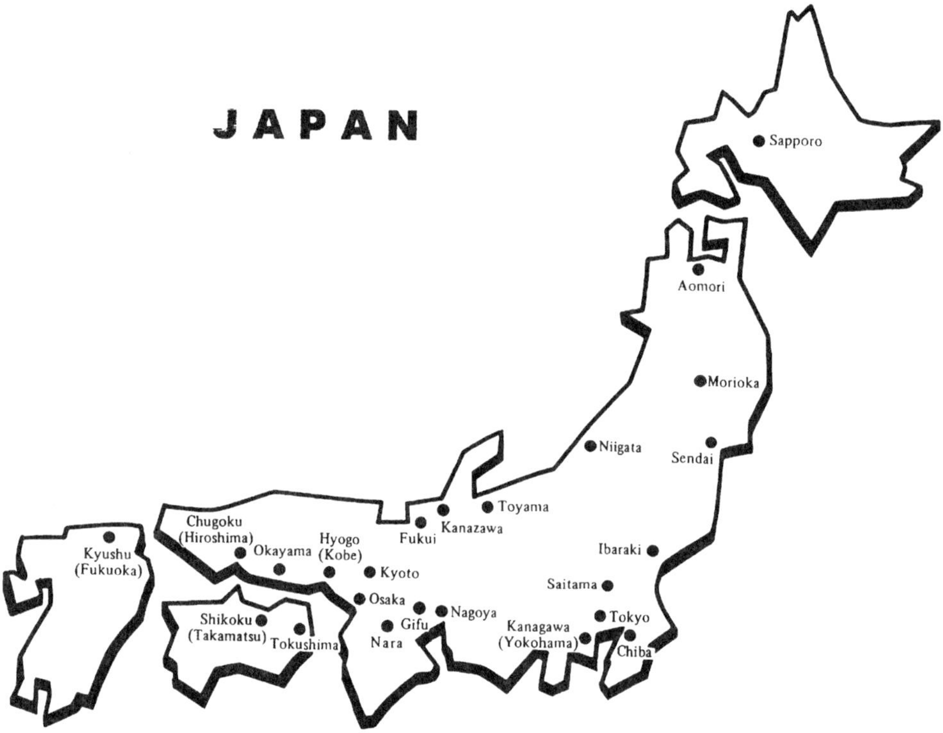

Source: Japan Building Owners & Managers Association (B.O.M.A.), ''Extracts from Annual Survey on Japan B.O.M.A. Member Buildings, 1997'' (Tokyo: B.O.M.A.). Reprinted with permission.

JAPAN REAL ESTATE INVESTMENT

M. A. Hines

Q

QUORUM BOOKS
Westport, Connecticut • London

Library of Congress Cataloging-in-Publication Data

Hines, Mary Alice.
Japan real estate investment / M.A. Hines.
p. cm.
Includes bibliographical references and index.
ISBN 1–56720–374–4 (alk. paper)
1. Real estate investment—Japan. I. Hines, Mary Alice. II. Title.
HD918.H55 2001
332.63'24'0952—dc21 00–032811

British Library Cataloguing in Publication Data is available.

Library of Congress Catalog Card Number: 00–032811
ISBN: 1–56720–374–4

First published in 2001

Quorum Books, 88 Post Road West, Westport, CT 06881
An imprint of Greenwood Publishing Group, Inc.
www.quorumbooks.com

Printed in the United States of America

The paper used in this book complies with the Permanent Paper Standard issued by the National Information Standards Organization (Z39.48–1984).

10 9 8 7 6 5 4 3 2 1

Contents

Preface and Acknowledgments

Japan Real Estate Investment is designed to assist readers to understand the characteristics of Japanese real estate that affect investment potential. Prospective and current Japanese investors do not seem to have a book about Japanese real estate investment that adequately serves their interests in either the Japanese or English language. Foreign investors who have been analyzing Japanese real estate opportunities have not had available to them a summary of the investment characteristics that this book offers. For example, many foreign investors have ventured into the Japanese real estate market with little knowledge of the unique features of the Japanese real estate market and working relationships. Some of the problems of these foreign investors have been voiced. Some of these problems originate from a lack of basic knowledge about this important national real estate market. The Japanese real estate market has attributes that are similar to those of the United States, Western Europe, and Asia; likewise, there are attributes that are very different from those in other regions of the world. The unique attributes that may spell success or failure in investment in Japanese real estate are the focal points of this book.

Besides prospective domestic and foreign investors in Japanese real estate and Japanese real estate–related securities, people who are interested in business systems other than that of their home countries will be interested in the Japanese methods, relationships, and trends promising change that are surveyed in this book. Students of international business including international real estate will be attracted to this up-to-date book. The book surveys the Japanese economic changes and the new investment climate in terms of culture and environment. The short history of Japanese land tenure is of interest to those who compare the development of international cultural systems.

Most multinational corporate executives seek locations in Japan, the second-ranked industrial power of the world, for the marketing and perhaps production of their products. One part of their Japanese market surveys is selection of office, warehouse, plant, and expatriate employee residential locations. Commercial locations are important when the marketing of goods and services is involved in the Japanese business decision. As an example, shopping center locations and attributes are important to those who normally distribute goods and services through shopping center storerooms.

Urban planners, land developers, construction company executives, and real estate leasing personnel who wish to profit from entry into this dynamic Asian real estate market need a basic understanding of the real estate market mechanism, regulations, conventional methods of doing business, and areas undergoing slow change. People involved in the finance of Japanese real estate ownership need to survey the whole system to see how their particular services fit so importantly into the overall real estate system. Bankers involved with real estate finance at the city banks, trust banks, long-term credit banks, postal savings banks, and other public and private financial institutions may need an overview of the current Japanese real estate system in order to plan for the future.

Appraisers who anticipate work associated with Japanese properties require a wide knowledge of the Japanese real estate system and its environment. This book reviews typical Japanese appraisal methods of past decades and then reviews the change in appraisal methods required by the new market environment and newly designed lease and property management contracts. As appraisers analyze the various property parameters to arrive at appropriate capitalization rates for the use of income capitalization methods, they must be aware of the changes occurring in the Japanese market and changing property investment yield expectations. This book aids with this important appraisal process.

Since the Japanese tax environment is an important component of real estate investment analysis, the highlights of tax features that vitally affect Japanese real estate investment are presented for the reader's benefit. The tax regime affects real estate investment planning and analysis. The tax benefits that may be available for foreign investors are included in the discussion of the tax environment.

Many real estate authorities have provided information for the development of this book. Multinational real estate companies headquartered in Japan, the United States, the United Kingdom, and Asia have contributed up-to-date information for the writing of this book. In Japan, executives from various divisions of the Mitsubishi Estate Co., Mitsui Fudosan, and CB Richard Ellis, which are large, multinational real estate companies, have contributed important current data. In addition, executives from the financial institutions, Citibank and Warburg Dillon Read, multinational investment banking houses, have provided a wide variety of Japanese financial information. In the United States and the United Kingdom, executives from Jones Lang LaSalle and Cushman & Wakefield/Healey and Baker have provided rent, investment yield, and occupancy data about Japan and other competitive real estate markets of the world. Colliers

Jardine, headquartered in Asia, has provided substantial background information for the book, particularly with respect to rents, investment yields, and occupancy levels.

The ongoing assistance of the Japan Real Estate Institute, the Building Owners and Managers Association of Japan, the Japan Council of Shopping Centers, and the Japan External Trade Organization has supported the multiple research efforts concerning Japanese real estate since 1985. Executives from these and many other Japanese companies have provided continuing hospitality during the many trips to Japan for the collection of research data, lecturing to business groups, and consulting to major companies.

The following people have particularly contributed to the research and writing of *Japan Real Estate Investment*: Takumi Watanabe, Syunichi Maekawa, and Yuji Hirato of the Japan Real Estate Institute; Professor Yukihide Okano of the University of Tokyo; Professors Musa Essayyad and G. Hayden Green of the University of Alaska; Ikunoshin Yoshida of Visual Japan; Masaji Miura, Ayako Komoda, and Susumu Inamura of the Japan Council of Shopping Centers; Ronald E. LaVoie of RTKL International; Takeshi Sakurai and Akira Nanakarage of the Real Estate Companies Association of Japan; Tumiko Kikuchi, Margaret Ng, and John Tofflemire of Ikoma/CB Richard Ellis; Akira Kojima and Hideo Koyama of the Semba Corporation; Ralph Inforzato of the Japan External Trade Relations Office–Chicago; Toshiyuki Kakinuma, Eiji Oda, Junichi Kogo, Atsushi Akimoto, Hiroshi Konno, and Mitsuo Honma of Mitsui Fudosan; Toshihiko Okino of Warburg Dillon Read–Japan; Makiko Hanabusa of Sanko Estate Co.; Donna O'Loughlin of the Appraisal Institute; Beth Meyer of Colliers USA; Takuo Kato, Tetsuya Watanabe, Junichi Tanisawa, Atsushi Nakajima, and Tetsuji Arimori of Mitsubishi Estate Co.; Tsamu Shishikura of the Japan Building Management Institute; Toshio Kawasaki and Kazuhisa Hirao of Laforet Harajuku Co.; Toru Inoue and Chiemi Kaneko of Cititrust; Ichisuke Okumura, Koji Ohara Sr., and Yuichi Igarashi of Aeon Kosan; Jiro Hattori and Eisaku Kaneko Sr. of the Nippon Credit Bank; Shunji Seko of the Takanaka Corporation; and Taeko Nagatsuka of Japan UNI Agency. Other valuable research contributors were Hiroyuki Isobe of Hiro & Associates; Masakiyo Miura and Takumi Ishii of Vivre International; Guy J. Cubitt of K. K. Halifax Associates; Koeichi Toyomaru of the Nippon Life Insurance Company; Yasuhiko Hatano, Kunio Osawa, and Shizuo Makamura of the Sumitomo Corporation; Akihiko Suzuki of the Long-Term Credit Bank; Susumu Nishimura of the Misubishi Corporation; and Kuzuo Horino of Mitsui & Co. The following people from PW Financial Advisory Services contributed to the research for this book: Takehito Sasaki, Kenneth V. Burd, Sachiko Hata, Takuya Watanabe, Michiyo Matsumoto, Midori Suzuki, Tetsuya Kato, Hisao Tateishi, Yoshikazu Kanakubo, Yasushi Katsuno, and Joshua D. Thornton Sr.

My mother, Alberta Elsie Hines, continues to support the comprehensive research of Japanese real estate with her daily presence and support of my writing and publishing activities, which require voluminous amounts of time. My father also encouraged the international research and writing until his death in 1992. Washburn University continues to encourage research and publication as the School of Business supports the research, writing, and publication by the maintenance and financial support of its Clarence W. King Endowed Professorship, which the book's author has held since 1982—a 19-year span of time so far. Washburn University should be honored for granting a female Professor of Finance and Real Estate the first endowed professor of finance and/or real estate in the United States in 1982.

JAPAN REAL ESTATE INVESTMENT

1

Introduction

Many investors look to Japan for opportunities. They want to participate in the future success of one of the most dynamic and most highly developed countries in the world. They want to diversify their investment portfolios with securities, company ownership, and/or real property interests from an East Asian country that is part of one of the most promising regions of the world. After surviving World War II, Japan immediately regained its world industrial position by concentrating on what it had to do. Industrial growth and development were Japan's keys to the world economic dominance that came about in the 1970s and 1980s. The highly educated people of this small island grouping have the wherewithal to make things happen when the country is united in pursuing a national objective. Today the people, business, and industry of Japan are determined to regain economic prosperity from the period of economic decline that started in the early 1990s and lasted until the new millennium.

THE NEED OF THE FOREIGN INVESTOR FOR KNOWLEDGE ABOUT JAPANESE REAL ESTATE

As the English-reading and -speaking investor scrutinizes Japan for possibilities for profitable investment returns, that person—who may represent himself or herself, an investment group, or a financial institution—usually finds that little is known about investment property in Japan. That person may assume that Japan's income property characteristics are much like those at home or may rightly try to learn more about Japan's income properties before forming a comparison with income properties of other highly developed or perhaps less-developed countries. Recently, investors have sought information about this highly complicated subject in well-organized sources of information. Since the first edition of this book, which was entitled *Investing in Japanese Real Estate*, was said to be the first and only book on the subject in the English language as of late 1999, the prospective investor needed to discover the original edition of this book, which was published in 1987, after appropriate research in 1985 and the immediately preceding years and after having been written in 1986. Fourteen years after the first edition, in 2001, the revised book, entitled *Japan Real Estate Investment*, is designed for the investor who wishes to learn more about Japanese real estate through one organized source of information. The book discloses that real estate investment in Japan has things in common with real estate investment in other parts of the world but has many unique attributes that the unsuspecting, non-Japanese investor would never suspect. The Japanese real estate market is generally different from the real estate markets of Western Europe or of the United States, where many major investors are domiciled. When non-Japanese persons—particularly persons who speak only the English language—try to directly access Japanese real estate information, they find a language barrier as well as company privacy barriers that compound the problems of information retrieval. For example, full disclosure by individual companies—even for stock and bond exchange listings and marketing—is still not commonplace in Japan, where closely held and managed *keiretsu* industrial and commercial groups still exist. This book is based on timely information from government, trade associations, and private companies that was drawn from seven research trips to Japan starting in the 1980s and continuing through late 1999.

THE FOCUS OF THE BOOK IS ON INVESTMENT IN JAPANESE REAL ESTATE, NOT JAPANESE INVESTMENT IN FOREIGN REAL ESTATE

There are two distinct views of the term "Japanese real estate investment": (1) investment in domestic and foreign real estate by Japanese individuals, investment funds, institutions, and companies and (2) investment in Japanese real estate by foreign individuals, investment funds, institutions, and companies. Some of these foreign investors may be Japanese by earlier national origin, such as the Brazilian and Peruvian investors of Japanese origin who may invest in real estate in Japan.

Both of these Japanese real estate investment phenomena are significant. Their individual financial significance in terms of huge capital flows depends on the period of time being analyzed. For example, in the 1970s and 1980s, large amounts of capital left Japan bound for investment in U.S. commercial, industrial, and residential real estate. At the same time, outbound Japanese funds were placed in real property investments of various types around the world. Starting in the latter part of the 1980s and the early part of the 1990s, investors in Japan started to sell their foreign real property holdings as foreign real estate recessions set in and more funds were needed in Japan. Today Japanese real estate investors still hold significant amounts of commercial, industrial, and residential real property in most parts of the world, but their holdings have diminished from the peak holdings of such periods as the 1980s. Japanese investment in real property abroad is a very significant topic, but many books, monographs, and articles cover this topic very well on a continuing spectrum. Foreign companies, investment funds, and individuals continue to seek commercial, industrial, and residential real estate in Japan for their individual purposes.

Very little information is available for English-speaking foreign investors who are attempting to invest in commercial, industrial, and residential real estate in Japan. Even institutional real estate investment in Japan has been a problem for non-Japanese governments. For example, the investment needed for an embassy in Tokyo amounts to an unusually large amount in global comparative terms. Therefore, the focus of the book is on foreign investment in Japanese real estate due to the problems that foreign real estate investors encounter and their need for information about the Japanese real estate market. The information also fits the needs of Japanese real estate investors when they invest in Japan. But most Japanese investors are more comfortable reading in the Japanese language.

BOOK COVERAGE OF JAPANESE REAL ESTATE SERVICES: METHODS AND PRACTICES

As the book provides the desired information, characteristics of Japanese real estate services and associated companies are discussed in brief. Most foreigners want to know more about Japanese real estate brokerage, consulting sources, and land development. They also usually want to know about the sources of real estate research studies and the nature of the ongoing studies. Construction practices, company situations, costs, and challenges also interest those who seek to build or redevelop their Japanese premises. Property management and architectural practices and sources of services are important to those foreign investors who anticipate need for those services.

As the foreign investor seeks to analyze individual Japanese real estate and related investment opportunities, that person needs to know the characteristics of the Japanese legal environment that may be unique to the country or at least different in part from the investor's accustomed legal circumstances. Japan's methods of real property appraisal, brokerage, land development, and investment analysis may be different from those of the foreigner's accustomed investment environment. Today, Japanese real estate practices and methods are said to be moving more toward those of the United States. The rationale expressed for this change is that U.S. investors have been actively analyzing major properties for possible investment. U.S. investors use their home country systems to evaluate Japanese real estate opportunities, even though traditional Japanese practices and methods differ from U.S. conventional practices and methods. Japanese real estate professionals may wish to better understand the investment analytical methods and criteria for real estate investment of this major, prospective client group.

THE IMPORTANCE OF REAL ESTATE IN JAPAN

As Chapter 4 (on the history of land tenure in Japan) explains, ownership of real estate has assumed great significance in the advancement of the society, the form of government, and the economy from early centuries. For example, the early period of feudalism in Japan had its social and economic foundations in the ownership and control of land. As the capitalistic form of government developed over the centuries, private ownership of property gradually grew out of the early industrial society where inheritance and sale of property were finally permitted by the emerging forms of government.

In the periods of rapidly rising land and building values that are highly exemplified by the "bubble era" of the 1980s in Japan, a person who sought great wealth considered that the shortest route to this financial success was to buy real property. Savings were deployed in real estate investment more often than bank and postal savings deposits or bank certificates of deposit. During these prosperous periods, land and building values generally climbed rapidly with no prospects of future value decline. The period of rapid property value increase was a lengthy one in the 1980s. The peak was finally reached in the early 1990s, when the decline in property values began (see Exhibit 1-1). Today that downward trend in property values continues after approximately seven years of value decline. Japanese property owners as well as foreign, prospective Japanese property owners wonder where the "bottom of the curve" is or when properties will bottom out and turn upward once again.

Real estate values have been called "hidden assets" of banks, other financial institutions, and industrial and commercial corporations. These values have been very important to these organizations, even though their true values—current market values—have not been shown on their corporate balance sheets. The reason that these values have been called "hidden values" is that the Japanese accounting system has been based on the acquisition prices of assets, including real estate. The international accounting system that requires "marking assets to market" or showing the market values of assets on financial statements has only recently been introduced and utilized in Japan. The market values of the "hidden assets" such as the real estate asset values are now being disclosed to company shareholders, *keiretsu* group members, and outsiders such as the investing public. The companies have long financed on the basis of hidden assets. Real estate has long been a revered asset of companies. Company holdings have been expected to constantly increase in value by lenders, shareholders, and others.

In Japan real estate holdings have been a symbol of corporate leadership. Many of the major Japanese businesses have large real estate holdings—far beyond their corporate headquarters and branch offices and industrial plants around the world. For example, the privatized Japan National Railways has only

Exhibit 1-1
National Land Agency's Nationwide Land Price Forecasts

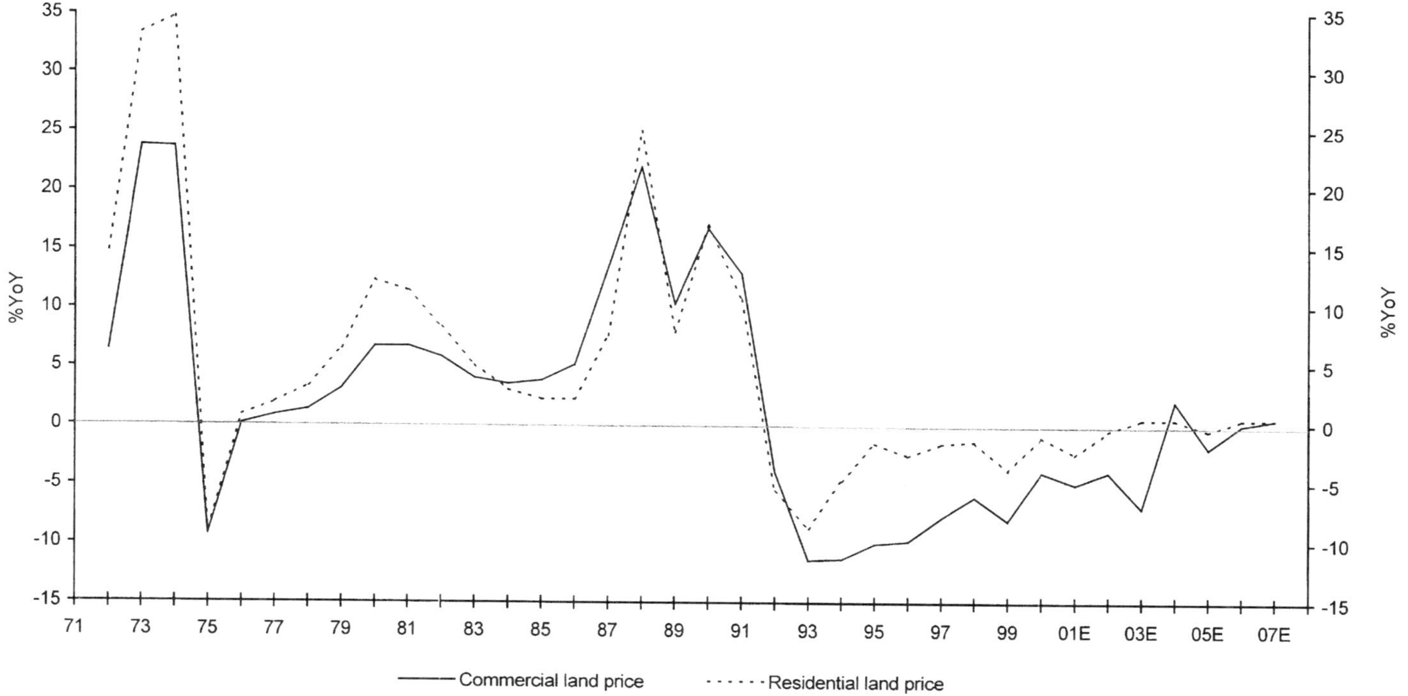

Note: E = National Land Agency and Warburg Dillon Read Estimates.
Source: Warburg Dillon Read, Research Department, *Japan's Real Estate Sector* (Tokyo: Warburg Dillon Read, October 1999). Reprinted with permission.

recently sold a very small part of its large portfolio of Japanese real estate. The railways with their large property holdings have been dominant companies of the Japanese business world. The major trading companies have also represented large and perhaps increasing real estate holdings. For example, Mitsubishi Corporation, one of Japan's largest trading companies, has a large, independently financed real estate subsidiary within its *keiretsu*, Mitsubishi Estate Co. Ltd. The same thing is true of Mitsui Corporation and Jusco Corporation. Mitsui Fudosan, the independently financed real estate subsidiary of the Mitsui trading company, is said to be currently the largest real estate owner in Japan. Jusco, another large Japanese trading company, has within its *keiretsu* a large real estate subsidiary called Aeon Kosan. The trading companies usually maintain large and expanding holdings of commercial, industrial, and residential real estate beyond their direct corporate real estate needs.

Historically, when a borrower from a bank closes a loan, the borrower offers real estate in addition to the borrower's corporate credit and position in its *keiretsu*. The Japanese bank lender has not actually underwritten the loan with the real estate as formal collateral but has merely taken the real estate as a supplementary pledged asset. The loan has not been considered a "mortgage" loan, but only a commercial loan with real estate given to close the deal.

Most Japanese real property owners hold their properties for the long term. As property values rose so quickly during the "bubble era" of the 1980s, property owners who considered selling certain properties and realizing their gains discovered that their tax burdens would have been overwhelming in a country where tax rates are comparatively high according to world standards. Therefore, property owners tended to retain their ownership and redeveloped their properties, perhaps in joint ventures with real estate companies, so that they would gain greater net cash flows from the original land, which became very highly valued. Short-term capital gains were taxed at particularly high rates at the end of the decade of the 1980s as the government discouraged any thoughts of short-term profit taking. At present, while land and building values are either continuing to decline or have stabilized, long-term holding is encouraged as owners await a market upturn and value return to or approaching earlier levels. Therefore, real estate is generally considered a long-term asset in Japan.

Land is scarce for urban development purposes in Japan. Land use controls preserve much of the land of the multi-island nation that is not mountainous and wooded for agricultural land use. The government has tried in past decades to assure enough rice and other food production on land of the Japanese island grouping to assure an adequate domestic food supply in case of war or other emergency. Therefore, land retains its high value due to its scarcity for agricultural, industrial, commercial, institutional, and residential purposes. A large portion of the island grouping is mountainous and devoted to rivers and streams, highways, toll roads, narrow local roads, bridges, domestic and international airports, military reservations, and other government land developments. The major Japanese cities—Tokyo, Osaka, and Nagoya, for example—cover a minimal number of hectares for such large populations. The number of residents per hectare, on average, is relatively high in terms of population density comparisons among global cities.

LARGE LANDOWNERS, THEIR MOTIVATIONS, AND CIRCUMSTANCES OVER TIME

The history of Japan shows large landholdings during each definitive era. During the feudal system royalty owned the land and let citizens cultivate it in return for military protection and administrative functions from royalty. Before World War II a more participative society lived within a very socialistic government system where the imperial family sat at the head of the government and controlled the government administration and the citizenry. Private property ownership was permitted during an extensive period before World War II. Landownership was still dominated by a select group. Many of the large landowners were industrial corporations within their particular *keiretsu*. Before World War II, the imperial government pursued a government policy that put industrial supremacy first and foremost; therefore, the industrial establishment was given the land that it needed to thrive and develop to new heights of production. All other land use and development took secondary importance. During this time, residential space was quickly provided near the industrial plants to provide proximity to work for the homes of the workers. The homes were small since the needed industrial workforce was large and since the space within reasonable travel time was very limited. The bullet trains and their special rail systems were not developed until many years after the massive destruction of Japan during World War II.

After World War II, under the military guidance of General MacArthur and his staff during the occupation of Japan, many reforms were promulgated and carried out. Land reform permitted more private land-ownership with inheritance and sale rights. Eventually, land reform of a different type was initiated. Small, individual landowners were permitted tax relief to reconstitute rural neighborhoods, in particular, so that better-organized transportation arteries and green space could become a part of better-functioning rural neighborhoods. On a joint basis, the owners of small farms could replan their neighborhoods and redesign roads, housing areas, and farm plots. They were permitted to sell certain portions of land and buy certain portions of land with tax relief so that land development would be more orderly for modern infrastructure and foreseen changes of the future. The same land reform for more orderly land development was applied to the major cities with less successful results. Purchase and sale of parts of owners' real estate with tax relief for the improvement of the infrastructure and protection of citizens in case of disaster were less effective due to the major structures in place and the government's lack of adequate financing to acquire selected properties under its power of eminent domain. At this point in Japanese history, urban property values were already very high; an immense government budget with higher taxes would be required in order to promote the necessary eminent domain projects for the public good.

Since World War II, the government has devoted sizable land parcels to military reservations that are primarily occupied by military forces from the United States. The U.S.–Japanese military agreements still promote U.S. military protection of Japan in case of invasion on land, from the sea, and/or from the air by possible hostile invading forces from China, North Korea, the Republic of Korea, Russia, or other countries. Therefore, large land parcels, particularly on Japan's island of Okinawa, which lies south of the island of Kyushu, are devoted to the U.S. military occupying forces; a large part of Okinawa is devoted to the military establishment. Military reservations occupied by U.S. forces are also located in other parts of Japan, including areas near Tokyo, the capital city. New agreements provide for their continued occupation into the new millennium.

Since World War II, the Japanese government again turned its focus on redevelopment of the industrial establishment to become once again a world power. Its objective has been reached; Japan is the second highest economic power in the world. At this stage of the new millennium, the industrial establishment of Japan continues to undergo redevelopment with the emphasis on technology development that involves computer software and telecommunications.

Industrial complexes occupy large sites in all prefectures of Japan but are particularly centered in waterfront locations of southern and central Japan. "Science cities" have been developed to further industrial research and development as well as production of industrial goods. For example, one of the special industrial "science cities" lies to the northeast of Tokyo approximately 100 kilometers (approximately 60 miles).

Nuclear and geothermal plants are spread across Japan, but primarily along the coastline. The land that the power plants occupy tends to be in close proximity to the various centers of industrial production and industrial research and development. The 52 existing and operating nuclear plants produce 35 percent of Japan's total energy output each year. Recently, a nuclear accident at the nuclear Conversion Testing Facility in Tokaimura, 70 miles northeast of Tokyo, caused nuclear contamination of a number of power plant workers and perhaps residents of nearby neighborhoods. Therefore, the safety systems for nuclear power plant workers and neighborhood residents are again undergoing scrutiny for causes of the recent accident and for methods of preventing the recurrence of such accidents.

Sports are very important to the Japanese. Therefore, sports complexes and associated land use are very significant. For example, almost every large neighborhood has at least one golf driving range with high and ample netting systems to keep golf balls from the many driving positions on multiple levels from straying into adjacent neighborhood locations. Large areas are also devoted to soccer fields and softball and baseball fields and stadiums. Large subsidiaries of the main trading companies tend to own separate baseball clubs and related land development. Subsidiaries of the main trading companies such as the real estate subsidiaries also tend to own the numerous golf clubs and courses. They finance their continuing holdings of large tracts with golf courses designed by world-renowned golfers by selling memberships to affluent domestic and foreign people who are largely businesspeople.

Large landowners continue to own large tracts in major cities and in suburban areas. Many of these tracts were assembled before land prices started to soar in the aftermath of World War II. As smaller landowners sold part of their tracts to raise funds for rebuilding their makeshift homes following World War II destruction, many of the larger landlords acquired additional space tract by tract over time, particularly in the suburbs, where the expanding population could find more affordable homes. The *keiretsu* often include construction companies and real estate companies that can continually pursue property acquisition and land development through the financing that has normally been available from the *keiretsu* bank.

The large landowners in the new millennium face the need to accommodate the space acquisition requirements of the expanding service industries and the space divestment requirements of basic industry that is accounting for a declining portion of the gross national product. The telecommunications industry is global in nature; fixed-line telephony is rapidly being replaced by mobile phones and telephony associated with computers and television sets. In Japan alone the number of purchasers of cell phones is rapidly increasing; the space devoted to fixed-line phones is decreasing; the space devoted to fiber-optic cables, satellite systems, and underwater cables is increasing. As new office buildings are being planned and as older office buildings are being redeveloped, the growth in managers and employees of computer software companies must be accommodated. This growth industry has its particular land and building space requirements. The same thing can be said about the legal, accounting, and financial services sectors, whose employment is growing by leaps and bounds; the land and other space requirements of these sectors must be met in the appropriate urban and rural locations of Japan. The landowners may profit from these changes in land use. They must manage and market surplus space and develop new space where necessary and desirable.

THE CLIMATE, GEOGRAPHY, AND GEOLOGY OF JAPAN IN GENERAL

The climate, geography, and geology of Japan may tell us something about the land use environment. The climate tends to differ among the various islands of the Japanese country grouping. The geography, of course, is different for the four main islands—if we exclude Okinawa and other smaller islands to the south of Kyushu Island Prefecture, which include Sakishima, Amami-O-Shima and Osumi Islands. These smaller islands lie immediately to the north of the Tropic of Cancer between the 31st degree and the 24th degree of latitude. The geology of the four main islands is similar.

Geography

Hokkaido Island lies between the 45th degree and the 42nd degree of latitude. Sapporo, the capital of Hokkaido Prefecture, lies on about the same latitude as Vladivostok, Russia, which lies to the west across the Sea of Japan. Honshu, the largest island of the Japan island grouping, lies between the 42nd degree of latitude and the 34th degree of latitude. The smallest island, Shikoku, lies on the east side of Honshu Island in a curve formed by the waterfronts of Osaka, Kobe, and Kure. The Inland Sea lies between Shikoku Island and Honshu Island. The Kii Channel separates the east coast of Shikoku from a southern peninsula of Honshu, where the city of Wakayama is situated. The Bungo Strait separates Shikoku Island from Kyushu Island, which lies to the south and west of Honshu Island. Kyushu Island lies a short distance across the Korea Strait from the Republic of Korea (South Korea). Kyushu Prefecture lies between the 34th degree and the 31st degree of latitude.

Japan is located geographically on the same longitude as the southern and middle portions of the United States—between the 31st degree of latitude and the 45th degree of latitude. Most of the United States lies between these same degrees of latitude. Japan's latitude, is approximately equivalent to that of Southern Europe and North Africa and, generally, to that of the northern two-thirds of India and the middle part of China and southern Russia.

Japan, the second highest economic superpower in the world, has few natural resources. It cannot even produce its total food supply. Even though Japan produces many hectares of rice, it still imports rice from countries such as China across the East China Sea. The growing demand for meat products is satisfied by imports from South America, including Brazil, and from Australia. Fruits and iron ore for its steel plants are imported from Brazil, also. Japanese-produced steel is used for high-rise building construction, train car manufacturing, and shipbuilding. Special strains of cattle are imported from the United States, including from the state of Kansas.

To satisfy its energy needs, the country must import most of its oil, coal, and natural gas to run its non-nuclear power plants. Most of its oil comes from Iran, Indonesia, and other countries of the Middle East. Natural gas is imported mainly from the Middle East, too. Uranium must be imported for its many nuclear power plants.

Japan has timber reserves on its many hills and mountains, but the vast majority of its lumber and pulpwood for paper manufacturing is imported from such countries as Canada and Australia. The trees of the hills and mountains are protected for recreational areas for residents of the densely populated urban areas and for emergency use in case of foreign invasion or embargo that cuts off imported goods including lumber and pulpwood. Generally imported, fire-resistant lumber is imported for housing construction. Granite, marble, limestone, and other office building exterior materials are imported from Italy and other countries. Coal and other minerals are drawn from Australia.

Climate

The central part of Japan, which includes most of Honshu Island, has temperate weather with four definite seasons as in the Midwest of the United States. The lower elevations in the coastal areas are hot and humid in midsummer, experience change of color in the foliage in the fall, are cold with some snow in the winter, and enjoy a moderate, rainy climate in the spring.

In the hilly and mountainous areas of Honshu Island, which comprise the majority of the land coverage of Japan, the summer weather is more moderate, and the spring, fall, and winter are cooler. There is so much snow in the mountains surrounding Nagano that the 1998 Winter Olympics were staged there. Hokkaido Island is cooler than central Honshu Island at all times of the year; the winters are characterized by cold and snowy conditions. In contrast, the island of Kyushu has warmer conditions than central Honshu Island in general. In fact, palm trees, which reflect tropical conditions, dot the landscape on the east coast of Kyushu Island. In the southern part of central Honshu Island near the Ise-Shima National Park, palm trees beautify the resort area. The currents associated with the Pacific Ocean that border this peninsula area give the national park area its tropical climate.

Geology and City Population Density

Approximately 70 percent of the Japanese island grouping is hilly and mountainous. The remaining 30 percent of the country is highly developed, with one of the densest residential populations on a square-meter basis. The population of Japan, approximately 130 million people, lives and generally works in only 30 percent of the land surface. The population of the city of Tokyo, on the Kanto Plain, approximates 28 million. It has been a relatively large city for centuries. The highly populated capital city is surrounded on the south, west, and northwest by mountains; Mt. Fuji, whose peak reaches 12,389 feet in height, lies to the southwest of Tokyo.

Japan is located on a fault line for earthquakes; Tokyo, for example, continually experiences minor earthquakes. The country experienced the great Kanto earthquake in 1923 and then recently, in 1995, experienced the great Kobe earthquake, which also had devastating consequences.

The shoreline to the east of Tokyo around Katsuura has a beach of volcanic lava. The Pacific Ocean provides surf for surfboarders who inhabit the area.

Typhoons hit the southern reaches of Japan. Precautions have been taken to reduce the water and wind damage that might occur from these periodic events.

TERMINOLOGY

The metric system is used by Japan for the measurement and description of space. Building rents, expenses, and construction costs may be quoted in both the metric and the English systems of space measurement. The currencies used for comparative purposes may be both the Japanese yen and the U.S. dollar.

Some of the most familiar Japanese spatial terms may be compared to English spatial terms. Some examples follow from the Japanese real estate market:

Tsubo (the traditional housing plot measuring standard in Japan) = 6 × 6 feet, where 50 *tsubo* = 1,800 square feet = 165 square meters or approximately one-twenty-fifth of an acre = 3.3 square meters

Meter = 39.37 inches

Square Meter = 1.20 square yards or approximately 10 square feet

Kilometer = 0.62 mile

Hectare = 10,000 square meters or 2.47 acres

Acre = 0.4047 hectares or approximately 0.4 hectares

CHAPTER SUMMARY

Foreign property analysts and investors may wish to know how Japanese real estate varies from real estate of their home countries. This book provides an important source for the analyst's and the investor's introduction to the Japanese real estate system, areas of change, methods and practices, and cultural patterns associated with real estate investment and land use.

This book is focused on foreign and domestic investment in Japanese real estate; the book does not focus on Japanese investment in foreign real estate. The book chapters include information about the offering of Japanese real estate services and about the prevailing real estate methods and practices associated with marketing, investment yield analysis, construction, land development, financing, securitization, appraisal, and leasing. The history of land tenure in Japan is linked with the new investment climate for Japanese real estate investment and government land planning and control.

The importance of real estate in Japan is shown by the nature of institutional, government, corporate, and consumer investment in Japanese real estate. The "bubble era" in real property is associated with the preoccupation of the Japanese people with investment in real property. Japanese individuals and companies have long thought that their fortunes could be made through real estate investment and that if they could only continue acquisition of real estate, they could assure themselves increased wealth in the future. The recent heavy decline in real property values has shaken this cultural concept to some extent, but many still await the turnaround in the property market so that wealth can again be gained through real property acquisition.

Many large landowners who continue to be motivated by continued property acquisition and development loom large in the culture of Japan. These large landowners have generally withdrawn from international real estate participation to gain more liquidity for renewed activity in Japan as the recessionary conditions tend to fade.

The combination of the climate, geography, and geology of Japan tends to form a distinctive country that remains ranked second in the industrialized countries of the world behind the United States. These conditions tend to affirm that land will continue to be relatively expensive due to the crowded residential, commercial, institutional, and agricultural conditions imposed by the climate, geography, and geology.

The terminology of the Japanese real estate market is partly related to the metric system, which is utilized in most countries of the world, and partly related to distinctive Japanese terms such as the *tsubo*. Many countries, including Japan, have distinctive real estate terms that have developed internally over time. The *tsubo* is equivalent to 3.3 square meters.

REFERENCES

Farrell, Roger. *Organisation, Motivations and Case Studies of Japanese Direct Investment in Real Estate 1985–94*. Pacific Economic Paper No. 282. Canberra, Australia: Australia–Japan Research Centre, Australian National University, August 1998.

Golany, Gideon S., Keisuke Hanaki, and Osamu Koide, eds. *Japanese Urban Environment*. Oxford, England: Pergamon, 1998.

Hanayama, Yuzuru. *Land Markets and Land Policy in a Metropolitan Area: A Case Study of Tokyo*. Boston: Oelgeschlager, Gunn & Hain, 1986.

Hines, M. A. *Investing in Japanese Real Estate*. Westport, CT: Quorum Books, 1987.

Japan: Eyes on the Country: Views of the 47 Prefectures. Tokyo: Foreign Press Center, 1997.

Landers, Peter. "Chain Reaction in Japan: Diary of Nuclear Accident: Japan Wasn't Ready: Critical Equipment Was Missing, Medical Treatment Delayed." *Financial Times*, October 8, 1999, p. A17.

Nakamoto, Michiyo. "N-Accident May Be Upgraded to Three-Mile Island Level." *Financial Times*, October 8, 1999, p. 8.

2

The Japanese Economy

Japan's place in world business and economic affairs is well established. Even during the recession of the 1990s, Japan's economy was ranked second only to the United States. As a world economic power, Japan's government is trying to use monetary and fiscal policy to regain its former domestic economic growth. Japan's multinational business is providing growth in many cases to support the decline in Japanese domestic business. Most of Japan's leading companies are positioned across the world. Japan's businesses in economic growth markets such as Europe and the United States grow while its businesses in economically slow or no-growth markets such as recession-prone South America, Africa, and South Asia produce little in profits or earnings growth. The worldwide diversification of many of Japan's largest companies again gives corporate earnings stability to some Japanese multinational companies. In some cases, the worldwide diversification has not worked to inhibit the overall corporate business decline and, perhaps, bankruptcy. For example, the multinational Japanese banks that are widely diversified in world geographic terms still have suffered greatly from non-performing loans. The largest Japanese bank, Dai-ichi Kangyo, has become bankrupt along with other large multinational Japanese banks. Japanese business in the growth markets balances, to some degree, its business in the slow or no-growth markets; the balance may or may not have proven adequate to forestall bankruptcy or near bankruptcy.

BALANCE OF TRADE

Japan is ranked very high in both worldwide exports and global imports. Japan has recently been mentioned as the third largest exporter of goods and services. The European Union leads in exporting. The United States comes second behind the European Union. While Canada is the fourth largest exporting country of the world, China is ranked in fifth place. Looking to Japan's import position in world trade, it ranks third behind the United States, which is in first place with the highest share of world imports, and the European Union, which is in second place. Although Japan is ranked in third place, its share of the world import market is quite distant from that of both the United States and the European Union. Fourth place is held by Canada, as it does in export share of the world market. But the fifth place in importing is held by Hong Kong, not China. China holds sixth place, with a share of the world import market of a little more than 3 percent.

Japan is encouraged by the economic growth forecasts for its main trading partners for the coming years. The principal trading partners of Japan over recent years, according to the *Europa World Year Book*, continue to be—in general rank order from the highest annual export trade volume to the lowest—the United States, the Republic of Korea, Taiwan, Hong Kong, the People's Republic of China, the Philippines, and Germany. The rank order in terms of highest annual import volume to the lowest for recent years is the United States, the People's Republic of China, the Republic of Korea, Taiwan, Indonesia, Australia, and Germany. The trading partners vary according to export and import trade and yen volume per country. Japan's trade surplus in general has declined due to a fall in exports that outpaced the decline in imports. Exports have been encouraged by the economic growth of the United States and Germany; Japanese exports were affected by the Asian financial crisis that hit the Republic of Korea, Taiwan, Hong Kong, the People's Republic of China, and the Philippines in the mid-1990s. The Asian countries other than Japan and Indonesia have generally pulled out of the economic slump caused by the Asian financial crisis. One recent economic forecast called for Asian economic growth of more than 5 percent in year 2000. Both the manufacturing and the service sectors of Asia are in major expansion modes. For example, manufacturing production has leaped upward in Indonesia, Malaysia, South Korea, and Thailand, even though political turmoil and financial reform prevailed in these countries, which are strong trading partners and recipients of foreign direct investment of Japan. The economic growth of Western Europe is predicted to continue its upward momentum in the early part of the new millennium. Therefore, the economic growth that ranges from slow upward to rapid upward movement within Japan's major trading partners fosters future economic growth for Japan through effects on both its export and its import trade.

Japan's trade surplus has declined, but the positive trade balances with most of its trading partners, including the United States, will probably stay positive in the near term. The amount of Japan's trade surplus with individual countries may continue below the high previous levels in the next few years.

The visible trade balance of Japan was positive through the decade of the 1990s, as was generally true of other members of the six leading economic powers of the world except for the United States and the United Kingdom. The

United States and the United Kingdom have continued to run negative trade balances overall with their trading partners since the late 1980s as their exports have been outrun by their imports. As Japan's exports continue to exceed its imports, its exports grew to more than 300 billion ecus by the mid-1990s. In comparison, the exports of the United States exceeded 300 billion ecus by the early 1990s. With the decline in Japan's economy and the strengthening of the economy of the United States, the exports of the United States almost doubled those of Japan by 1998. Germany's exports were roughly the same as those of the United States in the early 1990s, but U.S. exports almost doubled in a 10-year period, while Germany's rose approximately 50 percent. While the U.S. exports almost doubled within the decade of the 1990s, Italy's exports doubled, but its exports were only about two-thirds of the total exports of Japan and about one-third of total U.S. exports. Italy showed more economic growth during the decade than the usual Western European economic powerhouse, Germany. German economic recovery was strong in the 1990s, but has been overshadowed by the economic prosperity of the United States.

GROSS NATIONAL PRODUCT

In the world rankings by gross national product (GNP), Japan generally comes in third, as it does in world export share and world import share. As the United States attempts to assist the People's Republic of China in its wish to enter the World Trade Organization as a full-fledged member, the People's Republic of China (PRC) ranks second in the world on the basis of GNP figures. The GNP of the United States is double that of China, which is ranked in second place. The GNP represents the total value of a nation's output of goods and services. Japan's GNP, calculated in U.S. dollars, the international currency for statistics, is approximately three-fourths that of the United States' GNP. Germany, in fourth place, has a GNP that is approximately 55 percent of the GNP of Japan.

GNP figures are often interpreted in terms of the population of the country subject to the world ranking. Even though the GNP of the United States far surpasses the GNP of the PRC, the population of China (approximately 1.26 billion) is roughly four-and-one-half times larger than the population of the United States (approximately 276 million residents). Japan's population is less than one-half the size of the U.S. population.

GROSS DOMESTIC PRODUCT TRENDS

Looking to the trends in Japan's real gross domestic product (GDP) since the mid-1980s, we note the strength of the economy from the 1980s until 1991. The real GDP plunged to a low in early 1993 and finally turned upward at the end of 1995. Then it plunged downward again to new depths in 1998. The economic decline per annum continued until 1999, when the real GDP stabilized. It is, therefore, not surprising that the Japanese government debt rose from 1991 through 1999. Company capital spending declined in 1992, rose in the mid-1990s, and then turned downward again. Inflation has been contained at a relatively low level, while private capital spending tends to be on hold.

Japan has recently exhibited very low economic growth as measured by the real GDP growth rate. Before the Asian financial crisis, most of the East and Southeast Asian countries produced much higher growth rates than did Japan. The PRC has led the way in this area.

Looking back a few decades, the average rate of change of the real GDP of Japan was relatively high during the 1950s and 1960s. A slump to half that of the two preceding decades occurred in the 1970s. The decline continued in the first half of the 1980s. In the second half of the 1980s, an economic boom called "Heisei Keiki" occurred. Then the real GDP dropped about 3 percent from 1990 to 1991; the recession had started.

BUSINESS INVESTMENT TREND

Historically, Japan has maintained a relatively high capital expenditure per worker. Its recent figure exceeds $36,000, while American spending was a little over $24,000, and European spending was approximately $22,000. Japan's recent decline in capital spending still puts the country ahead of North America and Europe.

Business investment by major companies in all regions slowed during the 1998–1999 period, according to the United Kingdom Trade and Industry Department. Capital expenditure in the Pacific Basin declined about 5 percent; this decline partly reflects the slowdown in Japanese capital investment with the economic decline. Japan has slowed its replacement of fixed tangible assets. This action may decrease its competitiveness in world commerce. But Japan's gross tangible fixed assets per employee of $460,000 are still much higher than the comparable figure in Europe and in North America. The wide differential may be due to the higher-priced real estate in Japan in comparison with European and North American real estate.

In recent quarters capital investment has been negative. End-user demand is weak, and capacity utilization is low. Companies may have little reason to buy new plants and equipment. Also, corporate profitability continues to be low. Many companies cannot afford to invest in capital equipment and plants. At the same time, banks are examining loan applications for business investment more closely to assure themselves that the new loans will lead to profits. The profit motive has become far more important among Japanese companies as companies restructure and as financial reforms are pursued.

GOVERNMENT FUNDING TO STIMULATE THE ECONOMY

Since the early fall of 1999, the Japanese government has announced $1,150 billion—the equivalent of $1.15 trillion—in 10 supplementary spending packages in order to stop the economic decline and to encourage the return of economic prosperity. The most recent spending package of roughly $175 billion took effect in early 2000. The two chief foci of the spending packages have been public capital investment such as bridge building in Kyushu Prefecture and purchase of non-accruing loans from financial institutions, mainly banks. A subsidized mortgage program also stimulated home buying while the program was in effect; that short-period program is no longer in effect. Housing starts fell as the subsidy program ended. Some analysts comment that the Japanese economy is dependent on the injections of government funding; without the government funding, the economy again falters.

The economic malaise appears to stem from massive misallocation of capital, labor, land, and technology from the long-term government–business partnership that once impelled Japan's economy to become the second largest in the world. More capitalistic elements may be needed to guide the allocation of these factors of production.

THE STATUS OF THE GOVERNMENT DEBT AND ITS TREND

In the early 1990s, the Japanese government debt was less than 60 percent of the GDP. Now the debt surpasses 130 percent of the GDP, which is the worst country debt position of the OECD (Organization for Economic Cooperation and Development) countries. The debt continues to rise with each capital infusion. Fiscal policy is difficult to employ due to the economic distress of taxpayers, whether households or businesses, and the announced employee layoffs of the immediate future. The last increase in selected tax rates by a previous prime minister is reportedly the cause of the economy's sinking into recession.

The Ministry of Finance is preparing to publish its first set of consolidated national accounts. As the finance ministry publishes the national accounts during 2000, it will point out the difficulties in measuring pension liabilities and government asset values. Even though the first attempt at national account publication may be rather crude, the scale of Japan's debt problems may become more apparent. This publication will add transparency to government accounting, which is beneficial to the world financial system.

INFLATION TREND

Concerning the trend of inflation in Japan, we may note the minimal annual change in the low inflation in Japan from the late 1980s to the middle of the 1990s. Japan's trading partners, including Italy, Canada, France, the United Kingdom, the United States, and Germany, also had higher inflation than did Japan during this period as measured by wholesale prices. Inflation in Japan rose to more than 3 percent in the opening years of the decade of the 1990s as measured by consumer prices but subsided to low rates in the mid-1990s that were similar to the rates of the late 1980s. Japan's European and North American trading partners generally experienced higher levels of inflation than Japan based on consumer and wholesale prices. Japan's wholesale price index has shown vastly more volatility than Japan's consumer price index. For example, while the consumer price index was stable and low, the wholesale price index rose significantly from 1978 to a peak in 1980; from 1985 the wholesale price index plunged to a low in 1986 and then revived slowly to another higher plateau in 1989.

EXCHANGE RATES AND TRENDS

The Japanese yen–U.S. dollar exchange rate has followed a volatile path since 1971. This exchange rate has moved from 349.67 yen to the U.S. dollar when the U.S. dollar was very strong in 1971, to 104 yen to the U.S. dollar when the Japanese yen was very strong as the new millennium appeared. The exchange rate has been even lower; the rate published for 1995 was 94 yen to the U.S. dollar. The yen was particularly strong in comparison to the U.S. dollar in 1995.

Taking a longer historical view, we note that the U.S. dollar was particularly strong in the first half of the 1980s, when the yen–U.S. dollar exchange rate hovered between 200 and 275. Then the U.S. dollar weakened significantly against the yen so that the exchange rate reached the area of 150 at the time of the Plaza Accord, the Louvre Accord, and Black Monday. The yen gradually strengthened until the exchange rate reached 80 yen to the U.S. dollar in 1995. The dollar strengthened somewhat in the latter half of the decade of the 1990s when more than 145 yen was exchanged for the U.S. dollar in 1998, according to the Japan Economic Planning Agency, which tracks the yen–dollar exchange rate. Then the yen strengthened from June to the fall of 1999; the U.S. dollar exchanged for roughly 105 yen in the fall.

As the new millennium approached, the euro, the yen, and the U.S. dollar converged at 100 for the first time. The euro had weakened against the U.S. dollar, while the yen was much stronger than the U.S. dollar. This situation has occurred even though Japan's monetary authorities at the Bank of Japan and the Japan Ministry of Finance preferred a weaker yen to encourage exports and better domestic business conditions. Domestic goods could be sold at lower prices to foreign customers if the yen were weaker.

JAPANESE COMPANIES IN THE TOP-RANKED GLOBAL 500 COMPANIES

Japanese companies continue to be listed in the top 500 companies of the world, as reported by the *Financial Times*. Japan's National Telephone and Telegraph (NTT) was ranked 11th in 1998 and 7th in 1997. Toyota dropped from 9th place in 1997, to 26th place in 1998. The Bank of Tokyo–Mitsubishi dropped from 15th place in 1997, to 102nd place in 1998. Honda Motor Co.

dropped less dramatically than the Bank of Tokyo–Mitsubishi from 1997 to 1998—from 85th place in 1997, to 105th place in 1998. Matsushita Electric was reduced in rank from 69th place in 1997, to 111th place in 1998.

The rankings of leading Japanese companies according to market capitalization changed even between 1997 and 1998, as reported in early 1999. Mitsubishi Estate Co., the real estate subsidiary of the Mitsubishi Corporation, is ranked higher by market capitalization today than Mitsubishi Corporation itself. Mitsubishi Estate Co. dropped from a ranking in 25th place in the Japan 500 in 1997, to 40th place in 1998. The opposite was true for Mitsui Fudosan, the real estate subsidiary of Mitsui & Company. Mitsui Co. dropped from 44th place in 1997, to 62nd place in 1998, while Mitsui Fudosan fell in the rankings from 57th place in 1997, to 104th place in 1998. Sumitomo Bank, in the Japan 500 rankings, went from 4th place in 1997, to 10th place in 1998. The largest Japanese bank before the extended recession is now reported by the media to be bankrupt and is being merged with Fuji Bank and the Industrial Credit Bank, which are also technically bankrupt as they go into the merger.

JAPANESE COMPANIES AMONG THE WORLD'S MOST RESPECTED COMPANIES

In a new ranking by the *Financial Times* newspaper and Pricewaterhouse-Coopers, Sony of Japan was ranked 6th in the total survey of world companies. Among the world's most respected consumer goods companies, Sony ranked 2nd behind the 3M company from the United States. Toyota ranked 10th in the total listing of companies; this company ranked first among the most respected engineering companies. Honda ranked 38th in the total listing of companies and 3rd among the most respected engineering companies, behind Toyota and Daimler/Chrysler. Matsushita Electric Industrial ranked 2nd among the world's most respected electrical companies, behind General Electric, in 1st place. Seven-Eleven Japan ranked 2nd among the world's most respected retail companies; Wal-Mart was ranked number one in this area.

FOREIGN DIRECT INVESTMENT

While Japan's GDP in real and current currency terms and company capital spending plans are still depressed, the United Nations Conference on Trade and Development (UNCTAD) has estimated that foreign direct investment (FDI) into Japan rose nearly five times to $14 billion in 1999, from $3 billion in 1998. The liberalization of the mergers and acquisitions regime in Japan is given credit for the dramatic increase in FDI into Japan. Part of this recent FDI is foreign purchase of loans that are backed by Japanese real estate and foreign direct purchase of Japanese real estate investment with or without Japanese and/or foreign partners.

World FDI inflows rose significantly between 1997 and 1999. Cross-border mergers and acquisitions by companies from developed countries are given the primary credit for the FDI inflows reaching over $1,100 billion. In 1998 FDI rose over 40 percent to $660 billion from 1997. Therefore, there was a near doubling of international investment flows within just two years (1997–1999). The vast majority of the investment inflows were experienced by developed countries. Developing countries received approximately one-third of the total investment flow by 1997 and 1998, but Central and Eastern Europe received a very small portion of the FDI funds.

Japan has received a good portion of the FDI as the values of its companies and real properties have declined. The United States and Germany have continued their investment in Japan. Even though the Netherlands directly invests in Japan most years, that country particularly represented an unusually high amount of investment in 1990. Switzerland and the United Kingdom also invest continually in Japan. In the mid-1990s, total FDI in Japan was less than one-tenth of the amount of Japan's direct investment overseas, which approximated $50 billion.

FDI into Japan reached a very high level for the full year ending March 1999—a total of ¥1,340 billion, or approximately U.S.$13 billion. But, during the *first six months* of the fiscal year ending in September 1999, the inflow of FDI reached approximately U.S.$13 billion, with big investments in the automotive, financial services, and telecommunications sectors. France is the biggest single country source of this huge FDI. Renault spent more than U.S.$6 billion for a roughly one-third stake in Nissan, the auto company. Valeo, the French auto parts company, set up a joint venture with Zexel in air conditioning. Axa, the French insurance group that not long ago bought the Equitable Life Assurance Co. of the United States, invested about U.S.$2 billion in Nippon Dantai, the Japanese life insurance company. AT&T and British Telecom each bought 15 percent of Japan Telecom. Cable and Wireless acquired IDC, a Japanese domestic telecom company, in a hostile takeover that is rare in Japanese business dealings. Japan is deregulating most industry sectors, including the telecommunications and financial sectors. Other industry sectors have companies that have liquidity problems, heavy debt problems, and heavy portfolios of delinquent and defaulted loans. These companies are particularly good prospects for FDI.

Japan has contributed far less to FDI than the country did in the heydays of the 1980s. In the mid-1990s, Japan increased its share of total FDI in the United States to more than 40 percent. Japan continues to directly invest overseas in the following order. The United States is the top overseas destination for direct investment. Asia is generally the second ranked region after North America, of which the United States is the leading destination. In Asia most of the Japanese FDI is placed in China, Indonesia, Thailand, Singapore, and Hong Kong. Behind Asia in third place is usually Europe, with the primary focus on the United Kingdom, France, and the Netherlands. In Latin America, Panama receives the greatest amount of direct investment from Japan. In Oceania, Australia receives the greatest amount of Japanese direct investment.

FOREIGN DEVELOPMENT ASSISTANCE BY JAPAN

Japan continues to provide development assistance to countries that require financial assistance to support their economic growth. In the first half of the 1990s, Japan was the world's top source of official development assistance. In 1996 Japan disbursed approximately $10 billion or about one-sixth of the world total of official development assistance. This amount represented less than 1 percent of Japan's GNP.

Japan particularly gives financial aid to Asian countries, usually with financial assistance from other countries, also. For example, Japan has given assistance to Indonesia along with many other countries of the Association of Southeast Asian Nations and the Asian Development Bank. Indonesia has sought assistance in the refinancing of its particularly heavy foreign debt and in the return to political stability after the riots related to the recent general election and the events that led to the military and political turmoil in East Timor and Ache. Other countries that have recently received financial assistance for economic development have included Indonesia, the PRC, Thailand, India, the Philippines, Pakistan, Mexico, Egypt, Bangladesh, and Sri Lanka. These countries have been listed in the order of the funding given, starting with Indonesia, which was the recipient of the highest amount of funding in the mid-1990s. Japan's financial assistance is often associated with the growth of Japanese business and industry in the countries that are designated aid recipients.

Later in the decade of the 1990s, the government of Japan had to reduce the normal amount of yen associated with official development assistance. In late 1997, the government enacted the Fiscal Reform Law, which provided for the reduction of the fiscal deficit to no more than 3 percent of the GDP. The official development assistance budget had to be reduced to satisfy the requirements of the 1997 Fiscal Reform Law.

TAX RECEIPTS AND THE PORTION OF PROFITABLE COMPANIES

The National Tax Administration of Japan confirmed in the fall of 1999 that only one-third of Japanese companies were profitable. Tax revenues were substantially less in 1999 than the previous year's low tax collections. The bankrupt companies have caused the recent record low levels in tax collections. Corporate incomes continued to drop in 1999. For eight straight tax years, low tax revenues have marked the extended recession in Japan.

THE TREND IN THE CONSUMER CONFIDENCE INDEX

The consumer confidence index of Japan shows that consumers felt the deep recession in 1996 and then gained confidence in the middle of 1997. They tended to feel that the extended recession had run its course. But the economic indicators of late 1997 again deflated consumer confidence. The consumer confidence index hit a low point in mid-1998, followed by an upsurge again in early 1999. This extreme vacillation may continue a while longer since the economic indicators in late 1999 showed only a minor upturn in the economy in the first year of the new century.

HOUSEHOLD SAVINGS RATE AND AVERAGE HOUSEHOLD PORTFOLIOS

Historically, a large portion of the household budget has been represented by savings in the Asian countries. In Japan the household savings rate declined with the progress of the long recession of the 1990s from about 15 percent in the mid-1980s, to roughly 13 percent in the mid-1990s. The average household of the United Kingdom and the United States saves half of what the average Japanese household saves. The average Japanese household invests more in currency and demand deposits than does the average household in the United States or Germany. Most of the Japanese household savings are invested in time deposits, and often these time deposits are purchased from postal savings institutions. The purchase of insurance and annuities with the savings constitutes one-quarter of the household portfolio. Approximately 10 percent of the portfolio is devoted to securities. In comparison, the average U.S. household devotes far less of the lesser amount of savings in currency and demand and time deposits; two-thirds of the household savings are placed in insurance, annuities, and securities. An increasing motivation for the investment of the typical Japanese household savings is a retirement fund. Saving for emergencies is still the prime motivation for the accumulated savings. Saving for children's education is becoming less important over time, but it is still a tertiary motivation for accumulated savings. Some continue to save to purchase land or a house or to pay for future weddings for children.

FINANCIAL INSTITUTIONS, LOAN COLLECTION PRACTICES, AND LOANS IN DEFAULT

Collection policies of consumer and commercial loan companies are being investigated by the Financial Reconstruction Commission, which was established to implement the new financial reform policies of the federal government. Very high levels of company bankruptcies have been experienced in recent years. Some companies have found that they could not pay their bills due to high levels of debt, high levels of associated debt service payments, and high levels of non-performing loans and delinquent accounts receivable. Some loan companies have resorted to some unethical methods of collecting overdue loans. The federal government is asking banks to decrease lending to "*shoko*" commercial loan companies in general and in particular to the companies that are using unethical methods of debt collection.

Financial institutions of various kinds and classifications continue to request bad-loan bailout from the Resolution and Collection Corporation, a new, semi-governmental corporation that was established to purchase defaulted loans from still-operating financial institutions. The bad-loan bailout program is designed to reduce the bankruptcies among the financial institutions and prompt their reorganization and consolidation during the financial reform period. This governmental program has been in operation in recent years to alleviate the Japanese financial crisis that was impacted by the Asian financial crisis of the period 1995–1998 and the Russian financial crisis of 1997. The agency's functions are similar to the functions of the Resolution Trust Corporation during the savings and loan and banking crises of the United States. Even though this bad-loan bailout program has been in effect for a few years, during the fall of 1999 many financial institutions were still requesting bad-loan bailout. Most of the types of Japanese banks and thrift institutions were in this group: city banks, regional banks, second-tier regional banks, *shinkin* banks (credit associations that make loans only to members), and credit cooperatives. At this time, the long-term credit banks, the trust banks, and the postal savings banks—important classifications of the total system of financial institutions—did not seem to be in line for financial assistance from the federal government. All of the long-term credit banks were nationalized earlier. Mergers and consolidations are occurring among the trust banks and other types of financial institutions to prompt future profitability in the financial sector.

Bank lending may have started its recovery. The bad-loan bailout program has already provided government funding for many of the city, trust, and other banks. During 1999 these stabilized banks have been characterized by (1) mergers and acquisitions, (2) announcements of employee layoffs, and (3) lack of demand for bank loans.

One of the reasons for the lack of consumer confidence and the minimal demand for bank loans is the extent of the bankruptcies being filed, the minimal profitability of the one-third of the companies that are still "above water," and the continuing announcements of job cutbacks. As an example of falling profitability, we can note that four of the major Japanese trading companies, including Itochu Corp., Marubeni Corp., Mitsubishi Corp., and Mitsui & Co., experienced large declines in profits during the first half of their 1999 fiscal years. In contrast, Sumitomo Corporation reported that its group profit increased by more than 6 percent during the same six-month period. Another example may be taken from the banking sector. The central bank of Japan, the Bank of Japan, has announced a reduction in its workforce of 500 jobs or more by the year 2004. Japan's leading telecoms operator and one of the country's largest

Exhibit 2-1
Labor Cut Plan by Major Japanese Company

Company Name	Business	Number of Employees as of Sept. 1998 (parent only)	Planned Employee Reduction Rate (%)	Plans Announced (reported on)
NKK	Steel	15,725	22	12/18/98
Asahi Glass	Glass	8,309	11	2/9/99
NSK	Bearings	9,387	11	2/16/99
Oji Paper	Paper	13,789	8	2/17/99
Mitsukoshi	Department stores	9,956	6	2/18/99
NEC	Electronics	39,774	7	2/19/99
Hino Motors	Trucks	9,629	4	3/2/99
Chiyoda	Plant engineering	2,737	30	3/3/99
Toyo Tire & Rubber	Tires	3,764	20	3/5/99
Dainippon Ink and Chemicals	Chemicals	6,697	10	3/5/99
Sony	Electronics	21,296	10	3/9/99
Cosmo Oil	Oil refinement/ distribution	2,809	47	3/24/99
Daiei	Retail chain	16,554	18	3/25/99
Mitsubishi Electric	Electronics	46,450	10	3/31/99

Source: Warburg Dillon Read, Research Department, *Japan's Real Estate Sector* (Tokyo: Warburg Dillon Read, October 1999). Reprinted with permission.

employers, NTT, has publicly announced plans to cut 21,000 jobs by the year 2003. Many companies have been announcing prospective employee layoffs in the near future (see Exhibit 2-1).

STOCK MARKET TRENDS AND RECENT FINANCIAL REFORMS

Portfolio investments in Japan by foreigners generally increased for both stocks and bonds in the 1990s. Net stock and bond purchases by foreigners increased as the decade passed. Sales of Japanese stock and bonds tended to decline from the opening of the decade to the middle of the decade and then tended to increase. Foreigners ended the 1990–1996 period with less Japanese bond holdings than their holdings at the opening of the period.

On the First Section of the Tokyo Stock Exchange trading volume rose to high levels at the end of the 1980s and then declined sharply in the first half of the 1990s as business activity in Japan declined. Transaction value and the Nikkei stock average price index generally followed the same path. In the latter half of the decade, the Nikkei 225 average rose to a peak in early 1996 from a low in mid-1995 and then proceeded to decline to a new low in the fall of 1998. Then this index rose through 1999.

The Japanese stock markets have responded to future financial uncertainty caused by financial reforms. For example, in June 1992 laws were revised that regulate the financial system. In June 1993 interest rates on time deposits were fully liberalized; interest rates on demand deposits were fully liberalized in October 1994. Then in October 1996 subsidiaries of life and non-life insurance companies were allowed to enter each other's business spheres. In April 1997 the Foreign Exchange Law was revised. A year later, the Foreign Exchange Law was revised, and the Foreign Trade Control Law came into effect.

UNEMPLOYMENT, COMPENSATION, WORKING TIME, AND OTHER LABOR MATTERS

Japan is accustomed to very low unemployment rates. The unemployment rates typically reported have been 2 percent. The reporting of 2.5 percent was an embarrassment to the Japanese people, its companies, and its government. Now the Japanese official unemployment rate exceeds 4 percent. This rate is higher at present than the rate of unemployment of the United States. The rate for the European Union continues to hover around 10 percent. The unemployment of Germany, France, and Italy, which far exceeds the European Union average, remains a very important economic and political problem. The number of beneficiaries of Japanese unemployment insurance continues to climb toward 1 million people.

Japanese unemployment differs by age group. The unemployment rate is the highest for the extreme groups of the age scale: those potential workers under 20 years of age and those over 60 years of age. The retirement age has generally been moved up this decade from 55 years of age to 60 years of age. Higher than average unemployment rates are also experienced by potential workers in the 20-to-24 age group and the 25-to-29 age group. Recent university graduates are having hard times finding employment on the usual low tiers of corporate management. Women in general and new women university graduates reportedly have a harder time finding employment than men in general and new male university graduates.

Following global trends, the proportion of Japanese workers employed in primary industry declined from one-third of the labor force in 1960 to a little less than 5.5 percent in the last part of the 1990s. Secondary industry, which is mainly services, has represented about one-third of Japanese employees for the last 30 years; this sector is decreasing as a proportion while tertiary industry has expanded to over 60 percent of the labor force. Tertiary industry includes high-technology personnel such as computer software designers and telecommunications engineer-system designers.

The real rate of unemployment in Japan is estimated to be much higher than the official rate of 4 percent. Many Japanese people are underemployed. For example, in the last few years, university graduates have had great difficulty finding jobs. Companies have reduced their normal quotas for university graduates on an annual basis. Female graduates have suffered more than male university graduates in this reduction in corporate demand for entrance-level management trainees. The real rate of Japanese unemployment may be 15 or 20 percent rather than the official rate of 4 percent. At the same time that there are two or more applicants on average for every job offer, employee compensation is rising as a portion of the GDP.

Average wage increases per year have substantially surpassed the increase in consumer prices since the 1980s. Real wages on average continue to see positive increases, except for 1993, when real wages declined about one-half of 1 percent, according to the Japan Ministry of Labor. Employee compensation is said to be moving toward 60 percent of the GDP. This is perhaps one of the reasons that companies that are restructuring for increased profitability are attempting to counter the trend and reduce their payrolls.

In the 1970s and 1980s per capita income in Japan was less than the U.S. per capita income in terms of U.S. dollars. In the same decades, the wide spread between the total nominal GDP of Japan and that of the United States narrowed as time passed. By the middle of the 1990s, per capita income of Japan surpassed that of the United States, and the U.S. nominal GDP was less than twice the GDP of Japan in terms of U.S. dollars. German and French per capita income in U.S. dollars exceeded U.S. per capita income in 1980; in the mid-1990s, German and Japanese per capita incomes exceeded the U.S. comparable figure, but the French per capita income did not surpass the comparable U.S. figure.

The highest average monthly earnings in Japan tend to be associated with hospital physicians ($8,300), whose average age is now less than 40 years old, according to the Japan Management and Coordination Agency. The average salaries of office department managers tend to rank second, but the average age of such personnel approximates 50 years old. University professors, unlike in the United States and the United Kingdom, are ranked third by Japanese average monthly earnings, and their average age approximates 55 years. On the bottom of the earnings scale lie occupations that are predominantly held by females: telephone operators, who may average $2,630 and whose average age is 37 years; office clerks, whose monthly earnings average $2,850 and whose average age approximates 30 years; nurses, whose monthly income averages about $3,100 and whose average age is 33 years. Skilled personnel today in high-technology businesses, including the global telecommunications business, may be attaining new levels of average monthly compensation in Japan as they are in countries around the world.

Returning to the employment situation, Japan impacts local employment when the Japanese subsidiaries that are operating overseas hire local people. Generally the workforces of Asia and North America are increased as Japanese subsidiaries hire local people as managers and other personnel. Employment is also increasing in Europe, Latin America, and other regions as Japanese companies directly invest in these areas.

Looking to average working hours and days, we may note that total working hours continue higher than "official" working hours. The average Japanese worker puts in at least 8 hours a day, down from about 8½ hours a day in the 1960s. In the mid-1990s two-thirds of employees worked 5-day weeks during some weeks, but not every week. One-quarter of Japanese employees worked 5 days every week. About 10 percent of all employees worked 6 days or 5 ½ days a week. The shortened workweek in the 1990s is reflected in the number of average working days per month. This number declined from 24 in the 1960s, to a little less than 20 at the start of the new millennium, according to the Ministry of Labor.

A "Happy Mondays" holiday plan was established in January 2000. When a holiday falls within the week or on a weekend, the holiday vacation from here on will be celebrated on Monday. At the present time, the government is trying to promote consumer spending to resuscitate the anemic economic recovery. It is assumed that employees will spend their holidays on ski slopes, at hot spring resorts, and other such places where they will spend part of their large savings.

"Regular" working hours per week approximate 34, but total working hours per week are somewhat higher at about 37. In the mid-1990s the average weekly working hours for Japan were very comparable to those of Germany and France and less than those of the United States (over 42 hours) and the United Kingdom (over 43).

About 23 percent of Japanese workers are unionized. The trend is downward as the increasing number of part-time workers and young workers is not interested in becoming a member of a union. Generally, Japan's unions are company-based. The proportion of workers in the United States who are union members is far less than that of Japan—around 15 percent. But the United Kingdom and Germany had more than one-third of their labor forces among the ranks of unionized workers as of the mid-1990s. The number of labor disputes, the number of Japanese workers involved in labor disputes, and the worker-days lost are declining significantly over time in Japan.

The number of female workers increased by over 50 percent between 1980 and the middle of the 1990s, while the number of employed men rose only half that much. Women have recently accounted for at least 40 percent of the workforce in Japan. The increasing number of women in the workforce is related to the desire of women to work, the passage of the Equal Employment Opportunity Law in 1986, and the Family Care Leave Law, passed in 1995. Companies have been slow to implement the gender equality laws and the Family Care Leave Law.

Women represent less than 10 percent of all administrative and managerial employees in Japan, but 44 percent in the United States and 36 percent in Germany. Women represent a lower percentage of all professional and technical workers in Japan than in the United States or Sweden. In the United States, women represent about 80 percent of all clerical workers but only about 60 percent of all clerical workers in Sweden, Germany, and Japan. In Japan the occupations that attract the most women are clerical and service; the third-ranked occupational designation is professional and technical.

Part-time employment has grown significantly during the multiyear Japanese recession. Recently, females have made up one-third of the growing part-time employee group.

The mandatory retirement age has gradually increased over recent decades. Today 80 percent of business employees face mandatory retirement at age 60, according to the Japan Ministry of Labor. A very small percent face retirement at ages higher than 60, but approximately 10 percent face mandatory retirement at an age less than 60.

ELECTRICITY DEMAND AND SUPPLY

As the standard of living of Japanese consumers rises, the demand for energy has been rising. Since industry and commerce also demand more energy over time, Japan's total electricity demand has continued to increase. Most industrial, business, and household consumers purchase their electricity from power companies, rather than self-generate their needed energy. Company self-generation of energy represented only 12 percent of the total energy consumed, according to the Japan Agency of National Resources and Energy.

In the mid-1990s more than half of Japan's energy production was based on oil. The use of coal for the production of energy was similar in proportion to the use of nuclear plants for the generation of energy. About 10 percent of the power plants operate on coal supplies; hydroelectric plants that use water supplies for the production of energy represent a very minor portion of the total energy produced in Japan. The per capita consumption of energy in Japan (4%) is about one-half the per capita consumption of energy in the United States. But Japan must import at least 80 percent of its fuel for power plants, while the United States imports only 20 percent of its needed fuel supply. Japan is similar to Germany and France in that it is almost totally dependent on the importation of oil. As the Japanese consumption of crude oil has risen, its imports of crude oil have risen in lockstep. The main source of crude oil for Japan is the Middle East. The United Arab Emirates is the supplier of the largest share of the crude oil and is followed in ranking by Saudi Arabia, Iran, Qatar, and other Middle Eastern countries, according to the Japan Agency of Natural Resources and Energy. China and Indonesia supply Japan with a small portion of its total crude oil needs.

PENSION FUNDS AND MEDICAL CARE

The population of Japan is aging rapidly, as in North America and Europe. As a result, the ratio of total expenditures for social security to national income rose rapidly from about 5 percent in the mid-1960s to more than 15 percent in the mid-1990s. Total payments toward pensions and medical care have been rising rapidly each year. During the extended recession, companies continued their policies of underfunding their pension fund responsibilities, according to media reports. When mergers and acquisitions of Japanese companies are considered by both domestic and foreign prospective acquirers, often the prospective purchasers see underfunded pension liabilities and back off from further consideration of merger or acquisition. Seventy percent of social security expenditures are pension and insurance payments; pension payments exceed insurance payments. Pension payments have doubled in 20 years in terms of share of total social security expenditures; pension payments constitute one-third of the total expenditures. Then, in terms of percentage of the total social security expenditures, come elderly health care, then public health, social welfare, and, lastly, public assistance. Welfare and public assistance make up only 7 percent of total social security payments, according to the Japan Management and Coordination Agency. The amount of social security expenditures for the elderly in Japan has more than doubled within 10 years.

Japan's national medical care expenditures in total and on a per capita basis are rising with time. The share of the national income consumed in the mid-1990s was 7 percent, according to the Japan Ministry of Health and Welfare. Generally, the corporate worker is required to pay 20 percent of his or her medical bills; earlier, the corporate worker was required to pay only 10 percent.

CHAPTER SUMMARY

Japan normally has a balance of trade surplus with the majority of its trading partners. China has been one exception to this general situation. The recession has reduced this positive trade position with most countries. The GNP and the GDP of Japan have declined during the long recession of the 1990s and early 2000s. Business investment has slumped during the recession. Some of the FDI of Japan has been reduced in order to aid domestic business. The sale of foreign businesses and real properties has provided more cash and reserves to the domestic businesses that have been hit by declining sales. Not all business investment has declined. Increased investment has been characteristic of the growth industries such as telecommunications and computer software development. Government investment has grown significantly to promote more employment and to renovate, rebuild, and build needed public infrastructure. The government funding of public projects has caused the level of government debt in comparison to GDP to rise to precipitous levels, perhaps the highest percentage level among the industrialized nations of the world. Businesses and consumers now are worried about the rise in future tax rates in order to lower the government debt position. The tax rates during the recession have been lowered in several steps by the government.

The Japanese government considers its foreign exchange rates with its major trading partners' currencies to be unduly high, which tends to reduce international trade. The government is asking for the cooperation of the major industrialized countries in reducing the value of the Japanese currency.

Many Japanese companies appear in the top-ranked global 500 companies and among the world's most respected companies. Part of this success results from the continuing FDI of Japan around the world. The Japanese government and its major banks have actively supported Japan's FDI over many years. Japan is considered the second ranked world industrial power, after the United States.

Tax receipts are associated with public financing programs of many types of governmental units, including the national, prefectural, and city governments. During the lengthy recession, these tax receipts have been lower than they would have been without the recessionary conditions. As a result, some local governmental units, including the city government of Tokyo, have experienced financial troubles. Tax receipts continue to be relatively low because a large portion of private companies have not been profitable.

As companies have begun to restructure to gain higher levels of profitability and as the government has instituted some reforms in anticipation of even more reforms later, many employee layoffs have been announced for future periods. As a result, consumers have reduced their spending and have accumulated more reserves in case of company layoffs. The government is trying to counter the declining consumer confidence index by instituting and implementing more government programs to create higher levels of employment and economic growth. The household savings rate is normally relatively high; in this uncertain period, the rate tends to rise.

Average household investment portfolios tend to be concentrated in account balances at Japanese banks, account balances at the branches of the postal savings system, and perhaps the ownership of homes. As personal incomes have risen faster than the relatively low rate of inflation and as residential property prices have fallen significantly, many households have found the acquisition of a home feasible and have proceeded to buy an apartment or a house.

Japanese financial institutions are trying to recoup their former profitability through mergers and consolidations. Most major financial institutions have experienced high loan default rates among business, consumer, and real estate loans. When the collection of loan balances due has not been possible, they have resorted to the sale of loans in default. They have found a ready market for defaulted loans for which major real estate was given as collateral. Foreign investors have noted profit opportunities in the purchase of large packages of deeply discounted loans and the possibilities of acquiring major income properties through the forfeiture of the properties by the borrowers.

The stock market has benefited from Japanese investors' seeking investment returns higher than the relatively low yields offered by bank and postal savings system certificates of deposit, which have recently approximated zero. Both foreign and domestic investors have purchased stock that has impelled the Japanese market indices upward. Foreign pension funds and other institutional and personal funds have been investing in Japanese equities, while the stock prices are viewed as relatively low. Once the recession is behind the market, Japanese stock prices should rise with earnings from the streamlined, restructured Japanese firms, which may have more profit opportunities within the government-reformed economy. The Nikkei index has recently reached new peaks due to the recent foreign and domestic demand for Japanese company shares.

Unemployment rates continue relatively high for Japan. Worker compensation has risen faster in recent years than the rate of inflation. Working hours per day and per week have declined. Companies that have long sought more worker productivity and compensation plans approved by the government that would reward worker productivity rather than worker longevity with the company are looking forward to the time when they can reduce their workforces. Even though many companies have announced impending reductions in their workforces, most of those companies have not implemented these plans due to numerous pressures, including that of the national government, where elections to the lower and higher houses of the Diet are impending in 2000.

Electricity demand tends to exceed supply in Japan, a nation of minimal natural fuel sources. As the economic recovery takes place, energy demand should rise. The government and the energy companies would generally like to reduce the costs of energy to the consumer, but oil, coal, and uranium must continue to be imported from distant sources. Nuclear plant problems lately have decreased consumer acceptance for increased nuclear energy production in Japan.

Private pension funds are accumulating in Japan. Japanese private pension funds are a relatively recent phenomenon. Not long ago a retiring employee from a Japanese company would receive a watch for retirement; now employee and employer contributions are being made to pension funds for the financial security of retiring workers. The deferral of the problem of underfunded company pension funds has resulted from the raising of the normal retirement age from 55 to 60.

Affordable medical care for Japanese senior citizens is one of the major problems for this country, which anticipates a large portion of its citizens to be over retirement age in the near term. The future government and private medical expense of the aging population of Japan is similar to the medical affordability problems of other industrialized nations, including the United States.

REFERENCES

Abrahams, Paul. "Central Bank Chief Moves to Stem Yen's Appreciation." *Financial Times*, December 2, 1999, p. 6.

———. "Foreign Investment in Japan Increases to Record Levels." *Financial Times*, December 10, 1999, p. 16.

———. "Japan Sounds Warning on Economic Data." *Financial Times*, November 25, 1999, p. 6.

———. "Japanese Trade Surplus Tumbles as Exports Slip." *Financial Times*, May 25, 1999, p. 8.

———. "Japan's Junkie Economy Is in Need of Another Fix." *Financial Times*, December 7, 1999, p. 20.

———. "Tokyo Admits Economy Is Back in Decline." *Financial Times*, Weekend July 24/25, 1999, p. 2.

"Activities of Foreign Affiliates in Japan." *Investment News* (A Publication of the Japan External Trade Organization), Issue No. 16, 1999, pp. 4–5.

Barrell, Ray, and Nigel Pain. "Trade Restraints and Japanese Direct Investment Flows." *European Economic Review*, 43:1 (January 1999), pp. 29–45.

Bremner, Brian, Emily Thornton, Ireme M. Kunii, and Miki Tanikawa. "A New Japan." *Business Week*, 3652 (October 25, 1999), pp. 68–74.

Brown, Kevin. "Business Investment Slows in All Regions Says Report." *Financial Times*, December 6, 1999, p. 1.

Burton, John. "Economic Squeeze Calls for Change: Occupying Vulnerable Middle Ground between High-Tech Japan and Low-Wage China, the Country Needs to Establish a New Industrial Model to Secure Its Role as a Regional Economic Power." *Financial Times* (Financial Times Survey: South Korea), October 20, 1999, p. 1.

"Corporate Failures: Japan Bankruptcies Fall for 12th Month in a Row." *Financial Times*, November 16, 1999, p. 6.

Corrigan, Tracy. "Reputations in Business Can Be a Fragile Commodity." *Financial Times* (Financial Times Survey: World's Most Respected Companies), December 7, 1999, p. 1.

Cortes, Bienvenido S. "Trends in Industrial Concentration in Japan, 1983–91." *International Review of Applied Economics*, 12:2 (May 1998), pp. 271–281.

Cragnolin, Darel. "Downward Spiral of Japanese Bond Market." *Global Investor*, 126 (October 1999), pp. 58–60.

Cullen, Lisa Reilly. "The Rebirth of Japan Inc." *Money*, 28:9 (September 1999), pp. 50A–50C.

De Jonquieres, Guy. "Foreign Direct Investment: Worldwide Capital Flows Rose 39 Per Cent Last Year: Global Takeovers Fuel Investment Surge." *Financial Times*, June 23, 1999, p. 8.

Dornbusch, Rudi. "On the Edge." *Far Eastern Economic Review*, 161:9 (February 26, 1998), pp. 52–53.

"EIU Forecasts: Asia: 1999–2003." *Country Monitor*, 7:34 (August 25, 1999), p. 7.

Facts and Figures of Japan. Tokyo: Foreign Press Center, 1998.

"Finance and Economics: Is Japan Learning to Smile?" *Economist*, 352:8136 (September 11, 1999), pp. 75–76.

"Global 500, The World's Top Companies: The Top 500 Companies in the World, Europe, U.S., Japan, and U.K. The Top Asia-Pacific, Middle East, Africa, Latin America and Canadian Companies." *Financial Times* (Financial Times Survey: FT 500), January 28, 1999, pp. FT500 4, 6, 8–9.

Gutner, Toddi. "Japan: Everybody Back in the Pool." *Business Week*, 3644 (August 30, 1999), p. 226.

Harney, Alexandra. "Care Scheme Brings Confusion for Japan's Elderly." *Financial Times*, September 28, 1999, p. 6.

———. "Happy Mondays Holidays Plan to Stave Off Recession in Japan." *Financial Times*, January 10, 2000, p. 14.

———. "Honda Hit by Stronger Yen." *Financial Times*, August 12, 1999, p. 16.

———. "Japan's Jobs Subsidy Prop Stymies Industrial Restructuring: Extra Golfing Days Are Not Seen as a Real Solution to Sunset Industry Unemployment." *Financial Times*, August 10, 1999, p. 4.

———. "Nissan to Cut 1,000 U.S. Jobs as Part of Global Restructuring: Carmaker Will Merge Manufacturing and Sales Operations after Heavy Losses." *Financial Times*, December 2, 1999, p. 16.

———. "Retailing: Ailing Seiyu Plans Capital Increase to Saison Group." *Financial Times*, August 12, 1999, p. 16.

Hayashibara, Mariko. "The Right to Buy?" *Asian Business*, 34:11 (November 1998), pp. 56–57.

Huffman, James L., ed. *Modern Japan: An Encyclopedia of History, Culture, and Nationalism*. New York: Garland, 1998.

"Inconspicuous Consumption." *Financial Times*, September 10, 1999, p. 11.

"International Economy: Japan." *Barclays Economic Review* (Third Quarter 1999), pp. 26–27.

Intriligator, Michael D., Serguey Braguinsky, Jewell Ray Bowen II, Gordon Tullock, and Hilton L. Root. "Role of Market Institutions in Pacific Rim Development and Transition." *Contemporary Economic Policy*, 17:1 (January 1999), pp. 109–137.

"Itochu Lost $1.42 Billion in Half; Net Fell at Rival Trading Houses." *Wall Street Journal*, November 19, 1999, p. A18.

"Japan: Introductory Survey." *The Europa World Year Book 1998*, Vol. I, Part Two, pp. 1866–1894.

Japan Economic Planning Agency. "Japan's Economy 'Improving.' " *Financial Times*, July 14, 1999, p. 4.

Japan, Eyes on the Country: Views of the 47 Prefectures. Tokyo: Foreign Press Center, 1997.

"Japan Telecom Reports 8-Month Profit." *Wall Street Journal*, November 19, 1999, p. A16.

Japanese Real Estate Statistics 1999. Tokyo: Mitsui Fudosan Co., January 1999.

"Jobless Rate Registers Second Month of Decline." *Japan Times*, October 30, 1999, p. 9.

LaPier, Terrence. *Competition, Growth Strategies and the Globalization of Services: Real Estate Advisory Services in Japan, Europe, and the United States*. London: Routledge, 1998.

Lewis, Nathan. "Real Estate: Buyers Continue to Stand on Sidelines." *Financial Times*, June 21, 1999, p. 26.

Linsk, Michael. "Mixed Signals Spell Slow Going in Japanese Real Estate Recovery."

Global Real Estate Now (A PricewaterhouseCoopers Publication) (Fall 1999), pp. 28–31.

Martin, Neil A. "Is Asia's Rebound Real?" *Barron's*, 79:45 (November 8, 1999), pp. 42–46.

Mertens, Brian. "Baby Boomers." *Asian Business*, 35:7 (July 1999), pp. 40–41.

"Mitsubishi Restructuring to Cut 12,400 Jobs by 2003." *Japan Times*, October 27, 1999, p. 1.

Montagnon, Peter, and Rahul Jacob. "Banking on Borrowed Time: Manufacturing in Asia Is Powering Ahead despite the Fragility of the Region's Banks. Is the Recovery Sustainable without Them?" *Financial Times*, November 18, 1999, p. 16.

Nakamae, Naoko. "Bankruptcies Hit Record in Japan as Recession Persists." *Financial Times*, January 27, 2000, p. 1.

———. "Direct Investment: Small Town, Bright Lights." *Financial Times* (Special Supplement: Foreign Investment in Japan), October 19, 1999, p. iv.

———. "Japanese Politics: Obuchi Stresses Economy in Reshuffle." *Financial Times*, October 6, 1999, p. 4.

———. "Last into Recession, Hiroshima's Lateness Starts to Hurt." *Financial Times*, August 6, 1999, p. 3.

Nakamae, Naoko, and Paul Abrahams. "U.S. Group Set to Buy LTCB." *Financial Times*, September 28, 1999, p. 20.

Nakamoto, Michiyo. "NTT Planning to Cut 21,000 Jobs by 2003." *Financial Times*, November 18, 1999, p. 1.

———. "Worst of the Recession Is Over, Says Japan's PM." *Financial Times*, March 18, 1999, p. 1

Nashima, Mitsuko. "It's Prime Time to Invest in Property, Exec Says." *Japan Times Weekly International Edition*, 38:9 (March 2–8, 1998), p. 13.

"Overseas Companies Bullish on Japanese Real Estate." *Focus Japan*, 25:5 (May 1998), pp. 1–5.

Plender, John. "Land of the Rising Yen: Currency Markets, Rather than Policy Makers, Hold the Key to the Future of the World's Two Largest Economies." *Financial Times*, September 21, 1999, p. 17.

———. "Weak Euro, No Problem." *Financial Times*, November 23, 1999, p. 14.

"Profitable Firms Only 31% of Nation's Total." *Japan Times*, October 28, 1999, p. 15.

Sanghera, Sathnam. "BMW Benefits from Demand in Japan." *Financial Times*, November 23, 1999, p. 28.

Selected World Development Indicators. "The State in a Changing World." *World Development Report 1997*, pp. 215–231.

Sender, Henny. "Stemming the Flood." *Far Eastern Economic Review*, 162:30 (July 29, 1999), pp. 52–54.

Shirouzu, Norihiko. "Urban Blight: For a Struggling Japan, Tokyo Is Redefining Notion of Capital Loss: City's Huge Debts, a Legacy of Grand Public Projects, Hobble Nation's Recovery." *Wall Street Journal*, April 2, 1999, pp. A1, A7.

Silverman, Gary. "The Slowest Fire Sale on Earth." *Business Week*, 3588 (July 27, 1998), p. 42.

"Some Companies Shift to Merit-Based Pay Systems." *Focus Japan*, 25:5 (May 1998), pp. 8–9.

Spindle, Bill. "Japan Faces Three-Pronged Dilemma." *Wall Street Journal*, March 31, 1999, p. A19.

Tett, Gillian. "The Economy: Foreign Investors Sniff Recovery." *Financial Times* (Financial Times Survey: Japan), July 13, 1999, p. 10.

———. "Facing Up to a Wave of Foreign Competitors: Reform Spurred by Crisis Means the Financial Sector Will Be Opened to an Extent Only Recently Considered Almost Unthinkable." *Financial Times* (Financial Times Survey: Japanese Financial Markets), June 21, 1999, pp. 23, 26.

———. "Fear of a Fall on Wall Street Gives Japan the Jitters." *Financial Times*, October 26, 1999, p. 6.

———. "Japan to Go Ahead with Spending Plan." *Financial Times*, September 10, 1999, p. 4.

———. "Japan Zeros in on Cutting the Yen Down to Size." *Financial Times*, November 19, 1999, p. 18.

———. "Japanese Coalition Promises Big Public Spending Package." *Financial Times*, October 8, 1999, p. 8.

———. "Pressing Need for a Second 'Restoration: Not Long Ago the Country Enjoyed One of the World's Most Dynamic and Powerful Economies. Now the Story Is One of Corporate Bankruptcies and Social Strain.' " *Financial Times* (Financial Times Survey: Japan), July 13, 1999, pp. 9–10.

———. "Ripplewood Backs Japanese Recovery: The U.S. Group Is Set to Pay More than $1bn for the Troubled LTCB." *Financial Times*, September 28, 1999, p. 20.

———. "Sakakibara's Successor Will Not Seek to Keep Currency within a Set Range against the Dollar: 'Managed Float' Rate for the Yen." *Financial Times*, July 15, 1999, p. 1.

———. "Yen Hits Seven-Month High as Tokyo Hints at Improved Growth: Surge against Dollar Prompts Speculation over Intervention." *Financial Times*, September 1, 1999, p. 1.

Tett, Gillian, and Paul Abrahams. "Japan's Currency Tsar Is Left Walking on Eggshells." *Financial Times*, October 6, 1999, p. 4.

Tett, Gillian, and Naoko Nakamae. "Merrill Lynch Joins Top Japanese Employers." *Financial Times*, November 20/21, 1999, p. 4.

Tett, Gillian, Naoko Nakamae, and Alexandra Harney. "Down and Out in Japan." *Financial Times*, July 8, 1999, p. 15.

Urban Land Price Index. Tokyo: Japan Real Estate Institute, September 1997.

"Y2K Will Not Be a Problem in Japan, Government Says." *Japan Times*, October 27, 1999, p. 1.

Yamagiwa, Hiroshi. "Euro Is Unveiled: Should Japan Be Worried?" *Japan Times Weekly International Edition*, 39:1 (January 1–15, 1999), p. 8.

"Yen's Strength Hurts Toyota despite Net Rise." *Wall Street Journal*, November 19, 1999, p. A18.

3

The New Investment Climate: Culture and Environment

Major investors from across the world are observing investment opportunities in Japan as asset values reflect the economic slump. They wonder how long the "window of opportunity" will be available. The "vulture funds," sometimes called "hedge funds," have been expressing their investment enthusiasm by investing large sums for reportedly short-term yields. More conservative investment funds, major global financial institutions, and major global industrial corporations are more quietly analyzing the potential investment performance of multiple types of assets, and some have already invested sizable sums in global terms.

The new investment climate of Japan is growing out of the previously well-entrenched culture and environment for real estate investment. The previous culture of Japan is slow to change. The attitudes and social perceptions from long associations are entrenched. For example, Japanese real property owners are slow to sell even partial interests of their total property ownership to foreign entities. Japanese multinational investors are quick at times to purchase assets overseas to diversify their portfolios, but they are slow to permit assets in their homeland to be purchased by foreign multinational investors.

The legal and other infrastructure that supports real estate investment is slow to change in some respects and quick to change in other areas. For example, the rapidly changing telecommunications products are quickly adopted for personal and business use.

HEDGE FUND ACTIVITY IN TOKYO

Recently, the foreign hedge fund activity in Japan has been "the talk of the town." This investment activity is spectacular; hundreds of millions of dollars or their equivalent in yen or foreign currencies—perhaps a total of $1 billion or $2 billion—has been invested in Japan in defaulted real estate loans and partial interests of some major real properties. This money reportedly has been invested for only a two- to three-year period. This is "hot money"—in today and out tomorrow. But this is not unexpected in global terms. When high-quality assets are available at bargain-basement prices anywhere in the world for possibly high short-term yields, venture capital, alias hedge funds, is attracted to such assets. Recently, such "hot money" has invaded Paris due to the perceived low point in values of high-quality real properties as economic rejuvenation of Paris and the rest of France is expected.

THE BUSINESS CULTURE

The investor who is unfamiliar with the business culture of Japan but is interested in investing in Japanese real estate should know something of the Japanese business culture. The culture is associated with some perceptions that are changing with the times. The perceptions include the common feeling that "real estate will make you wealthy," the idea that investment is always long-term in nature, and the idea that *keiretsu* members must always protect other members of the same *keiretsu*. From past experience and current conditions, employees expect certain business–government relationships, certain working conditions, and certain retirement benefits. Citizens have certain expectations concerning corruption, croneyism, theft, crime, and the need for security systems. As foreign-language competence is expected where international business is involved, the adoption of the mobile phone with its access to the Internet and electronic mail is expected, particularly by younger working people. Immigration to Japan by foreigners is a phenomenon that is becoming part of the domestic and business culture.

Real Estate Will Make You Wealthy

In the recent speculative real estate period, the society felt that real estate acquisition would make one wealthy. In case after case, this was proven to be true in that era. Therefore, savings were put aside for real estate acquisition when enough money was accumulated for that purpose. Much of the money on deposit in banks and the postal savings institutions was associated with that purpose.

Long-Term Business Perspective

The government–business economic form that created policy by consensus focused on long-run revenues and earnings. Companies focused on capturing increasing shares of the market for their goods and services rather than increasing the return on their shareholders' investment. Both government and business policies were focused on long-term results. These policies were successful in creating the world's second largest economy. The country generated positive trade balances with the vast majority of its trading partners, even though the country continues to be highly dependent on imports of natural resources. Since the United States occupied Japan for many years after its military victory over Japan, the United States has continued, with Japanese acquiescence, to defend Japan against any possible attack or encroachment on its territories by any challenger from Asia or elsewhere.

Protection of *Keiretsu* Members

The group of companies whose members represented most major industries of Japan that is called a *keiretsu* agreed to give market and financial protection to all members within the group. The interlocking shareholdings assured this protection from all domestic and foreign intruders into the affairs of the group and its individual members. The government respected the interests of each of the *keiretsu* as the government and business worked together to bring about economic growth on a worldwide scale. Today these *keiretsu* are being threatened or restructured as mergers and acquisitions take place among the banks that led each of the *keiretsu*. For example, as Sumitomo Bank merges with Sakura Bank, the merger is disturbing the normal *keiretsu* structures. Sumitomo Bank headed the Sumitomo *keiretsu*, and Sakura Bank headed the Mitsui *keiretsu*.

Government–Business Relationship Has Retirement Implications

The long-term business–government cooperation and coordination led to many valuable consequences in previous economic periods. The economic growth of Japan has been phenomenal. The high-quality products developed by Japanese manufacturers have been prototypes for the development of high-quality products by manufacturers of the United States, for example. Employment relations were impacted by this strong government–business relationship, which was condoned by the citizens of Japan due to its favorable economic results. A pattern was set for government officials to retire to high-ranking private company positions. As retirement of government officials and business executives was expected at age 55, the business executives who retired officially from the companies within the various *keiretsu* were often reassigned to employment with related trade associations or other subsidiaries of the same *keiretsu* for another period of years. Their usefulness to the companies was continued for additional years, perhaps to age 60 or so. In contrast, over the last 10 to 15 years, the retirement age has been extended to age 60; the companies within the *keiretsu*, as a reflection of their financial situation, may or may not extend company-associated employment for another period of years, assuming that the retiring company executives are in a good state of health.

Work Period Expectations

Turning to the length of the official workday, workweek, and work year, the length of the workday has declined to approximately seven to eight hours. The workweek has declined to less than five days for the majority of workers. The time spent at work during the work year has declined. But Japanese workers still have more vacation time than they feel that they can take and still meet their employers' expectations about performance.

Lifetime Employment with One Organization

The business culture of Japan has long promised lifetime employment with a single organization where promotion and other advancement have been heavily tied to longevity of employment, with minor emphasis on employee productivity. With the initiation of financial reforms and the institution of corporate focus on profitability in the short run, the "promise" of lifetime employment is being threatened as companies have announced sizable layoffs from their corporate workforce. Since the culture is so entrenched in this area, since the government lacks funds for greater contributions to unemployment compensation, and since the political parties see the possible effects of higher unemployment on their success at the ballot box, the announced corporate layoffs are very slow to materialize. Corporate structural and financial reform has resulted in more rhetoric than action. The delay in the economic revival of the Japanese economy is partially associated with the delay in implementing the promised corporate and financial reforms and associated labor market reforms.

Retirement Benefits

Not long ago, when a Japanese person retired, he or she was given a "gold watch." Today companies have developed retirement plans with accumulated employee and employer contributions over the working life of the employee. Social security payments are also received by the retired person. In fact, the government has noticed the upward trend in social security payments and the higher proportion of retired Japanese citizens. The government budget must accommodate this steadily rising transfer payment. Companies seek money managers who will invest the employer–employee contributions to realize reasonable returns. Foreign as well as domestic asset management firms have developed to accommodate this need. Their investment returns may be measured against returns from portfolios managed worldwide by asset managers. The capital market is a global one.

Corruption and "Cronyism"

Japanese companies have had to live with the influences of the Japanese mafia. The mafia continues to exist and impact business operations and development. The changes recently have been prosecution of government and company officials who have conspired with the various mafia group members in business operations and development. The exposés have rocked the business and government communities. A film entitled *Cursed—the Financially Corrupt Islands*, which was released for showing in the fall of 1999, deals with the vices plaguing Japan's business sector—corruption, arrests, suicides, the struggles of a bank teetering on the verge of collapse. The public is flocking to see this film, which was adapted from a novel by Ryo Takasugi. It gives a stark portrayal of the problems embedded within corporate Japan, such as complicity between supposed competitors, the threat of disintegration of lifetime employment, and the threat to the strict seniority system. Some of today's vices were once corporate virtues that helped Japan to become an economic power in the 1960s and 1970s. The disintegration or restructuring of the *keiretsu* may assist in fighting the associations that are considered vices rather than virtues. The mafia is still a strong element that is difficult to counteract by the government and the companies.

Theft, Crime, and Security Systems

White-collar crime called corruption is endemic in society regardless of the country undergoing scrutiny; corruption and mafia operation continue to be a problem in Japan. Theft and other crime in general have not been major problems for the various levels of the police force of Japan until recent years. More police protection is needed. Historically, city or metropolitan police forces supplemented the police protection provided to the local government establishment, the federal government establishment, and leading political figures in particular. Neighborhood and community police protection was weak in comparison to that of other industrially developed countries. Today the neighborhood and community police force is taking on more significance as theft and other crime increase in neighborhoods within wider communities.

The increase in crime in Japan is blamed on (1) the change in the culture, which has become more impersonal and less family-oriented, (2) the weakening influence of the family, and (3) less acquaintance with neighbors in the large apartment blocks and more turnover of residents. More neighborhood watch groups have been established, particularly for residential neighborhoods. Home security systems are selling well in today's Japan.

Office building security systems tend to be minimal in Japan. Corporate security is lax in most of the major office buildings of midtown Tokyo, for example, in comparison to major office buildings in midtown locations of such major cities as New York, London, Paris, and Milan. The terrorism in the Tokyo subway system not long ago may lead to more examination of appropriate security systems for government and private high-rise office buildings in the many urban areas of Japan.

Adoption of the Mobile Phone and Its Internet and E-Mail Capability

Japanese workers have readily adopted the mobile phone technology. Increasing sales of mobile phones have impelled upward the demand for NTT DoCoMo and other mobile phone company products. Profits in the Japanese industry are rapidly rising due to the acceptance of the product, which has recently offered Internet and electronic mail service as well as general telephony service. Many customers would like Internet service via this telecommunications medium.

As women in Japan increasingly use the Internet, female Internet subscribers have doubled from 10 percent in the mid-1990s to 20 percent before the start of the new millennium. Even though Japan is considered to be three years behind the United States in Internet development, this female use of the Internet at the present time in Japan has attracted the attention of e-commerce sponsors. Several Web sites are focused on female buying by Internet.

The logistics of running an international organization have become much easier for Japanese companies that use company intranets and the public Internet. Communications by computer electronic mail make regional and global company management much easier and cheaper.

Foreign-Language Competence

Computer programs have been developed that translate one language into another with some efficiency and accuracy. Japanese companies have been in the middle of this particular type of computer development. Since these computer programs need more development for widespread use, the translation services of people who speak, read, and write foreign languages are still very valuable for correspondence and contract negotiation and execution.

Among the 128 million Japanese citizens, many people in business, in particular, have learned one or more foreign languages. The second language may be associated with the person's domestic work assignment or foreign tour of duty assignment. Before a Japanese company sends an employee overseas for an established tour of duty, it may train the employee in the associated language(s), or the employee may try to individually learn the language(s) of the foreign country of the coming work assignment. For example, a young real estate professional from Japan may be sent for a two- or three-year tour of duty to Brazil. That person becomes acquainted with the fact that Brazilians use the Portuguese language in daily intercourse. To be successful in Brazilian real estate work, the person will have to learn the Portuguese language before or after going to Brazil. The language instruction may start in Japan and then be continued in Brazil at the company location.

Most Japanese people do not speak English or any foreign language, but they may learn English or another foreign language in Japanese schools and universities. Reading a foreign language is much easier than speaking or writing that language. Therefore, many major Japanese companies have international departments where employees who speak foreign languages are placed on assignment. Other departments of the major company may have personnel, particularly on the top executive levels, who speak the foreign languages most often used by the company in its international business. English-language-speaking employees are in the minority in most Japanese companies; they are valuable to the company in their many company encounters with English-speaking people from the United States, the United Kingdom, Australia, and Canada. Japanese companies find that the international language is English in their multinational business around the globe.

Japanese Acceptance of Immigrants

Japanese society until recent years has been very homogeneous in comparison with most of the other advanced countries of the world. The society has been very slow to accept the integration of immigrants from Asia or elsewhere into the social fabric of the island grouping. But most Japanese citizens have realized that unskilled workers from abroad in certain fields and skilled workers from abroad in other areas may be necessary to attain the desired standard of living for many citizens and to attain the economic growth that is necessary to sustain the role as a world economic power. Therefore, many Japanese households have employed temporary or permanent workers from the Philippines and other parts of Asia as unskilled domestic workers. In certain business areas, skilled labor from abroad supplements the skilled labor in Japan. For example, financial and high-technology professionals from the United States are attracted to Japanese temporary and permanent residency. The four main sources of immigrants to Japan are China, the Philippines, Brazil, and the United States, in the order of magnitude of people involved, according to the OECD report *Trends in International Migration 1999*.

Japan has probably become more of a melting pot of nationalities since the end of World War II, when U.S. armed forces occupied Japan. A racial mixture was represented in the long-term occupation forces of the U.S. military establishment. But, today, few black persons, for example, are visible within the throngs of working people who flock to Japanese offices each workday. The Japanese workforce, for example, continues to be very homogeneous in its national origin and racial characteristics.

LEGAL ORIENTATION AND CULTURE

The role of consensus building in the cultural system of Japan needs to be reviewed in light of the availability of lawsuits and mediation. We also need to look at the basis for the Japanese legal system.

Consensus Building versus Lawsuits

The culture of Japan promotes decision making through consensus building. Legal action has been taken as a last resort. Even little mediation and arbitration have been used in past decades. Mediation and arbitration may have been employed sparingly due to the reportedly low number of practicing attorneys for the total population and for the large company population. Under the consensus-building system, few attorneys or solicitors were needed. This is in sharp contrast to the litigious society of the United States and its large number of attorneys in practice.

When major Japanese companies operate abroad, they tend to accept the business culture of the particular country. If the country encourages lawsuits rather than consensus building, the Japanese company may follow suit and file lawsuits in the appropriate situations. But, in the same company's operations in Japan, instead of bringing lawsuits, the company will again conform to the national culture with consensus building for decision making.

The Basis for the Japanese Legal System

Japan adopted a civil code for the foundation of its legal system rather than the common law, whose early beginnings are associated with England. For centuries, Japan was an isolated, inward-looking country with a feudal system, then with adaptations of a feudal system and military dictatorships, and then with socialistic-style governments. Since Japan had little early association with England and its global colonies of South Asia and Africa, a heavy influence from common law was not felt in Japan during its key development periods. Unlike Hong Kong and the PRC, Japan has retained its legal foundations in the civil code. The Japanese legal system has more affinity with the country legal systems of continental Europe, which are based on the civil code. Common law is associated with the development of a large legal community of many solicitors and attorneys, whereas the civil code may have less need for the large legal community.

MINISTRIES AND COMMISSIONS RELATED TO REAL ESTATE INVESTMENT

The Japan Ministry of Justice and the Financial Corporate Restructuring Commission are particularly active in the redevelopment, reform, and restructuring of the legal and financial system of Japan. Japan's Securities and Exchange Council is particularly involved in the trend toward more real estate securitization. Many other ministries and commissions are associated with today's real estate investment in Japan by Japanese citizens and foreigners.

The Japan Ministry of Justice maintains a legal recording system for real estate documents. The system assures the registration of private property rights and the protection of those rights that are shown in the recorded documents.

A Financial Corporate Restructuring Commission is working to implement the legislation that leads to the eventual restructuring of many corporations, including major banks that have experienced or are experiencing financial difficulty due to huge debt and/or large volume of loans in default.

As the real estate securitization program moves forward, Japan's equivalent of the U.S. Securities and Exchange Commission is functioning to protect investors against lack of public information for security investment purposes and against unethical and unscrupulous dealings with financial services providers.

INFRASTRUCTURE FOR REAL ESTATE INVESTMENT

At this point, we review the status of selected infrastructure associated with Japanese real estate investment. Let us review Japanese telecommunications service, energy provisions, clean water systems, sanitary and storm sewer systems, fire and police service, and mass transit service.

Telecommunications Service

When the telecommunications system was deregulated in 1985 with the privatization of the Nippon Telegraph and Telephone Company, this action ushered in great changes in the telecommunications product offerings and the foreign–domestic ownership of the mushrooming number of telecommunications companies that operate in Japan. The number of fixed-line phone subscribers has continued to grow to over 61 million people. At the end of 1997, there were over 28 million cell phone users, up from approximately 10 million cell phone users the previous year. The portable phone market consists of cell telephones and the simpler and less expensive personal handyphone system (PHS). In 1997 the number of PHS users reached 7 million.

The number of items carried by the mail service continues to grow; the number of items reached 25 billion in 1996, according to the Japan Ministry of Posts and Telecommunications. Telegram usage has declined from a peak in the early part of the 1990s. The number of pager subscribers continues to grow; roughly 10 million companies and individuals subscribe to this type of service, according to the last government survey.

Computer sales and usage continue to grow. During the recession, this business sector thrived. In 1996 over 7 million computers were sold; subscriptions to personal computer communications providers rose to roughly 8 million in the same year. Internet usage in Japan tends to lag behind that in Finland, the United States, Australia, the Netherlands, and the United Kingdom, but Japan's Internet usage surpasses that of Spain, according to the OECD's *Communications Outlook 1997*.

Energy Provisions

Japan uses most available types of energy generation systems and is continuing to do research and development in new energy generation areas. It is attempting to perfect the systems for the use of fuel cells, for example. The government pursues the interests of citizens in that it encourages research and development that would relieve the country of its dependence on foreign oil and nuclear power. Nuclear power threatens disaster, particularly when human errors cause failures in the management of Japan's 50 existing nuclear plants and when the periodic earthquakes could cause harmful conditions for employees and citizens living and working in the plant vicinities. Uranium and oil must be imported, which makes Japan highly susceptible to foreign political change and military threats that may cut off its strategic supplies of fuel.

Volatile Middle Eastern conditions threaten Japan's supplies of crude oil. Most of Japan's crude oil is imported from the United Arab Emirates, Saudi Arabia, Iran, Qatar, and other Middle Eastern countries. These countries are listed in order of their percentage provision of oil to Japan from highest to lowest.

Japan competes with Italy in the use of oil as a high percentage of fuel for power plants. The United States, Germany, France, Canada, and the United Kingdom are far less dependent on oil for fuel for power plants in percentage terms than Japan and Italy. Japan imports 99.7 percent of its oil due to only a few offshore oil-producing rigs, which have low volumes of production.

Nuclear power in Japan provides a little more in percentage terms (15.3%) than in most of the other highly industrialized countries, according to the Japan Agency of Natural Resources and Energy. In contrast, in the United States only 9 percent of its power is from nuclear energy, and Germany derives only 11.8 percent from nuclear power.

Japan is not a heavy user of energy, according to per capita figures of the Japan Agency of Natural Resources and Energy. Japanese citizens are well aware of their dependence on foreign oil, particularly Middle Eastern sources. Per capita consumption of oil is half that of the United States. The per capita oil consumption of Japan is close to that of Germany and France. These three countries individually consume more per capita than the United Kingdom, another highly developed country, does.

Clean Water and Sanitary and Storm Sewer Lines

The provision of clean water and the disposal of waste, rainwater, and other industrial and household refuse are major problems for the Japanese government on the various levels from cities and towns, to the prefectures and the federal government. Three factors that compound the government's problems are (1) the huge industrial establishment of this second-ranking economic power, which tends to pollute the water and air and promote unusually high levels of noise,

(2) the dense population of Japanese cities—not just Tokyo—which prompts waste collection problems, and (3) the presence of an abundance of water sources, including many rivers plus oceanfronts entirely around the island cluster that cause natural problems with their changing water volumes and levels.

Fire and Police Protection

Fire protection continues to be a problem due to the periodic earthquakes that at any time may cause the same or similar destruction that the Great Earthquake of 1923 did or the 1995 Kobe earthquake did. The outbreak of fire brings on the need for emergency routes for people who are living and working in the area affected by the fire. Police protection is needed for such fire disasters as well as the normal protection for the public from various forms of crime. Parks must continue to be designed into the urban landscape to provide evacuation points for people who are attempting to escape fire and building damage from earthquakes and other reasons.

Crime is increasing in this once "crime-free" country. More police protection is needed as family and other personal neighborhood relationships break down and as various forms of crime take place. Citizens have been supplementing the relatively scarce police protection by neighborhood watch groups similar to the neighborhood watch groups of the United States.

Mass Transit

The train system of Japan is reportedly 200 percent used, which means that the use of the train system is double its capacity. It is said that the only way that the existing train system works so effectively is the basic culture of the people, since the orderly behavior of the citizens, who are so highly dependent on the train system, permits the orderly use of the system. The above- and belowground trains tend to have older technology in effect; the government and the private rail system owners realize that the technology needs to be replaced. But it is difficult to comprehend the inconvenience to such a large commuting population to shut down trains for extended periods for their refurbishment. Many workers in the center of Tokyo ride the trains for an hour to two hours from home in outer urban areas to the office or plant each day. The refurbishment is closely associated with the underground systems in Tokyo that control the electrical generation and flow of electricity, wastewater and refuse disposal, and other underground municipal systems. Tokyo, as only one Japanese city, has realized its need to rehabilitate the older municipal systems under- and aboveground, but continuing general elections at relatively short intervals cause reluctance on the part of elected officials to disturb large portions of the electorate by the needed renovation.

Progress has been made in the privatization of the rail system. At least government finances have been bolstered through the influx of the purchase prices and the decline in repair and maintenance cost that have normally been relegated to the government.

CHAPTER SUMMARY

The new investment climate of Japan brings with it foreign and domestic hedge fund activity. Investment funds from across the world have scrutinized the Japanese property market; some have taken positions in loans with real estate given as collateral, and some have acquired real properties with and without Japanese partners.

The foreign investor needs to be aware of the characteristics of the business culture in Japan and how it is changing—if only slowly. From the real estate "bubble era," Japanese generally think that the ownership of real estate will make them wealthy. This belief may be slowly changing with the growing length of the recession. With the economic reform and its emphasis on business profitability, the long-term business perspective may be slowly changing to a shorter-term perspective. As the historical *keiretsu* break up with the major mergers among lead banks of multiple *keiretsu*, the phenomenon of *keiretsu* member protection of other *keiretsu* members may be disappearing.

The close relationship between government and business still seems to hold. For example, to accommodate the financial dilemma of underfunded corporate pension funds, government and business condoned the lengthening of age for retirement from age 55 to age 60. As a result, the corporations and the government have more time to accumulate reserves before more retirements take place in the gradually aging society. As good medical services and better lifestyles have led to longer lives for Japanese citizens, public and private retirement plans have felt the necessity to accumulate greater financial reserves for increased retirement payments. Retirement benefits have moved from the giving of a watch to the employee at retirement after lifetime employment at the company, to continued retirement benefits that afford financial security until death.

While company and perhaps government layoffs are impending, the Japanese workday and workweek are gradually shortening. The government is currently encouraging workers to take vacations and spend money that will invigorate the economy. Lifetime employment with one company is very slowly disintegrating as companies wish to reduce their payrolls and encourage the remaining workers to individually produce more toward the profitability of the organization. In the past, gaining increased share of market was the predominating goal of the company rather than profitability as the primary goal.

The Japanese have tolerated government and business corruption and "cronyism" for many decades. Today people who are found guilty of corruption are prosecuted, convicted, and punished according to the law. For example, the practice of Japanese companies of paying off the Japanese mafia has been discouraged by the courts and the press. As the Japanese society becomes more impersonal, business and personal theft and other crime have become more pervasive. The purchase and installation of security systems have become more common for homes and businesses; the owner of a business property tends to consider the need for such a system within the structural components.

The mobile phone has become very popular in Japan, even though fixed-line service is excellent and available within a relatively short period after application for service. Real estate communications will be enhanced as electronic mail and Internet service are available from the mobile phone handsets. Foreign-language competence is increasingly valued by the Japanese citizens who particularly are involved in international trade and other international business. As Japan permits a greater number of immigrants to supplement the existing Japanse workforce, the need for foreign-language competence becomes more obvious. Many immigrants to Japan come from Taiwan, the Philippines, and other Southeast Asian countries.

The legal culture of Japan is based on consensus building among parties to an agreement, less on confrontation and lawsuits. The Japanese legal establishment is being enlarged with the addition of international attorneys who have applied to practice law in Japan, particularly for their multinational clients who are doing business in Japan. Many international accounting firms are already doing business in Japan; as they each add international legal divisions, this legal staff will wish to serve both international and Japanese clients as their international accounting divisions do. The basis for the Japanese legal system is the civil code, not the common law.

Among the many ministries and commissions that work with foreign investors, the Ministry of Finance and the reconstruction finance commissions are particularly important to investors in real estate and real estate securities. The infrastructure for real estate operation needs extension, replacement, and reconstruction as time passes. In this deregulation era, telecommunications are improving so that more telecommunications service options are available from multiple domestic and foreign companies. Energy sources and costs to the business and personal consumer remain problems as Japan has minimal energy national sources and must import fuel from the Middle East, Southeast Asia, Alaska, or other sources. The systems for provision of clean water and sanitary and storm sewer service continually need updating to fit the current needs of the society. The urban populations continually change; business and industry locations continually change to fit current needs. As the basic industries decline, the infrastructure needs of the growth industries, including telecommunications, computer software applications, and other high-technology industries, must be met. Fire and police protection needs expansion as the various threats to safety change. The all-important mass transit is aging and needs replacement by newer systems that promise more safety with greater speed and reliability. As the culture of Japan changes, its services and infrastructure must change to fit the needs of this second-ranked world industrial society.

REFERENCES

Amaha, Eriko. "We Need You." *Far Eastern Economic Review*, 161:11 (March 12, 1998), pp. 44–45.

Balls, Andrew. "Essay: Evolving Populations: Sharing a Planet with 9bn Others." *Financial Times*, December 6, 1999, p. 12.

Bickers, Charles. "Off the Record." *Far Eastern Economic Review*, 162:33 (August 19, 1999), pp. 54–56.

Bremner, Brian. "Reform in Japan: Maybe This Time." *Business Week*, 3648 (September 27, 1999), p. 45.

Communications Outlook 1997. Vol. 1. Paris: Organization for Economic Cooperation and Development, pp. 56–57.

Crystal, David. "Essay: Language: English as She Is Spoke in the World." *Financial Times*, December 6, 1999, p. 4.

Easton, Thomas. "The Case for (Some) Japanese Stocks." *Forbes*, 164:7 (September 20, 1999), pp. 240–241.

Grice, Kevin. "Japan Faces Bleaker Economic Outlook." *Accountancy*, 121:1254 (February 1998), pp. 58–59.

Hamlin, Kevin. "The Eclipse of Mr. ¥." *Institutional Investor*, 33:10 (October 1999), pp. 37–44.

Johnson, Stewart, and Lynn McAlevey. "Stable Shareholdings and Japan's Bubble Economy: An Historical Overview." *Strategic Management Journal*, 19:11 (November 1998), pp. 1101–1107.

Kelly, Bruce. "International Adjustments." *Pensions & Investments*, 27:20 (October 4, 1999), p. 26.

Martin, Ellen James. "Bald-Hawk Investing." *Institutional Investor*, 32:6 (June 1998), p. 197.

Martin, Peter. "Multinationals Come into Their Own." *Financial Times*, December 6, 1999, p. 16.

Nakamae, Naoko. "Japanese Flock to See a Flim Showing How Corporate Virtues Have Become Vices." *Financial Times*, September 25/26, 1999, p. 3.

Nakamoto, Michiyo, and Gillian Tett. "Japanese Flock to Send e-mails by Mobile Phone." *Financial Times*, November 11, 1999, p. 6.

Nusbaum, Alexandra. "Women Take to the Internet in Japan." *Financial Times*, September 18/19, 1999, p. 4.

Ono, Yumiko. "These Boots Aren't Made for Walking but for Taking Stands." *Wall Street Journal*, November 19, 1999, p. A1.

Prasso, Sheri, Brian Bremner, Michael Shari, Mark L. Clifford, and Emily Thornton. "Asia Hits a Bump." *Business Week*, 3651 (October 18, 1999), pp. 168–169.

"Promoting Foreign Investment." *Focus Japan*, 26:7 (September 1999), pp. 3–5.

Roy, Sudip. "Life in the Fast Lane." *Global Investor*, 124 (September 1999), pp. 17–23.

Scherrer, Phillip Scott, and Chad Bolick. "Fire Sale in Asia: A Buyer's Market." *Real Estate Finance Journal*, 14:3 (Winter 1999), pp. 55–58.

Scott-Joynt, Jeremy. "Braced for the Big One." *Communications International*, 26:3 (March 1999), pp. 59–62.

Smith, Charles. "Can the Upstarts Topple the Giants?" *Institutional Investor*, 33:9 (September 1999), pp. 100–107.

"Success on Japan's Silicon Island." *Focus Japan*, 26:7 (September 1999), pp. 12–13.

Thomson, Andy. "Wendt Revs Up New Vehicle." *European Venture Capital Journal* (September 1, 1999), p. 7.

Trends in International Migration 1999. Paris: Organization for Economic Cooperation and Development, 1999.

Weinberg, Neil. "Master of the Internet." *Forbes*, 164:1 (July 5, 1999), pp. 146–151.

Yamigiwa, Hiroshi. "Finance Likely to Maintain Iron Grip on Policymaking." *Japan Times*, 39:8 (April 16–30, 1999), p. 10.

4

History of Land Tenure in Japan

Over the centuries Japan has experienced feudalism in various forms. But in the nineteenth century, leasehold estates developed with the entrance of private property rights. Instead of payment in the form of part of the crops from the farm, rent was due the landlord in the form of money. Private property ownership was fully protected and preserved. Land reform continued in many respects and even was fully protected and preserved, even through World War II. General Douglas MacArthur instituted land reforms after World War II that he and his advisers thought were needed. These reforms were instituted while the Allied Forces occupied Japan and reorganized the nation's economic system.

After reviewing briefly the many land reform movements from the seventh century forward to the twentieth century, the current status of Japanese landownership by corporations, financial institutions, government bodies, and households is reviewed. The nature of private and corporate land-ownership is noted. The reasons for corporate land acquisition are indicated. Finally, the trends in residential acquisition ability of households, the tenure status of dwellings, and housing starts by tenure are surveyed.

EARLY FEUDALISM TO THE CURRENT FREEHOLD-LEASEHOLD SYSTEM

The first major land reform occurred in the mid-seventh century. The Taika Reform amounted to a coordinated set of measures that attempted to strengthen the power of the imperial clan and those who governed in its name. A centralized administrative system that was created was patterned on that of T'ang China. All land originally the private preserve of the local clan chieftains was taken over by the central government. The land was to be allotted to each farm family according to the number and the ages of the individual family members. Taxes in the form of agricultural and textile products and labor were levied on the family-allotted land. These taxes were to be collected by local agents of the central government.

This reform did not take hold as designed. Many of the local chieftains reportedly retained their lands and their local supremacy with the labor of agricultural slaves and presented minimal tribute to the central authority. Even in the districts in which the land reform was implemented, the regular redistribution of land in accordance with changes in family composition broke down with time.

When tax exemptions were granted for certain types of land, a more complete form of private property rights evolved and challenged the central authority over land reallotment by family composition. Tax exemptions were granted for:

- Land belonging to shrines and temples;
- Land given to court nobles in reward for meritorious services; and
- Land newly reclaimed for fulfillment of the greater need for land from population increase.

The area of such privately controlled, tax-free land grew at the expense of the land area controlled by the central government. As the tax revenues of the central government declined, power passed from the central government to the new class of provincial, estate-owning warriors. The foundation was established for the feudal institutions that prevailed in one form or another from the twelfth to the nineteenth centuries.

The eight centuries from the twelfth to the nineteenth were denoted by great swings from centralization to decentralization. At first the feudal manors covered scattered tracts of land and were not necessarily under the exclusive dominance of a single knight. But the manors often were subjected to a multiplicity of fiscal obligations—called *shiki*—to members of the new military class and to the members of the old aristocracy. The coercive power behind these military and aristocratic rights came from the alliances between geographically separated knights whose alliances were usually based on family ties. When one of the important alliances—the Minamoto faction—reigned victorious over its Taira rivals, the first attempt at centralization occurred. Yoritomo's military government was established at Kamakura at the end of the twelfth century. The political stability and the consolidation of the military powers led to the formulation of a body of law governing property rights. Courts were established in Kamakura that were capable of passing judgment on the ownership of *shiki* rights in any part of Japan. An enforcement mechanism was designed by the central government to put into effect the judgments of the court. Agents, stewards, and constables were appointed in each province to carry out the court decisions across the land.

The Kamakura system did not last. Since the power of this central government depended on the personal and family loyalties that bound the provincial vassals to the central power, the central government's power declined with the passage of generations and the weakening of their loyalties. By the middle of the fourteenth century, the anarchy was complete. The right to collect taxes from the land depended on the power to defend physically the right rather than on the traditional right and custom. The old multiplayer *shiki* rights to a share in the produce of certain pieces of land by various powerful entities of the society were gradually replaced by *shiki* rights of a single feudal lord. This feudal lord was often a descendant of one of the Kamakura stewards. As the strong absorbed the weak during the next two centuries, the number of feudal lords grew smaller, and their domains increased in size.

The various domains were administered in various manners. Some domains were administered by bailiffs similar to the manner of the English feudal manors. In other domains a large number of smaller establishments were represented by owners who paid allegiance and tribute to the domain lord and cultivated the land by serf labor. At the height of the feudal wars of the fifteenth and sixteenth centuries, when the domains were rapidly changing hands, villages of more or less independent peasants had a high degree of local autonomy. They continued to be bound by their obligations to pay taxes to whoever happened to be the domain lord at the time.

As the number of feudal lords grew smaller under the system of the survival of the fittest, new alliances led to a reconcentration of power. The system established by the end of the sixteenth century became the forerunner of the modern Japanese agrarian structure. A single military authority was powerful enough to control the provincial feudal lords, adjudicating disputes among them and establishing legal principles necessary for the enforcement of ownership and cultivating right in land. Hideyoshi reigned in the sixteenth century until replaced at the beginning of the seventeenth century by the Tokugawa shogunate. Hideyoshi standardized the measurement methods and established a cadastral survey in the 1580s. He generally eliminated the samurai status of the country knights and divided the peasants in the villages from the non-landowning warrior class concentrated in the castle towns. The latter class was permitted the drawing of a rice stipend from the domain lord's granaries. The sale of peasant holdings was prohibited in 1643. Later, peasant land division on the basis of inheritance was prohibited by the Tokugawa government.

The Tokugawa land was partially administered by the shogunate directly and partially by the feudal lords over fiefs of varying size. About a quarter of the total land was administered directly by the shogunate. The remainder was divided into nearly 300 fiefs. Each of the feudal lords had his own army of samurai retainers and foot soldiers who lived in the fief's fortified castle town. The Tokugawa itself followed this pattern. The feudal lord of this period based his wealth on the rice tax levied in kind on the peasants of the fief. Out of the peasant rice payments, stipends of rice were paid to the lord's retainers, which were supplemented by income from fief enterprises such as mines and taxes on local industries. The cadastral register established land-ownership. The tax burden of each peasant household or family was determined by the amount of land and its quality as denoted on the land register. Peasant property rights were limited by the ban on land alienation, crop restrictions, and lack of freedom to leave the land.

The fief government, which was primarily a tax collection system, was administered from the castle town by locally stationed or itinerant samurai officials, district headmen, and village headmen. Generally, the district and village headmen were richer peasants appointed by the fief.

The rate of taxation was high. It tended to get higher as the standard of living of the tax-supported samurai class rose and as the Tokugawa regulations forced the feudal lords to spend half their time in the capital. Taxes commonly amounted to 60 percent of the peasant family's crop. Special levies and advance collections were frequent. In order for the feudal lords to spend half their time at the capital, they found it necessary to increase constantly the taxes and borrow from moneylending rice brokers. Peasant revolts recurred as peasant conditions deteriorated. The Tokugawa government thought highly of agriculture but thought little of the peasants who pursued agricultural work and supported the government system.

The Tokugawa rulers wished to establish a system that would last forever. A hereditary system overlaid the systems of allegiance and patronage with their forms of control and fiscal obligations. A disruptive element was the accumulation of debt by the rulers, the feudal lords, the samurai class, the district and village headmen, and the peasants. The rice merchants and moneylenders had to collect the overdue debts. While Yoshumune reaffirmed in the 1720s the ban on alienation, his reform system permitted the mortgaging of land. As the moneylenders and rice merchants acquired land through loan foreclosure, they became richer peasant and town merchants and members of an emerging class of small rural capitalists. The moneylenders were often village headmen, brewers, weavers, town merchants, and other such prosperous peasants and fief administrators. The middlemen administrators were in a position to see opportunities for profits from moneylending and to break fief regulations for their personal benefits. The moneylending town merchants acquired land in spite of the feudal regulations that prohibited such action. They were the creditors and financial advisers of the lords of the fiefs. In such a position the Homma family of Yamagata became Japan's biggest landowner in 1945.

When the customary ownership of land was transferred for debt collection, the new landowner might take over the cultivation of the land. Otherwise, the former owner might continue to cultivate the land. The tenant would retain responsibility for the original tax burden on the land and would assume a rent obligation to the new landlord or mortgagee. The rent could be considered the annual interest on the original mortgage that was still payable.

Another source of tenancy in the Tokugawa period was associated with the reclamation of land for more area for cultivation. To gain more income, the feudal rulers realized that more area under cultivation would lead to greater sources of income. The rice merchants had the capital resources for the costly irrigation and land clearance work. The rice merchants acquired the title to the land they reclaimed, and the peasants who actually did the reclamation work became the rice merchants' tenants. The country samurai and the non-samurai landlords of long standing often cultivated their lands through the labor of serfs who were allowed a small amount of land of their own. Since the landowner continued to hold title to all the land, the serf paid a form of rent on the land granted the serf household.

The Meiji Restoration sought to dismantle the old feudal regime and to build a new centralized administrative system. The government issued a decree in its first year that agricultural land was the property of the peasants. The government then started to resurvey the land. The productivity of each plot of land was evaluated in money terms. New land registers were compiled. This surveying and registration effort resulted in a 48 percent increase in the total amount of agricultural and residential land registered. Even though the peasants rioted in resistance to the effort, the new government accomplished its task. Title deeds were issued for each plot of land to those customarily considered to be in possession. The Tokugawa ban on the alienation of land and other such land-ownership restrictions were abolished. Private property rights were established. The land tax became an annual money tax of 3 percent of the assessed value of the land with an additional possible 1 percent tax for local government purposes.

The serfs became independent proprietors free to use and dispose of their land as they wished. They could change their occupation if they could find an appropriate alternative occupation. Since the privileged classes of the old regime and the officials associated with the new regime had to be paid along with the expenses of maintaining a military force to suppress local rebellions, the tax burden remained high. In some districts, the tax burden was lightened. On rice land, though, it still amounted to 35 percent of the value of an average crop. The 3 percent money tax was proclaimed a temporary measure that the government was imposing reluctantly. After a period of widespread rioting, the money tax for the central government was reduced to 2.5 percent, while the local tax was confined to 0.5 percent. Plans were established for the five-year revision of the land values for tax assessment purposes. After repeated postponement, the periodic tax assessment plan was abandoned in 1884. Gradually, the land tax was reduced to only 3 percent of the central government revenue by 1940.

The Meiji changes included confirmation of land-ownership by peasants and a takeover of village communal lands by the state or by rich and powerful individuals who influenced the commissioners in charge of title deeds. The fixed money land taxes had their disadvantages. When the land produced less crops than normal under poor weather conditions, the taxpayer was forced to borrow from moneylenders to pay the fixed taxes. In some instances, the poorer taxpayers had to sell crops at sacrifice prices to meet tax obligations rather than hold back the crops from the market until prices rose. The landlords could benefit from moneylending and rice brokerage under such circumstances.

The Meiji recognized only unconditional ownership; all other property rights were not recognized. Mortgagees were given title deeds to mortgaged land. The cultivators of tenanted land had essentially no property rights. Finally, the Civil Code of 1898 recognized the right of permanent tenancy as marketable property rights but imposed a maximum limit on their duration. Such claims were difficult to defend in a court of law.

Rents for tenanted land remained essentially the same; they were paid in kind and continued to represent about half of an average crop. Land taxes remained high. Debt continued to accumulate, land was mortgaged, and then title was transferred to the mortgagee when the debt was unpaid. As this transfer of title took place, the new landowner could cultivate his enlarged estate by himself, or he could lease the land to a tenant—quite often the former owner. The latter course was usually followed. Tenancy increased measurably, but the volume of hired laborers did not. Since the rents could be levied at a relatively high level due to the population pressure on the land, the landlord had a financial advantage to lease the excess land rather than hire labor for cultivation under the landlord's direction. As the high rent levels were maintained, the tax burden on the landlord was reduced. The rich got richer, and the poor got poorer.

By custom the peasant chose to remain on the land. High rents were paid due to the increased population pressure even on newly reclaimed land. As financial emergencies occurred, the peasant sold off his holdings parcel by parcel.

In the nineteenth century experiments were conducted in large-scale farming by enthusiastic ex-samurai newly returned from education in the West. Due to the high tenant rents, it was still more profitable for the landlord to rent the land than to use hired labor to cultivate the land on a large-scale basis. Rice production is not subject to cost savings through large-scale production methods. Rice production is labor-intensive.

Distress sale of land by farmers cultivating the land increased the prevalence of land tenancy. The financial distress often resulted from crop failures, illness, and a fall in the price of rice that coincided with the expense of a wedding or a funeral. Due to such distress sales of land the proportion of land cultivated by tenants reached 46 percent in 1941 and then stabilized. The stable tenancy relationships probably resulted from an increase in productivity through better crop strains, improved methods of cultivation, better pest control, and increased use of fertilizers. Yields per acre doubled between 1880 and 1940. Silkworm rearing began to provide high incomes per acre of mulberry trees.

When the government recognized the gradual demise of the peasant proprietor around the time of World War I, the government created credit facilities and encouraged the formation of agricultural associations and cooperatives that would help the tenant-cultivators to buy their cultivated land. The landlords were reaping most of the profits from rice and other agricultural production.

After the Rice Riots of 1918 and the growth of tenant unions, rent strikes, and numerous disputes, farm land investment became unattractive to many investors. Surplus agricultural labor was siphoned off the farms into the military service and war industries during World War II. After the war there was a scarcity of farm labor, and families and the government had to take steps to reorganize the agricultural community.

TRENDS IN LAND-OWNERSHIP

At the end of 1982, households owned two-thirds of the land in Japan. The government agencies, financial institutions, and cooperations other than financial institutions owned the remainder of the land. According to the Japan National Land Agency, the following land-ownership relationships exist:

Ownership Entity	**Percentage of Total Land Held**	**Billions of Yen**
Corporate bodies other than financial institutions	25.2	217,241.7
Financial institutions	1.5	12,523.6
Governments	5.9	50,810.8
Households	67.5	582,601.8

Private land-ownership increased more than 140 percent between 1973 and 1983. Most of the increase occurred with respect to "miscellaneous" land, which excludes housing land, farmland, and forestland and plains. Private ownership of housing land increased 167.5 percent over the 1973–1983 period. The Japanese people are eager to own their own homes.

In 1983 corporations owned 1.8 million hectares of land, an increase of 352,000 hectares compared with 1973. One hundred and one of these corporations were subject to taxation. Most of the corporate landholdings are found in forestland and plains. Only 25 percent of these landholdings is committed by corporations to housing land. About 70 percent of the land owned for selling by corporations with capital greater than 100 million yen was acquired more than 10 years ago. Of the land owned by corporations in 1983, 90 percent was held for business; only 10 percent was held for selling at profitable prices. Of the land owned for business purposes rather than for sales purposes, almost 90 percent was acquired 10 or more years ago, according to the Japan National Land Agency.

In 1977, according to the Tokyo metropolitan government, most of the corporate landholdings in the city area of 23 wards contained 5,000 square meters or more. In the Tokyo suburbs the corporate holdings generally surpassed 10,000 square meters.

TRENDS IN HOMEOWNERSHIP

The ability to purchase a home in Japan is reduced by the relationship between high residential land and building prices and average annual incomes. For example, the ratio between acquisition prices and incomes fluctuated between factors of 5 and 6.75 during the 1970s. That ratio remains high in comparison to U.S. home purchasing-power ratios; that is, it is more difficult for a young person to own a housing unit in Japan than it is in the United States. More time must be spent in saving money for this significant and costly expenditure.

From a high of 71 percent owner-occupied households in Japan in 1958, the early 1990s rate of owner-occupied households had fallen to 60 percent. The national homeownership rate was very stable around 60 percent during the decades of the 1970s and 1980s and the early 1990s, according to the "Housing Survey of Japan" (*Japan Real Estate Statistics 1999*), conducted by the Japan Management and Coordination Agency.

The homeownership rate for the greater Tokyo area continues to be considerably lower than the Japanese national homeownership rate. Since 1963, when the rate was 51 percent, the rate for the greater Tokyo area has fluctuated a little around the central rate of 50 percent. This situation is somewhat expected: Major cities usually exhibit much lower homeownership rates than rural or smaller city rates. In a relatively small area—the Kanto plain—the 28 million people of greater Tokyo live in densely developed housing areas.

In contrast, the homeownership rate of the United States continues to be 63 to 66 percent. A city such as New York would normally have a significantly lower rate due to the densely populated housing areas of greater New York.

CHAPTER SUMMARY

The current land-ownership and leasehold system is derived from earlier periods of land tenure. For example, land registration started in the early centuries. The cadastral system continued to the present. The feudal system gradually gave way to the private property system due to land financing and loan foreclosure.

Japanese land is owned today by government agencies, financial institutions, corporations, households, and other types of business organizations. More households seek to own their own homes; even more households wish to live in housing units with better residential environments. In Japan as a whole, the rate of owner-occupied housing runs 60 percent, while, within the greater Tokyo area, the same rate runs 50 percent; since 1968 both rates have been very stable.

REFERENCES

Building Construction Survey: Monthly Statistics of Japan. Tokyo: Japan Ministry of Construction (February 1984), table E-13.

Dore, R. P. "The Development of Japanese Agriculture." In *Land Reform in Japan*. London: Oxford University Press, 1959, ch. 1.

Hines, M. A. *Investing in Japanese Real Estate*. Westport, CT: Quorum Books, 1987.

Japan Real Estate Statistics 1999. Tokyo: Mitsui Fudosan Co., Corporate Planning and Research Department, January 1999, p. 20.

"Tenure of Dwellings, Japan, 1958–1983." In Statistics Bureau, *Housing Survey of Japan*. Tokyo: Japan Management and Coordination Agency.

5

Land Planning and Control: New Approaches

The well-organized land planning and control system of Japan continues to function well. The National Land Agency and other government ministries and agencies of Japan that deal with land planning and control matters continue to plan for the future in light of current conditions and prospective future changes. Where ample government funds were available for land planning and control by local governments, prefectures, and the federal government in earlier decades, funding for such government functions is now more stringent. With the revival of the economy, funds will be more readily available for implementing plans and programs.

This chapter on new approaches to land planning and control begins with the general status of land planning and control, the coordination of government land planning and control efforts, and the major problems currently faced by land planners. The chapter continues with a brief discussion of the system approach to land planning and control and the currently emphasized urbanization promotion and control areas. Discussion of the methods used, including land price approval and publication, expropriation, and environmental controls, follows. The grand design for the twenty-first century of Japan's new comprehensive national development plan is integrated into the chapter.

THE GENERAL STATUS OF LAND PLANNING AND CONTROL

An agency from the Prime Minister's Office heads the Japanese land planning and control system. The Japan National Land Agency works with prefectural and local government agencies to establish guidelines and action programs for nationwide land use programs. The major land uses that are subject to federal, prefectural, city, and neighborhood plans and controls are residential, commercial, industrial, institutional, forest, recreational, and agricultural land uses. One of the most important sectors of agricultural land use is the paddy field for rice production. Important areas of land planning include housing space, housing land supply, infrastructure planning and development, environment protection, earthquake precautions, and fire prevention and control. Transportation planning, control, and development are principal parts of the infrastructure planning and development. Highway and airport construction and redevelopment are important parts of transportation planning and control. For example, another runway is being added to the Narita International Airport east of Tokyo, and the authorities are considering the addition of international airports to the existing Osaka and Narita Airports. Other important areas of infrastructure decision making relate to water control and treatment, deregulation of railroads and the impact upon rail services, extension of rail and natural gas lines to more remote areas, and provision of community services and facilities for more remote areas.

Some of the infrastructure plans relate to the general government policy toward decentralization of the Japanese population. The dense concentration of people, businesses, and industries in the three major metropolitan areas—Tokyo, Osaka, and Kobe—continues to create major planning and control problems. For some time, the government has considered moving the government establishment—particularly the federal government establishment—from Tokyo to a site away from the existing capital city.

The "Grand Design for the 21st Century"

The fifth plan to be created under the Comprehensive National Land December Plan sets forth the "Grand Design for the 21st Century" (Appendix 5-1). In Part I, the basis for the planned national land development includes the major trends, the proposed, regionally distributed structure for Japan, the five basic objectives, and four initiatives toward the objectives. Part I also states that the New Plan advocates the importance of participation and cooperation in the restructuring of the land. In light of the severe economic climate and the need for a long-term decrease in public investment, the plan states that the public investment in the planned national infrastructure must be focused, efficient, and tailored to fit regional needs and promote investment that will benefit future generations. A new national land planning system will be developed from a complete review of the Comprehensive National Land Development Act and the National Land Use Planning Act and the need for a whole range of reforms to the existing system. Part I also contains proposals to deal with the problems that continue to confront the Tokyo metropolitan area and Okinawa.

Part B-6 (Specific Measures in the Plan), also displayed in Appendix 5-1, adds objectives for building a national land that is more environmentally friendly and for conserving land based on river basin spheres. Directions for urban development are summarized. Specific measures relate to (1) assuring people, including the growing group of elderly citizens, that they may lead secure and healthy lives, (2) assuring a favorable environment for new industries, (3) improving the transportation system, and (4) improving the information and communications systems.

As we consider the general status of land planning and control, we should take into account the social and cultural determinants of the Japanese urban and rural environments.

Social and Cultural Determinants

Let us start the review with the social determinants of Japan's urban and rural environments.

Social Determinants

The social determinants of Japan's urban and rural environments involve the changing age and income distributions, the change in family size over time, the gradual mixing of the races within the increasing population, and other social factors.

Due to improved health care, Japanese residents are living longer and are enjoying better lifestyles over their longer lifetimes. In the new millennium, the proportion of Japanese citizens over 60 years of age is relatively large, as it has become in Europe, the United States, and Canada. Unlike the rest of Asia and Africa, the proportion of young people is declining. But the decline in the proportion of young and middle-aged people in Japan is not due as much to the effects of AIDS (acquired immune deficiency syndrome) as it is in Africa and other parts of the world. Land planning is impacted by this change in age distribution. The relatively small apartments and houses may accommodate the residential demands of young people and the elderly. But the young people generally require residential land use in the central urban areas, while the elderly may prefer residential space in suburban areas with less traffic congestion and air pollution and more recreational opportunities, including golf courses and playing fields. As the elderly of Japan tend to seek suburban residential space, land in nearby areas needs to be set aside for medical, sports, and other elderly-related facilities to accommodate elderly demand for service. Hospitals, medical clinics, and retirement complexes, including nursing homes, need new locations for this expanding elderly population. The young people need shopping and recreational land development near their places of employment and residences.

The income distribution promises continued change from Japanese corporate restructuring and continued development of service and high-technology companies as traditional manufacturing companies decline in employment and land use. In past decades, the Japanese saved a relatively large portion of current income to establish reserves for eventual retirement, large-ticket items such as private passenger cars and vans, and other contingencies. The recession of the 1990s has reduced the size of the typical household savings and reserves as

Japanese prices of goods and services and government taxes have remained relatively high, while incomes have tended to decline. The outlook for the new millennium is higher unemployment, some reduction in personal and corporate taxation, personal earnings based on productivity and not seniority, and continued relatively high prices for goods and services, including medical and nursing home services. The accumulated savings of the typical household may decline further; incomes may decline outside the high-growth telecommunications and high-technology industries.

Family size started changing as the rural populations of Japan started moving into the major cities for employment. The households of many children who might assist with the farmwork in the rural areas now have changed, as the many households have moved to the major cities, to one- or two-child households. Now, to retain the accustomed lifestyles, both spouses of young couples must continue to work to buy the many assets that are a social necessity such as mobile phones, stylish clothing, and entertainment services in the increased leisure time. Marriages take place at older ages as female employees continue their work to finance "social necessities." Young couples put off childbearing until later years to accommodate two-spouse employment for a number of years. This occurs as the job market is providing higher-level positions for women. The newer employment positions for women that provide more enjoyment and more personal achievement in more managerial-type positions have attracted women to longer employment in the workplace.

The Japanese racial population mix in past centuries was very homogeneous. Interracial marriages were deeply frowned upon. Few foreigners of any race were allowed to migrate permanently or even temporarily to Japan. Policymakers recognized the restraints of the small land area of the multiple islands of Japan. Until recent decades, there was less of a scarcity of domestic and other unskilled labor in Japan. Recently, temporary and permanent immigrants of other races have been permitted entry to this highly industrialized country, mainly to fill the unskilled labor vacancies of the labor force. Immigrants from such countries as South Korea and the Philippines have filled these unskilled jobs in industry and have become domestic employees in homes. Immigrants of other races have recently been permitted to enter Japan temporarily and perhaps permanently to bring with them desired high technology and other advanced business and industry skills and knowledge. In this evolving process, the Japanese population has become a little more diverse. Businesspeople and educators from worldwide sources visit the country and work on relatively short tours of duty in Japan. The population of Japan is more diverse due to this steady flow of relatively temporary residents of multiple races.

Cultural Determinants

The cultural determinants of the Japanese urban and rural environments include the use of more leisure time with the shortened workweek and the care of elderly family members by the younger family members in retirement facilities separate from the homes of the younger family members. The cultural determinants of urban and rural environments also include the threat of the weakened corporate lifetime employment pattern, the change to promotion and advancement due to job productivity rather than longevity with the company, the acceptance of foreign workers for unskilled work positions, and the acceptance of relatively long commuting times to and from the workplace. Also involved are the continuing Westernization of the culture, the changing role of the female employee in the workplace, and the enduring attractions of the major urban places for entertainment, education, cultural enrichment, and employment opportunities.

The workweek is rapidly declining from a 10-hour-a-day, six-day standard workweek to more or less an eight-hour-a-day, five-day standard workweek. As companies restructure to survive in one of the longest recessions in Japan's economic history, permanent layoffs of many company employees are threatened in the future by many Japanese companies. Business and government have seen the need to shorten the workweek in order to create more jobs. The people who may lose their current employment at bankrupt or restructured companies may find other permanent and temporary employment as jobs are created in growth areas and as the normal workweek is shortened. If the same or more company and government work must be accomplished, more people may be employed.

Japan has long maintained a very low rate of unemployment in comparison with other highly industrialized countries. One reason for this low rate is the nature of the business–government culture up until the current time. For example, the major companies have continued for long periods to carry people on their payrolls for whom there was essentially no work. The lifetime employment culture led to this long-term situation. That cultural pattern is deteriorating. Companies that are seeking capitalistic investment returns on their stockholders' investments would like to purge their payrolls of unproductive personnel and to compensate their employees according to productivity as well as longevity with the firm. The ingrained culture of lifetime employment is slow to change. Therefore, it would be difficult in Japan to compensate employees only by their company productivity toward the company's goal of return on stockholder investment. It would be a major cultural deviation from past history—a history of high industrial productivity that has made Japan a world business leader.

Due to the economic prosperity of Japan, family support and care of elderly members are changing in terms of housing accommodations and medical insurance coverage for the elderly members. Instead of the older generation living in the same household with the younger generations of the family, the members of the older generation are tending to move to retirement complexes in the suburbs of major cities and other appropriate locations. At the same time, the Japanese federal government is changing the premiums and coverage of government-provided medical insurance coverage for Japanese citizens of the specified retirement age. Opportunities for real estate investment in Japanese retirement communities and nearby medical, entertainment, and shopping complexes that cater to the needs of retired Japanese people are being discovered and explored.

In addition to the cultural adaptation to the weakened corporate lifetime employment pattern and the very gradual change to promotion and workplace advancement based on job productivity rather than longevity, the society has grown to accept the presence of foreign workers who are needed for unskilled and skilled work. Instead of a highly homogeneous, single-race society, the Japanese society has grown more diverse with the increased presence of non-Japanese residents, including skilled and unskilled workers. Unskilled domestic, construction, manufacturing, and other workers are needed and are brought in from abroad. The culture of Japan is being infiltrated by the cultures of immigrants from the Republic of Korea, the Philippines, the People's Republic of China, other Asian countries, Europe, and North America. The growing, diverse permanent residents of Japan are causing a departure from the earlier homogeneous Japanese society.

There are repercussions for the Japanese culture from the continued growth of the major cities of Japan. The business culture accepts the inevitability of the long commuting time to and from the city workplace for a large percentage of Japanese businesspeople who live in distant suburbs and towns. As Japanese cities such as Osaka and Tokyo grow in population, single-family housing must be built in distant suburbs due to the lack of land closer to the center cities. To gain the increased space and privacy of single-family homes, the worker must live in the suburbs, where the commuting time to the center city is 1 to 1½ hours.

The Japanese culture continues to be greatly influenced by Western culture. For example, product advertisements constantly use Western models to market product advantages, benefits, and desirability. The consumer may favor mobile phones that are produced by U.S. or European companies; jewelry from Tiffany's of New York is highly preferred. At present, Japanese real estate professionals are greatly influenced by Western real estate practices such as investment yield calculation and real estate securitization methods.

The Japanese female has long observed a subservient role in the male-dominated society. The business culture has long been focused on the enterprising Japanese "company man" who holds a lifetime position with the company. The female company employee has been relegated for years to the role of secretary or hostess. The culture has emphasized the basic role of the female as one devoted to the home and the care of husband and children. The female employee has been hired with the general understanding that she will soon leave company employment to take her rightful place in the home. This cultural pattern is changing very slowly. It might have changed more rapidly in the decade of the 1990s if the long Japanese recession had not interfered in the evolutionary process. More women are being trained and educated for lifetime or at least longer-term jobs in more important positions in government and business. During the long recession of the 1990s, though, many college-educated women were hired after their male college-graduate colleagues had located employment. When jobs have been scarce even for newly minted college graduates, women have fared poorly in company recruiting efforts. As economic growth returns to Japan, more educated and trained women employees may gain better positions in larger numbers. More Japanese young people are marrying later in life and having fewer children so that both spouses may work to attain better lifestyles.

GOVERNMENT COORDINATION AND A SYSTEMS APPROACH

While federal land-planning policies are established by the federal government, local governments are expected to analyze their local area needs, devise alternative means for attacking the local problems, and request approval for action plans from prefectural and federal land-planning offices. The City Planning Act of 1968 (Appendixes 5-2, 5-3, and 5-4) provided procedures for the determination of city plans by the prefectural governor and by municipalities. The comprehensive approval system within the political and governmental bureaucratic hierarchy tends to assure full coordination of land planning and controls on all levels.

Since city planning involves changing land use patterns, numerous land use zones and districts, various project expediting areas, urban facilities and infrastructure, and urban development projects, a systems approach is utilized. An example of the Japanese government use of a systems approach to decision making and policy making applies to the housing sector (Appendix 5-5). Key policies lead to the improvement of housing conditions and improvement of residential environments. These two areas of housing improvement are integrated through a systems approach.

THE MAJOR PROBLEMS CURRENTLY FACED BY LAND PLANNERS

With the decline in land prices since 1991, land planning may be encouraged in the long run. At the present time, land is more affordable for government purchase for land use restructuring. The federal government has been spending freely for infrastructure development, for bank and other financial institution loans to keep loans available for businesses and consumers, and for consumer financing of homes and other necessary expenditures. The debt-to-GDP ratio has reached alarming heights in terms of comparison with other highly developed countries. While the federal government increases its spending, the tax receipts are very much reduced from previous levels for all levels of government. Business profits and consumer spending are down from previous levels so tax receipts tend to be lower during this recession. Since salaries and wages have risen in recent years far faster than the rate of inflation, income tax receipts from individual taxpayers may be more stable than business income and sales tax receipts. The expected decline in personal income from the expected company layoffs in the corporate restructuring movement will presage reduced tax receipts in future years.

The purchase of land by the government for infrastructure redevelopment is discouraged due to the growing government deficit spending but encouraged if a favorable economic impact is foreseen. In the longer run, the infrastructure redevelopment that has been delayed for so long due to relatively high land prices may be encouraged due to the relatively low land prices now. Of course, the government will want to wait until land prices stabilize at a new, low level. As long as land prices are expected to decline further, both public and private investors will refrain in general from further land purchases.

Since land prices are declining in both urban and rural areas, purchase price approvals by the government assume little significance. The speculation that led to the exorbitant land prices of the late 1980s and early 1990s is no longer present; the government price approval program is no longer needed as it once was. But the publication of land and building purchase prices for real estate appraisal purposes may still be needed. As the government continues to plan and control the use of land, the government needs all indications of property value in its deliberations.

Commercial tenant tenure has been a problem for owners who wished to redevelop or renovate their existing properties. Many land use changes are sought by government planners. But the planners and the building owners must recognize the tenant tenure rights. At present, when most building owners wish to redevelop or renovate their land improvements that are leased, they may find vacant space in the same building or nearby for the relocation of lessees due to the higher vacancy rates. The tenants may agree to such nearby relocation during the existing building renovation or redevelopment. At the same time, the Japanese court system is gradually moving to weaken the previous commercial tenant tenure rights in this area. In previous years, if tenants would not agree to the owner's planned tenant relocation program during reconstruction, the building owners and planners were blocked from implementing their reconstruction plans.

The aging of the population in general and the changes in the cultural patterns lead to new housing demand. The planners must anticipate the needs of retired persons whose retirement incomes may be rising with company and government establishment of pension funds. The management of pension fund moneys may bring higher investment returns with the financial restructuring and development of money management systems. At the same time, the culture seems to be moving away from multigenerational cohabitation in a single housing unit.

Housing for the elderly in separate and possibly community-center accommodations is a major planning issue at present.

Plans and programs for increased and improved transportation facilities are needed. Increased incomes have resulted in more vehicle purchases by households and companies. The increased use of vacation time will prompt more automobile traffic on the roadways in all parts of Japan. Mass transit needs extension to more remote parts of the island nation as part of the government's economic development programs. Adequate transportation facilities are desired by relocating business and industry.

Earthquake protection, water control, and environmental controls continue to be problems that need solutions. Earthquakes continue to shake Japan. Earthquake- and fireproof buildings are needed. Increased numbers of parks and recreational areas may be utilized as future evacuation areas in the case of disasters. Typhoons continue to cause destruction each year; the water control measures in effect are still inadequate for the continual problems. The pollution of major metropolitan areas that house pollutive industries will be less a problem as heavy industries are redeveloped into high-technology, non-polluting industries. But many sources of air, noise, water, and other pollution still exist. As automobile traffic increases, the pollution from automobile exhausts will increase even with advanced non-pollutive automobile designs. Extension of the railroads into more sections of Japan will increase noise pollution in the newly served areas.

One survey in land use in habitable areas indicated three of the most important perceived problems among those interviewed:

- Streets are irregularly arranged, and there are many narrow or winding roads.
- Farmland and forests were lost due to disorderly development of housing land.
- There are insufficient numbers of parks and green tracts.

Problems indicated by medium-level rankings were as follows:

- House lots are being developed too slowly, and there are still many vacant lots.
- Use and control of farmland and forests are being improperly performed.
- Houses are sprawled on poor ground, and the outbreak of disasters is feared.
- Houses and factories are mixed together, and the environment is poor.

THE METHODS USED IN LAND PLANNING AND CONTROL

Several devices and methods are utilized by the various levels of government to guide and control land use. Some of the devices and methods are used constantly; others are seldom used. These devices and methods include:

- Land price approval and publication
- Building codes

- Zoning ordinances
- Building permits
- Designations of urban promotion and urban control areas
- Expropriation
- Preemptive right
- Environmental controls

The planning and control measures that are constantly used include land price publication, building codes, zoning ordinances, building permits, and environmental controls. Since land prices have plummeted from the peaks in the late 1980s and early 1990s, there has been little need for the government to approve property prices to control speculation. The government seldom uses its preemptive right. It expropriates or condemns properties only when public purposes require its exercise and when there is consensus that use of the right of condemnation is appropriate. The designation of urban promotion and urban control areas for implementation of government programs was promulgated in the 1980s and may not be appropriate for the current land planning programs.

Land Price Approval and Publication

Land price approval and publication, a device for control of land speculation, were widely used and enforced by the government in the 1980s and early 1990s. At present, land prices for widespread properties across Japan are published for the indication of land value to prospective investors and real estate appraisers. Recently, land price publication has revealed the continuing decline of real property values in the six major metropolitan areas and other parts of Japan.

Building Codes

Since Japan is constantly threatened by disasters, building codes have long been important to the citizens for their ultimate protection from the consequences of disasters. Currently, building codes encourage the construction of fireproof and earthquake-proof buildings for housing, commercial, institutional, and industrial purposes. The fireproofing requirements for wooden structures are particularly stringent.

Use Zones and Districts

Numerous use zones and districts exist for land use control purposes. Explanations of the city planning classifications, the zoning objective for each zone and district, the restricting law, and the nature of the land use restrictions in effect in the late 1980s are indicated in Exhibit 5-1.

Building Permits

While building permits are seldom given for land development in urbanization control areas, they are normally issued in substantial volume in urbanization promotion areas. Building permits are issued for housing construction in "urbanizing" districts, urban improvement districts, and areas as yet without development plans.

Authorization from the government may be required for any building on surface area greater than 1,000 square meters. The criteria for the government authorization and issuance of a license are established by national law related to urban development, and the law is applied by the prefectures. Each prefecture has its own criteria for licensure. The prefecture views the development situation, the adequacy of the public utilities, and other such relevant factors. It may take two to three years to obtain the necessary license.

Expropriation

The parties that can employ the right of land expropriation or condemnation include municipalities, government departments, public institutions, concessionaires of public services, and private individuals. Private and public property of all parts of Japan is subject to expropriation. The expropriation is usually based on the legal reserve principle. A specific organization is utilized for the action when expropriation is declared appropriate through public necessity and use.

Recently, land and houses needed to be acquired in the path of the planned new runway for the Narita International Airport. The government could have used the power of eminent domain to involuntarily acquire the property. Due to the characteristics of the property owners and the lack of a consensus in the affected area that the power of eminent domain should be employed, the government declined to use its lawful power. The design for the new runway was altered so that the particular area was not affected.

Preemptive Right

The government may exercise its preemptive right in the purchase of real estate since the establishment of this legal right in Japan in 1963. The following entities may employ the preemptive right: municipalities and public, semipublic, and private persons and companies. The government takes note of the sale contract and generally pays the equivalent of the sale contract price that was drawn up by the other party. The government generally uses the preemptive right to buy property for the creation of green space, extension of public utility lines, acquisition of land for new and expanding industry, the renovation or creation of new districts, the creation of land reserves, and reduction of land speculation.

Exhibit 5-1

Use Zones and Districts Utilized in Japanese Land Planning and Control

Classification of City Planning	Objectives of the Plan	Restricting Law	Matters Restricted	Procedure	Decision Made: Number of Cities	Decision Made: Area (ha)
(1) Use zone		Articles 48, 52, 53, 54, 55, 56, and 56-2, Building Standards Law	Use of the building coverage, diagonal line limitation depending on the neighboring plot, restriction on the northern diagonal line, the height of multi-storied buildings by the sun shadow	Subject to confirmation by the construction examining body	1,358	1,619,179.7
Category 1 exclusive residential zone	To preserve the good environment of residential district of low-storied buildings					
Category 2 exclusive residential zone	To preserve the good environment of residential district of multi-storied buildings					
Residential zone	To preserve mainly the housing environment					
Neighborhood commercial zone	To promote commercial and other services, chiefly to provide the residents with daily necessities					
Commercial zone	To promote mainly commercial and other activities					

	Light-industrial zone	To promote industries which do not aggravate the living environment					
	Industrial zone	To promote mainly industries					
	Exclusive industrial zone	To promote industries					
(2)	Special use zone	To encourage the land utilization for special purposes and to preserve the environment in the use zone	Building Standards Law 49, municipal ordinances	Use of building	Subject to confirmation by the construction examining body	180	29,655.8
	Special industrial zone	(1) To preserve and nurture as a local industry the domestic industries, such as textile and woodworking, in the residential zone					
		(2) To limit, from the pollution prevention point of view, the types of industry to be established in the exclusive industrial zone, the light-industrial zone, or the industrial zone of the existing built-up area					
	School zone	To preserve the environment of the area where educational and cultural facilities, such as schools and research institutes, are concentrated					

Exhibit 5-1 (continued)

Classification of City Planning	Objectives of the Plan	Restricting Law	Matters Restricted	Procedure	Decision Made	
					Number of Cities	Area (ha)
Retail-shops zone	(1) To promote convenience of the retail-shop-concentrated area					
	(2) To encourage the establishment of specialty shops, in the commercial zone in particular					
Office zone	To protect and encourage the establishment of governmental and other office buildings					
Welfare zone	To preserve a good welfare environment where hospitals and other medical facilities are located					
Amusement and recreation zone	(1) To encourage the concentration of amusement facilities in large cities					
	(2) To protect and encourage the concentration of game facilities, such as bowling alleys and restaurants, in the residential zone					
	(3) To preserve the environment of recreation facilities, such as seaside resorts and large parks					

		(4) To protect and encourage the concentration of hotels, game facilities, etc. in summer resorts, hot spring resorts, etc.					
	Tourist industry zone	To protect and encourage the concentration of facilities, such as hotels necessary for the utilization of tourism resources, in tourist resorts					
	Special business zone	(1) To protect and encourage the concentration of wholesale related facilities, such as shops and offices, etc.					
		(2) To protect and encourage the concentration of distribution-related facilities, such as truck terminals					
		(3) To protect and encourage the concentration of wide-range service facilities, such as gas stations, in the areas along the trunk roads, etc.					
(3)	Building height control district	The upper and lower limits are established for the building height to maintain the environment of the urban area and to promote land utilization in the use zone	Building Standards Law § 58	Height of building	Subject to confirmation by the construction examining body	142	285,721.8

Exhibit 5-1 (continued)

Classification of City Planning	Objectives of the Plan	Restricting Law	Matters Restricted	Procedure	Decision Made: Number of Cities	Decision Made: Area (ha)
(4) Intensive-land utilization district	To make a rational, intensive use of land in the urban area in the use zone and to renovate the functions, the maximum and minimum floor-area ratio, the maximum building coverage, the minimum building area, and the restriction on the wall location are established	Building Standards Law § 59	Floor-area ratio and building coverage, building area and wall location	Subject to confirmation by the construction examining body	120	590.7
(5) Specified block	To improve the urban areas, zones are replotted and the new floor-area ratio, height limit, and wall location are established	Building Standards Law § 60	Floor-area ratio, building height, and wall location	Subject to confirmation by the construction examining body	13	112.1
(6) Fire-prevention district, Quasi-fire-prevention district	A zone provided to remove dangers of fire in urban areas	Building Standards Law § 61, § 62	The structure of building, etc.	Subject to confirmation by the construction examining body	590	19,796.9 215,193.3
(7) Urban aesthetic district	Established to maintain the orderly appearance of urban areas	Building Standards Law § 68, municipal ordinances	Lot, structure, and facilities of building	Subject to confirmation by the construction examining body and a procedure stipulated by ordinances	5	1,356.3

(8) Scenic beauty district	Established to maintain the scenic beauty of cities	City Planning Law § 58, the Cabinet orders postulating the basis for regulations on construction in scenic beauty district, municipal ordinances	Construction, land development, felling of trees	Regulated by ordinances	217	161,306.5
(9) District with parking facilities	A zone where automobile traffic is heavy in a commercial zone or neighboring commercial zone and where the utility of roads and smooth road traffic should be secured	Parking Space Act § 20, municipal ordinances	Installation of parking facilities for large buildings	Obligated by ordinances	66	12,624.7
(10) Port side district	Provided to operate harbors	Port and Harbor Law 40, 40-2, 41	Construction of buildings and structures	Municipal ordinances (restrictions apply when zones are specified)	276	38,965.6
(11) Special preservation district of historic landscape	A zone which is a component to the area where a historical place is preserved	Ancient Towns Law § 8	Installation of buildings and other structures, alteration of land, felling of trees, etc.	Subject to approval of a prefectural governor	7	3,786.1
(12) Category 1 preservation district of historic landscape	The Category 1 preservation district of historic landscape constitutes an important part of preserving a historical place and should be preserved by strictly limiting the alteration of the present state	Ancient Towns Law § 8	Installation of buildings and other structures, alteration of land, felling of trees, etc.	Subject to approval of a prefectural governor	1	125.6

Exhibit 5-1 (continued)

Classification of City Planning	Objectives of the Plan	Restricting Law	Matters Restricted	Procedure	Decision Made: Number of Cities	Decision Made: Area (ha)
Category 2 preservation district of historic landscape	The Category 2 preservation district of historic landscape is a zone which should be preserved by restricting a substantial change of the present state. (A certain part of Asuka-Mura is said to be delimited and specified as this type of zone.)				1	2,278.4
(13) Green space conservation district	This is a zone which makes up a good, natural environment in a city-planning area	Urban Green Space Conservation Law § 5	Almost same as above	Subject to approval of the prefectural governor	24	1,722.5
(14) Distribution business district	A zone which should be arranged as a distribution business area in view of the availability of trunk roads and railways in the specified area of a large city	Commercial Distribution Business Law § 5	Construction of buildings and other structures	Certain items are prohibited by law; buildings must be confirmed by the construction examining body and must be granted an approval of the prefectural governor	18	1,706.7

(15) Category 1 agricultural zone reserved in UPA	In areas of farming land, etc. of UPA, more than a certain size, the good living environment and land for public facilities are secured to prevent public hazards or disasters	Law Concerning the Agricultural Land § 8	Construction of buildings and other structures, change of land features by housing land formation, removal of soil or stones, etc., reclamation	Subject to approval of the mayor	22	335.5
Category 2 agricultural zone reserved in UPA					21	287.4
(16) District for preservation of traditional structures	To preserve the environment of traditional buildings, the value of which is formed with it	Cultural Properties Protection Law 83-3, ordinances of municipalities	Construction of buildings and other structures, changes of land features by housing land formation, etc., felling of trees	Subject to approval of the mayor and the municipal board of education	11	216.0
(17) Airplane noise pollution prevention zone and Special airplane noise pollution prevention zone	To prevent noise hazards and to promote rational land utilization in areas suffering from intense noise from airplanes in the vicinity of a specified airport (New Tokyo International Airport)	Special Airport Law § 5	Construction of schools, hospitals, houses, etc.	Airplane noise pollution prevention zone: subject to confirmation of the construction examining body; Special airplane noise pollution prevention zone: construction of schools, hospitals, and living houses is prohibited by law and must be granted an approval of the prefectural governor	—	—

Source: Government of Japan.

Environmental Assessment and Control

A system has been established for environmental assessment. Various levels of government are involved in the systematic environmental assessment of such projects as:

- Reclamation by public water bodies
- Port and harbor construction plans
- Locations of industrial complexes
- Establishment of specified facilities in the Seto Inland Sea
- Various public utility projects
- Thermal power stations
- Superhighway, driveway, national road, bypath, dam, lake, and drainage projects
- Building land development.

In 1965 the Pollution Control Council was set up in the Ministry of Health and Welfare as the first step toward the control of environmental pollution. At the same time the Environmental Pollution Control Service Corporation was established, and a Special Committee for Countermeasures against Industrial Pollution was organized in the national Diet. By 1967 the Diet passed the Basic Law for Environmental Pollution Control. This law provided for the establishment of Environmental Pollution Control Councils in each prefecture and a Central Council for Control of Environmental Pollution in the Prime Minister's Office. By 1970 a series of supplementary laws was passed that covered air pollution, water pollution, noise regulation, prevention of offensive odors, treatment of waste products, and safety of chemical substances.

CHAPTER SUMMARY

Japan has a well-organized land planning and control system that is changed to fit the circumstances of the times by the Japan National Land Agency and its associated agencies on the local and prefecture level. The implementation of the policies and regulations depends on the financing provided by the federal, prefecture, and local governments.

At any one time, a number of public projects associated with land planning and control are under way. When the economy reflects recessionary conditions, the government tends to spend more funds on infrastructure to create jobs and spending power while attacking the existing infrastructure problems. That situation exists at the present time. Such a situation may also exist when elections are pending for the lower and upper houses of the Diet. Under this circumstance, infrastructure spending also satisfies potential voters in the various districts where government funds are applied.

The 1998 passage of Japan's New Comprehensive National Development Plan, which has been labeled "the Grand Design for the 21st Century," reflects the adaptation to changing national conditions. From the establishment of the major trends leading to the adoption of the new law, the New Plan sets out five basic objectives that lead toward the alleviation of the currently identified problems and four initiatives that support the five objectives. The five objectives relate to the creation of independent regions, citizen safety and security, the relationship of people with the natural environment, the restructuring and deregulation of business, and regional interaction with other countries. The four initiatives deal with building nature-rich residential areas, renovation of urban areas, formation of regional cooperation corridors, and formation of international spheres of interaction on a large scale. These objectives and initiatives are associated with planned national infrastructure, establishment of a new national land planning system, dealing with the problems of the Tokyo Metropolitan Area, and dealing with the Okinawa problem. The specific measures relate to making the national land more environmentally friendly, conservation of the river basin spheres, direction of urban development, provisions for citizen security, creation of a favorable environment for new industries, improvement of transportation systems, and improvement of information and communications systems. These objectives will be implemented through the coordination of government on the various levels and utilization of a systems approach. The objectives and specific measures for meeting the objectives indicate the major problems currently facing land planners.

A number of methods are used in Japanese land planning and control. Building codes, zoning ordinances, building permits, the right of expropriation, the preemptive right, and environmental assessment and control are methods used in Japan that are similar to those used in industrialized and other less developed countries. Continual environmental assessment and control methods are also common to Japan, Europe, the United States, and many other countries of the world. The land price approval and publication system is unique to Japan. This system was created and implemented by the national government as an attempt to control the continued rise in national land prices in the 1980s and early 1990s.

Appendix 5-1. Japan's New Comprehensive National Development Plan: "Grand Design for the 21st Century" (Planning and Coordination Bureau, National Land Agency, Japan)

INTRODUCTION

Japan's New Comprehensive National Development Plan was approved by the Cabinet on March 31, 1998. This is the fifth plan under the Comprehensive National Land Development Act.

The Japanese economy has now reached a crucial turning point. With the collapse of the "bubble economy," the advent of an age of megacompetition, and an increasingly aging population, the people of Japan have begun to lose sight of their objectives and are concerned for the future of the nation. This plan, subtitled "Grand Design for the 21st Century," was formulated with a view to providing people with a perspective on the twenty-first century and helping to overcome the stagnation that Japan is currently facing.

PART I. BASIS OF THE PLANNING NATIONAL LAND DEVELOPMENT

Major Trends behind the New Plan

The people of Japan are facing new changes and trends, all of which must be accommodated as the background to the New Plan. They are as follows:

1. Lifestyles and values are diversifying; for instance, people increasingly place a higher value on mental, than on material, fulfillment.
2. Globalization has moved forward. In trade, the rise of the Asian economies coupled with the participation of East European nations in the global market has brought about an era of megacompetition between industries. Environmental issues that need to be tackled on a global scale have emerged and are likely to become more severe. In addition, we are likely to experience worldwide shortages of energy, food, and other natural resources as time moves on.
3. The number of elderly people is increasing, and the birthrate is among the lowest in the world. These factors are bringing us into an aging society. The population of Japan is predicted to start to decrease sometime soon after the beginning of the 21st Century.
4. The introduction of a highly informed society will help to overcome the constraints on money and time imposed by distance.

National Land Use in the 21st Century

Japan's population and functions have been highly concentrated in a Pacific belt, with Tokyo at the center. This has led to overpopulation and over-concentration in this single zone. Deliberation on a structure that will be suitable for the 21st century leads us to understand the necessity to transform this uni-axial/unipolar structure into one composed of self-reliant, multiple subregions.

The New Plan proposes a regionally distributed structure that consists of four subregions; a Northeastern Zone, a Japan Sea Coastal Zone, a New Pacific Ocean Coastal Zone, and a Western Zone.

Five Basic Objectives

The New Plan sets out five basic objectives that allow the major trends to be tackled and that build a basis for implementing the Grand Design for the 21st century by 2010 to 2015. These objectives are:

1. Create regions that are independent and that residents can take pride in.
2. Make Japan a safe place to live, protected against natural disasters including earthquakes, and guarantee its citizens a stable way of life through old age, without fear of shortages of resources.
3. Reorganize people's relationship with the natural environment so that they can enjoy nature's blessings and nourish them for future generations.
4. Restructure the economy, deregulate, and develop new business activities to create a society that is attractive and vibrant.
5. Enable all of Japan's regions to interact directly with other countries.

Four Initiatives toward the Objectives

The New Plan proposes four initiatives to attain the five basic objectives effectively. These initiatives are:

1. *Build nature-rich residential areas.* Regions including rural villages and small and medium-sized towns that are in areas of abundant greenery will become the sites of nature-rich communities. These residential areas will become self-reliant, with modern amenities in a green and pleasant living environment.
2. *Renovate metropolitan areas.* Metropolitan centers have become overcongested. These areas will be renovated and restored to a level where they operate efficiently once again, based on an advanced urban infrastructure.
3. *Form regional cooperation corridors.* Life in the regions will be revitalized and made self-reliant by forming regional cooperation corridors, in which regions are developed by the concerted efforts of local authorities. In these corridors, regions are able to complement each other and share resources and local features.
4. *Form international spheres of interaction on a large scale.* Large-scale international spheres of interaction will be formed that will make every part of Japan a possible partner capable of interaction with the rest of the world. Each sphere will make optimum use of its own regional characteristics and be independent from Tokyo. In order to make this possible, each sphere will have global communication capabilities (including international business and convention centers and international transport hubs, including airports, linked by high-speed trunk roads).

Participation and Cooperation as the Keys to National Land Development

The New Plan advocates the importance of participation and cooperation in restructuring the land. It is essential to encourage not only local governments but also private enterprises, non-profit organizations, and individuals to participate actively in discussions and the implementation of regional development. The promotion of further cooperation between local governments makes it possible to maximize achievement; such cooperation will enable them to combine the resources and local features that each of them possesses.

Investing in the Planned National Infrastructure

In the current severe fiscal climate and with the long-term decrease in investment potential in the public sector, it is important to ensure that investment will be truly effective and focused. The plan advocates the following proposals:

1. Focus investment into attaining the basic objectives outlined in this plan. Furthermore, to ensure that the investment is effective, direct it toward projects that directly contribute to the four initiatives.
2. Increase investment efficiency:
   a. Promote cooperative investment that extends beyond national ministries and local public entities.
   b. Introduce more competition to bring down construction costs.
   c. Maximize the use of the existing infrastructure, including reuse of existing facilities.
   d. Assign project investment priorities based on objective evaluations that include cost-benefit analyses.
   e. Promote private sector investment in the infrastructure based on studies of advanced models such as the Private Finance Initiative in the United Kingdom.
3. Tailor investments to suit regional characteristics; encourage investment in development that is tailored to particular regional characteristics, including providing equality of access to advanced urban facilities.
4. Promote investment that will benefit future generations:
   a. Develop new technologies that bring about new possibilities for development in the 21st century.
   b. Encourage investment that emphasizes new perspectives, including environmental concerns.
   c. Continue to study closely methods that ensure that investment is effective, including timely feedback on evaluation of completed projects and improvement of methods of cost-benefit analysis.
   d. Ensure that the burden of investment is shared appropriately between regions, the government, and the people.

Establishing a New National Land Planning System

Having reviewed trends in people's demands for national land planning over the past half century, the New Plan advocates the necessity for a complete review of the Comprehensive National Land Development Act and the National Land Use Planning Act and the establishment of a new national land planning system in their place. The review will be carried out from the following perspectives:

1. *Revised aims and concepts for national land planning.* National land planning embraces a wide range of ideas, not only related to development but also related to the

conservation and proper use of land. It is therefore necessary to establish clear definitions of the concepts and to develop a new comprehensive national land planning scheme.

2. *The range of the reforms.* The relationship between national planning and regional planning should be clarified as they relate to a whole range of reforms, including devolution and administrative reform. In addition, procedures should be improved to reflect the opinions of those affected as much as possible.

Proposals to Deal with Problems Related to the Tokyo Metropolitan Area

To solve the overconcentration of functions in the Tokyo Metropolitan Area and the resulting problems and to enable Tokyo to continue to fulfill its role as one of the major cities of the world, the New Plan makes the following proposals:

1. Efforts should be made to halt the excessive concentration of advanced urban functions in the center of Tokyo. These functions should be redistributed to the areas surrounding Tokyo and the other regions.
2. In the light of the national land policy, it will be effective to transfer the functions of the capital from Tokyo to the other regions. Positive consideration should be given to making this a reality. A precondition to the transfer is a national consensus under open and fair procedures, based on the Act for Relocation of the National Diet and Other Organizations.

Development of Okinawa Facing Garrison Base Problem

Since 1972, when Okinawa was returned to Japan, disparities between Okinawa and mainland Japan in income levels, unemployment rate, and so forth have been narrowed as a result of the Japanese government's policy of vigorous investment in the island. However, Okinawa still carries the major part of the burden of the U.S.–Japan Security Pact, with 75 percent of the U.S. military installations sited there.

In this age of globalization, the island's geographical and environmental features, together with its open-minded people and their unique traditions, must all be taken into account in any development plan for Okinawa. Under this plan, Okinawa will become a "Pacific Crossroads"—a center for the Pacific area and instrumental in promoting peace—and this will be a major cultural and socioeconomic contribution to the nation. Implementation of the Final Report of the Special Action Committee on Okinawa (SACO) will be an important step in reducing the number of military installations in Okinawa and the limitations on land usage that they impose.

PART B-6. SPECIFIC MEASURES IN THE PLAN

Building a National Land That Is More Environmentally Friendly

In order to leave to our children and grandchildren a country with a well-preserved and maintained natural environment, the New Plan proposes that the following tasks be carried out:

1. Securing areas of nature where wildlife can thrive.
2. Creating a network of these areas covering several prefectures.
3. Building a national land where the environment is valued and preserved by encouraging people to stop wasting resources and energy and creating a way of life that is more in harmony with the cycles of nature.

National Land Conservation Based on River Basin Spheres

National land conservation and maintenance can be carried out effectively by introducing policies tailored to the concept of a river basin sphere that includes the river basin, the floodplain, and other areas relating to a river. Issues such as water pollution, land erosion, floods, and unattended forests and farmland arising in river basin spheres and the interrelations between them will be addressed effectively. Urban areas that are supplied with water from a river will be included in its river basin sphere.

Direction of Urban Development

The New Plan puts forward the following proposals for the direction of urban development:

1. Urban development should focus on building and conserving advanced urban facilities that provide people with a comfortable living environment, thus contributing to improved quality of life and strengthening regional vitality.
2. In order to restructure the country into self-reliant subregions, functions that are presently overconcentrated in the Tokyo Metropolitan Area will be shared between major core city areas composed of the three major metropolitan areas, cities acting as provincial centers, and bigger cities in the prefectures across the whole nation. In these major core city areas, urban functions will be improved and will serve the needs of the suburban areas.
3. At the same time as the metropolitan areas are being renovated, the urban functions in local cities should be improved in relation to the size and the location of each city. This should be carried out with interregional cooperation, and each region should use its resources fully to revitalize its centers of commerce. Regions should establish the foundations for their own independent development and should create a living envi-

ronment with abundant greenery in which people can lead rich lives, integrating regional characteristics such as the history, culture, and industries of the region.

Enabling People to Lead Secure Lives

The New Plan advocates the following to enable people to lead secure lives:

1. In order to prepare for an aged society, it is necessary to construct a social support system that will enable elderly people to live with peace of mind. For this purpose, a system should be established to provide them with health and medical care and welfare services in an integrated and comprehensive manner. In addition, an infrastructure should be provided for long-term care services in the communities.
2. Welfare-conscious communities should be built that provide the elderly and the disabled with continuous barrier-free access to houses and public facilities.
3. Energy and food provision should be stabilized.

Creating a Favorable Environment for New Industries

Increased competition enhanced by globalization and very rapid technological change is compelling Japanese industry to restructure. In order that individuals and firms can adapt smoothly to these changes, the New Plan declares that the Japanese government will give support by providing an environment favorable to their activities.

The government will:

1. establish and improve research and development (R&D) facilities and strengthen its support for human resource development so that individuals and firms can produce technological innovation;
2. expand support for venture businesses by providing venture capital and encourage industry–government–university partnerships to help new start-ups;
3. create less-regulated markets in sectors such as telecommunications, transport, and energy supply to improve the business environment through cost reductions.

Proposals to Improve Transportation Systems

1. All regions of Japan are anticipated to communicate more with other countries, particularly with their East Asian neighbors. In light of this, the New Plan proposes the long-term creation of an "East Asian one-day zone," in which international airports and harbors will be improved and new ones constructed. Within this zone, people will be able to travel to their destination and conduct business within one day.
2. One of the main goals of improving transportation systems within Japan is to form a system that will support cooperation and active exchange between regions, providing people in every region with equal access. Against this background, the New Plan

proposes the long-term creation of "regional half-day trip zones," in which people can travel to another region and return within half a day. This concept aims at providing easier access from regional residential areas to cities with full urban amenities, including shopping malls, general hospitals, and the full range of educational facilities, by improving roads, highways, and railways.

Proposals to Improve Information and Communications Systems

In order to improve information and communications systems toward an "information-communications-based society," the New Plan advocates the following proposals:

1. Provide a nationwide advanced infrastructure including fiber-optic networks that can be accessed by everyone.
2. Encourage people to use the network fully by providing proper education and use the network for various services including teleworking and telemedicine so that people can remain active both in their personal lives and in business.

National Land Agency
1-2-2, Kasumigaseki, Chiyoda-ku
Tokyo 100-8972, Japan
e-mail: zensou@nla.go.jp

Appendix 5-2. City Planning Law

A City Planning Law, which abrogated the then existing law on this subject and the Law concerning Building Land Development Projects, was enacted in 1968. Briefly, the law provides for the designation as a unified urban area of any area, including a built-up section in a city, town, or village, for which integrated development, improvement, and construction is necessary. The criteria for the selection of such areas are provided by a cabinet order. A city planning area extending over two or more prefectures is designated by the minister of construction after hearing the opinions of the prefectural governor. A city planning area within a prefecture is designated by the prefectural governor after ascertaining the opinion of the cities, towns, and villages concerned and of the local city planning council.

Two types of planning areas are envisaged, the urbanization promotion area and the urbanization control area. The former refers to an existing built-up area or an area where preferential treatment has to be given for systematic urbanization to occur in the course of ten years or less. The latter is an area where urbanization or premature urban development should be curbed. Every city plan should decide zoning areas and districts and urban facilities as listed in the law. The city plan may contain one or more of the following types of built-up area development projects: land readjustment projects, new residential built-up area development projects, industrial estate development projects, and built-up area renewal projects.

The law requires that city plans conform to certain standards. Important among these are plans that shall conform to the National Comprehensive Program, the National Capital Region Development Program, and other regional development programs. They are also required to conform to the state's programs covering roads, rivers and railways, harbors, airports, and other facilities. If a public nuisance protection plan has been established in the city, the city plan must conform to it. In the application of standards due note should be taken of the results of the government's surveys on population, industry, housing, building, traffic, factory location, and so on.

Decisions on matters pertaining to the urbanization promotion areas and urbanization control areas, zoning areas and districts of certain types and areas and districts designated by cabinet order, basic urban facilities, and urban development projects are all taken by the prefectural governor after hearing the opinions of the cities, towns, villages, and the local city planning council. City plans, other than those decided by the governor, are decided by the cities, towns, and villages after obtaining the prefectural governor's approval. Such plans are required to conform to the basic principles contained in the plans for wider areas of which the city, town, or village may form a part. The governor, before giving his approval to such a plan, must refer it to the local city planning council. If a plan prepared by a city, town, or village is inconsistent with a city plan approved by the governor, the latter plan prevails over the former.

The prefectural governor or the city, town, or village, as the case may be, is required to open the draft plan for public inspection for a two-week period after the public notification to this effect. Within this period the inhabitants or any other persons or parties may submit their views in writing. Insofar as the plans for large cities or areas in their environs, city planning areas designated by a cabinet order, or a city plan seriously affecting national interest are concerned, the prefectural governor is required to refer them to the minister of construction.

The law provides that permission for land development must be obtained from the prefectural governor or the mayor of the city concerned. However, no such permission is required for the following specified land development activities within the urbanization promotion area:

a) Within an urbanization promotion area whose scale is smaller than the scale fixed by cabinet order;

b) For the purpose of constructing buildings and so on for the use of agriculture, forestry, or fishery;

c) Buildings necessary for public benefit, such as a railway station and social welfare facility;

d) Land development to be executed by the state, prefecture, city, or the like;

e) A city planning project;

f) A land readjustment project;

g) Land reclaimed from a public water area of which the reclamation completion has not yet been formally approved;

h) Other land development fixed by cabinet order.

No permission may be given for land development in an urbanization control area unless it is executed to construct buildings:

a) For shops, workshops which sell or process commodities for the everyday life of the inhabitants in and around the area to be developed;

b) For effective utilization of resources such as mineral resources and sightseeing resources;

c) For enterprises fixed by cabinet order requiring special conditions with respect to temperature, humidity, and air, which are difficult to construct in an urbanization promotion area;

d) For agricultural, forestry, or fishery uses or for the treating and processing of agricultural, forestry, or marine products;

e) For certain kinds of businesses which are conducive to joint management on the part of smaller enterprises and to group management of factories and shops of smaller enterprises;

f) For use in businesses having close connections with the business of factories now located in an urbanization control area as are necessary for improving the efficiency of such business activities;

g) For storing dangerous objects whose construction in an urbanization promotion area is inappropriate;

h) To be fixed by cabinet order, whose construction in an urbanization promotion area is difficult or inappropriate.

Permission also may not be given to the kinds of land development listed below concerning which the prefectural governor has previously consulted the land development council:

a) Such land development covering an area not smaller than the area fixed by cabinet order as is deemed to present no obstacle to the promotion of planned urbanization in the light of the urbanization status in the urbanization promotion area;

b) Land development involving no fear of accelerating urbanization of the surrounding areas whose execution in an urbanization promotion area is difficult or extremely inappropriate and whose execution in an urbanization control area is unavoidable.

The provisions concerning the regulations of the type mentioned above do not for the time being apply to city planning areas except the ones designated by cabinet order as, for example, those involving large cities and their environs.

The law provides for the imposition of restrictions on construction in areas designated for city planning facilities. Where permission for construction is refused by the governor and when he is requested to purchase the land because its utilization is extremely hindered by such refusal, the governor is legally bound to purchase the land. The law also empowers the governor to exercise the right of preemption in a city planning facility area and in built-up area development projects.

The law requires the city, town, or village concerned to execute the city planning projects after obtaining the governor's approval. Where it is difficult or inappropriate for the city, town, or village to do so, the governor may execute the project after obtaining the approval of the minister of construction. In case of a city planning project having an important bearing on the interests of the state, the state itself executes the project. Besides these authorities, any other person may also execute a city planning project if approved by the governor. The law authorizes that any land to be used for a city planning project may be expropriated for that purpose.

When the minister of construction deems that a matter has an important bearing on the interest of the state, he may give instructions to a governor or to a city, town, or village (through the governor) to take necessary steps for the designation of a city planning area. The minister of construction may also do this upon a request to this effect by the head of a state organ. If a governor or a city, town, or village defaults in carrying out the instructions within the time limit prescribed, the minister may himself take necessary steps after obtaining the confirmation of the Central City Planning Council.

The minister of construction or the prefectural governors are required to consult the minister of agriculture and forestry before designating or deciding a city plan concerning an urbanization promotion area. The minister of construction is also required to hear the opinions of the ministers of international trade and industry, transport, and health and welfare in regard to the urbanization promotion area or a specified use area. Similarly, the minister of construction, before he approves a city plan connected with a city facility, must first consult the head of the national administrative organ authorized to grant licenses, permission, approval, and so on for the establishment of the facility.

An interesting provision is that the prefecture or a designated city may establish a land fund for the purpose of purchasing land and former factory sites within a city planning facility area or within an area for executing an urban development project, for purchasing land on the owner's request where permission for construction is denied to the owner, and for exercising the right of preemption. The law enjoins the state and the local public bodies to take measures and other pertinent steps for the promotion of effective use of land within the urbanization promotion area and for controlling land speculation. Any person who loses his living as a result of being dispossessed by the execution of a city planning project may request the project developer for rehabilitation assistance which according to law must be provided.

The law establishes in the Ministry of Construction a Central Planning Council, which is an advisory body both of the minister of construction and, at the level of the prefecture, the local city planning councils. Another organization established at the level of each prefecture is the development review council, whose function is to decide appeals in connection with land development.

Land readjustment projects are an important urban planning and development measure in Japan. The law on this subject requires that where a land readjustment project is being carried out by a private organization, a sokai or general meeting involving all owners and right holders in the area should be held at least once a year and all important decisions pertaining to the project must be approved by the group. Where a government or public organization carries out such a project, a land readjustment advisory commission consisting of members elected from among the landowners, other right holders, and persons of learning and experience is constituted. The project executor is required to take into consideration the commission's views and opinions after which a plan to replot the land is worked out. The allocation of replotted land has to be done in such a manner that the land allocated corresponds to the value of the right originally held, also taking into consideration the original situation and advantages or disadvantages of the owner's land. After determining the replotting, construction works relating to public facilities are executed. Buildings or structures that prevent the execution of such works are removed for which compensation is paid by the project executor. After the installation of the necessary facilities, building lots are allocated in accordance with the replotting plan and all rights to the former lots are legally converted into the newly allocated plots. Any excess or deficiency arising out of the difference in the value of the original and the reallocated plot is settled through cash payments which are determined on the basis of assessments made before and after the execution of the project.

The expenses of land readjustment projects are borne by the project executor. The executor's financial burden is mitigated to the extent that the reserved land is sold outright. In addition, the national and local governments advance loans to private organizations and also offer them technical assistance in the execution of the projects. For projects executed by local governments, the national government extends them loan assistance. If a costly land readjustment project is carried out for urban renewal, the national government may subsidize up to two-thirds of the total cost.

Appendix 5-3. Decision Making in City Planning

	City Planning	Decision by Prefectural Governor	Decision by Municipality
Urbanization promotion area and urbanization control area		All cases	No
Districts and zones	Use zone	In city planning area of large cities	Areas other than shown at left
	Urban aesthetic district	All cases	No
	Port side district, green space conservation district, special preservation district of historic landscape (Including categories I and II districts) distribution business district, airplane noise pollution prevention district and special airplane noise pollution prevention district		
	Other districts and zones	No	All cases
Project Expediting Area	Urban redevelopment Expediting Area Land readjustment Expediting Area Residential blocks construction Expediting Area	No	All cases
Urban facilities	Roads	National highways, prefectural roads 16 m wide or over (22 m for specified cities), roads exclusively for motor vehicles	Roads other than shown at left
	Urban expressways	All cases	No
	Automobile terminals	General automobile terminals	Terminals other than shown at left
	Airports	Types 1 to 3 airports	Those other than shown at left
	Parks, green belts, open spaces	4 ha (10 ha for specified cities) or over, but 1 ha for the time being	Those other than shown at left

Appendix 5-3. (continued)

City Planning		Decision by Prefectural Governor	Decision by Municipality
Urban facilities (continued)	Cemeteries	10 ha or over	Less than 10 ha
	Sewerages	Regional sewerage systems or public sewerage systems with drainage area covering 2 or more municipalities	Those other than shown at left
	Rivers	Class 1 rivers, Class 2 rivers	Those other than shown at left
	Canals	All cases	No
	Schools	Universities and technical colleges	Those other than shown at left
	Group Housing Facilities	A group of 1,000 households or above	Those other than shown at left
	Group government and public office facilities	All cases	No
	Distribution business centers	All cases	No
	Title preventive facilities	All cases	No
	Other urban facilities	No	All cases
Urban development Projects	Land readjustment projects	Area of more than 20 ha	Area of 20 ha or less
	Other urban development projects	All cases	No
Areas where Urban Development, etc. is to be Undertaken		All cases	No
District plan, etc.		No	All cases

Source: Government of Japan.

Appendix 5-4. Procedure for Making a City Plan

a. Procedure for Determination of the City Plan by the Prefectural Governor

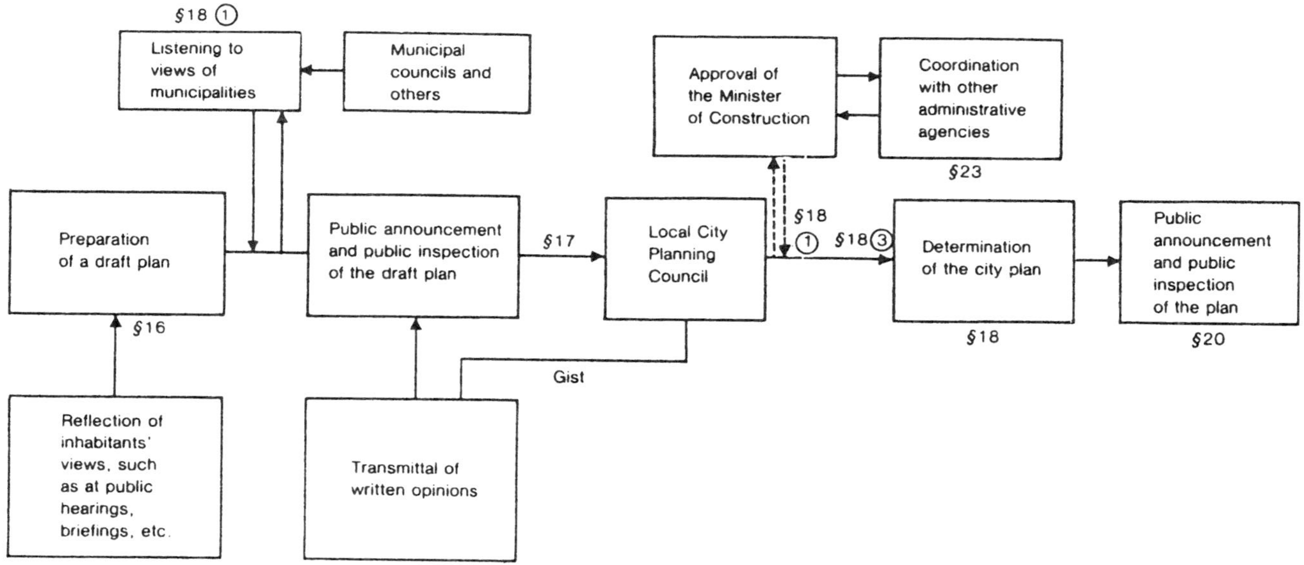

Appendix 5-4. (continued)

b. Procedure for Determination of the City Plan by Municipalities

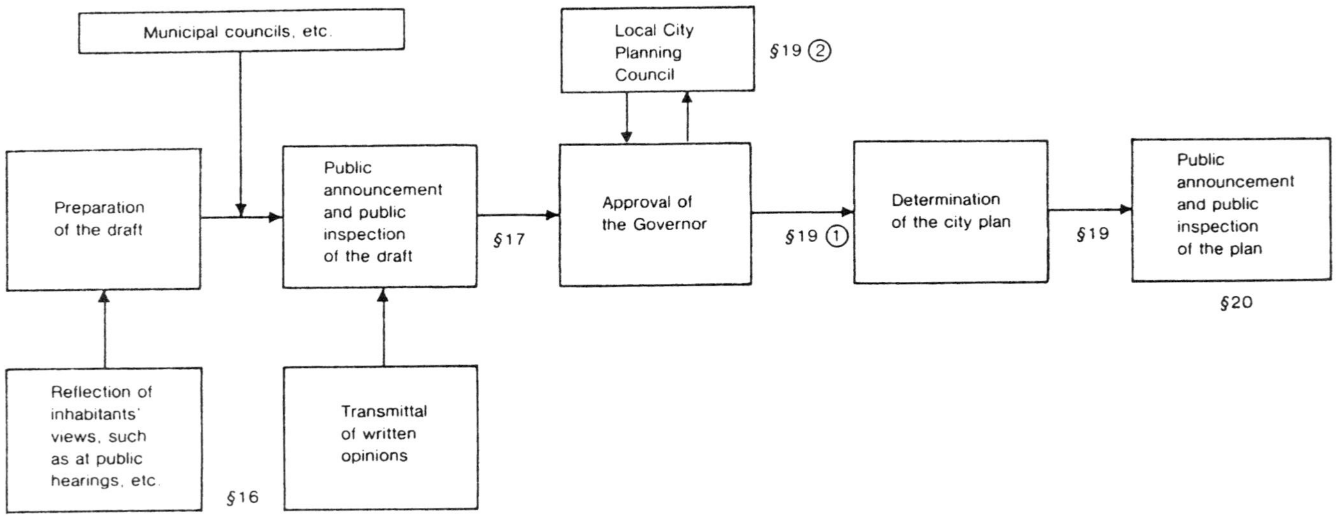

Note: "§18 ①" represents Article 18, Paragraph 1, City Planning Act.
Source: Government of Japan.

Appendix 5-5. A Systems Approach to Policy Making in the Housing Sector

Improving housing conditions	Housing supply through public funding	Direct housing supply	Public-operated houses Improvement houses Houses by Housing and Urban Development Corporation Houses by the Local Housing Supply Corporation
		Indirect housing supply	Housing Loan Corporation
	Promotion of housing construction and acquisition	Saving system for housing Private housing loans Tax system for housing	
	Rationalization of housing production and supply		

Appendix 5-5. **(continued)**

Improving residential environment	Residential environment improvement project	Residential district improvement project Model project for residential environment improvement Comprehensive improvement promotion project for wooden rental housing district
	Purposeful development of housing complex	
	Urban development project	Land readjustment project
		New town development project
		Urban redevelopment project
		Residential blocks development project
		Comprehensive improvement promotion project for specific residential urban area
	Development of public facilities	
	City planning regulation, building regulation	

Source: Government of Japan.

REFERENCES

Department of the Environment and Government Office for London. *Four World Cities: A Comparative Study of London, Paris, New York and Tokyo*. London: Llewelyn-Davies, 1996.

Foreign Press Center, Japan. *Japan: Eyes on the Country: View of the 47 Prefectures*. Tokyo: Foreign Press Center, Japan, November 1, 1997.

Golany, Gideon S., Keisuke Hanaki, and Osamu Koide, eds. *Japanese Urban Environment*. Tokyo: Elsevier Science Japan, 1998.

Hanayama, Yuzuru. *Land Markets and Land Policy in a Metropolitan Area*. Boston: Oelgeschlager, Gunn, & Hain, 1986.

Hines, M. A. *Investing in Japanese Real Estate*. Westport, CT: Quorum Books, 1987.

6

Leasing and Marketing Japanese Real Estate

Two of the keys to Japanese property profitability are good leasing and marketing of property. Good leasing practices assure a good cash inflow from the tenants over the terms of their leases. Good marketing practices assure a stable, long-run stream of cash inflow from real property sales and leases. This chapter considers ground leases in general, shopping center and office building leases in particular, and the changes occurring in the leasing of property. The discussion of the marketing of real estate includes information about the currently expanding use of the Internet and electronic mail for communications.

THE TENANT–LANDLORD BALANCE IN LEASE TERMS

In Japan the owners of office buildings say that office building leases and the legal system favor the tenant. Some office building tenants and real estate analysts say that office building leases and the legal system favor the landlord. Some foreign retailers who would like to lease shopping center space in Japan say that shopping center leases favor the landlord and would like to see Western-style leases that lean in favor of the tenant. Some shopping center landlords who would like to profit more from their properties would like to see more lease clauses that work in their favor. Therefore, we must review typical lease provisions in order to decide for ourselves which party—lessor or lessee—is favored by current leases. Maybe both parties benefit equally.

GROUND LEASES

A large portion of the land in Japan is not available for purchase, as many prospective foreign buyers are finding out. Prospective foreign buyers are generally looking for (1) industrial properties—both land and buildings—for production and distribution of goods, (2) office buildings—both land and buildings—for the administration of foreign companies that are doing business in Japan, (3) office buildings for investment—short- or long-term, (4) apartment buildings for expatriate personnel who are working for the companies in Japan permanently or on relatively short tours of duty, (5) apartment buildings for investment—short- or long-term, and (6) land for residential, commercial, and industrial property development. Prospective foreign purchasers find that land and buildings are not available for purchase for various reasons: (1) if the land and existing land improvements were sold, the profits derived would be taxed heavily, and cash might not be available to pay the current taxes due, (2) the owner dreams of the return of the rapid increase in land and building prices like that experienced in the 1980s, (3) the owner plans to develop the land in a highly profitable land use once the deep recession ends, (4) a government unit may own the land and have plans for infrastructure redevelopment once funds and a favorable political climate appear, and (5) the property owner may wish to pass the property down to heirs without letting the property ownership leave the family and without paying heavy taxes on the family estate transfer.

On the other hand, the property that may not be available for sale may be available for lease. The ground may be leased for industrial, commercial, or residential purposes for relatively long periods. Or the land may be leased for only a short period depending on the motivations of the landlord.

Currently, the financial distress of many levels of government from the decline in tax collections during the long recession has led various government units to lease certain land parcels for relatively short terms. For example, the bankruptcy of the Tokyo municipal government has been highly publicized in the global press. This government entity owns property that would support currently profitable land use. For example, many shopping center developers have leased waterfront and other well-positioned government land for factory outlet malls for periods of 10 to 20 years on advantageous terms because the government unit seeks near-term revenue to cover projected expenditures. The governmental unit may have plans for the space after the relatively short-term lease expires. The developer may agree to the governmental ground lease terms if the proposed land development is expected to return the capital invested in the land improvements plus a reasonable profit within the relatively short lease period.

SHOPPING CENTER LEASES

Once the landlord acquires the development rights or ownership of land that is located at a major mass transit hub or other such prime location, the Japanese and foreign retail tenants seek storeroom space on such a competitive basis in the new shopping center that they will agree to the usual Japanese-style lease terms. If Japanese or foreign retail tenants wish to expand their locations in Japan, they will find well-established leasing patterns in existing shopping centers. The publicly listed property companies, the major department stores, the real estate subsidiaries of the major railway companies, or other such shopping center owners will usually require non-interest-earning key money deposits, advance payment of rent quoted in Japanese yen per square meter of at least one year, security deposit, common area maintenance fee payable periodically, three- or four-year leases that are perhaps subject to renewal, and six-month notice of vacation of the premises before the lease expiration. The lease may or may not have a restriction on the line of business permitted in the storeroom. The lease may or may not restrict the operation of the retail storeroom business within the confines of the official storeroom space; the retailer's merchandise display may be permitted to extend into the common area walkway in front of the storeroom. The retailer's square footage of leasable space may be less than the square footage of total retail space once the merchandise overflows the storeroom into the public walkway of the shopping center.

The tenant usually pays the commission of the marketing person who helps to locate the leasable retail space. The commission may be equal to one-month's rent at the new shopping center location.

The tenant has tenure in the space and cannot be evicted if the tenant has met the provisions of the lease. The landlord has difficulty redesigning the tenant operating spaces within the shopping center due to tenant rights to their occupancy of the center. In a lawsuit in the Japanese courts, the tenant's rights usually win out over landlord rights, as has historically been the case in Western Europe.

OFFICE BUILDING LEASES

The office building lease usually specifies the square meters and *tsubo* of the leased space. The office building structure may be given a title such as the "Millennium Tower." This title becomes a part of the leased premises description. The term of the office building lease is usually two years with advance payment of the lease in its totality plus non-interest-bearing key money deposit and advance payment of the security deposit. Exhibit 6-1 shows a sample office building lease that also has provisions for liability for damages and repairs, the purchase of and payment for fixtures, the payment of the consumption tax on the lease payments, adherence to building regulations, and provisions for the settlement of disputes between the lessor and the lessee.

Generally, the office building tenant has tenure rights similar to those of shopping center storeroom tenants. If the landlord wishes to redevelop or remodel office building space, the landlord must provide temporary relocation space for each tenant whose space falls within the purview of the redevelopment building project. If office building space comparable in quality and location to the tenant space is difficult to find in a tight office building market, the landlord may find it difficult to proceed with the building renovation or redevelopment until comparable temporary space is found for each existing building tenant.

Exhibit 6-1
Sample Lease Agreement

This Agreement (hereinafter referred to as the "Lease Agreement") is made and entered into by and between ____________ (hereinafter referred to as the "Lessor") and ________________ (hereinafter referred to as the "Lessee"), concerning the lease of the premises defined below. Upon consultation between the Lessor and the Lessee, the parties have agreed to as set forth below.

Article 1 Lease Premises

The Lessor shall lease to the Lessee the premises defined below (hereinafter referred to as the "Premises") and the Lessee shall take the Premises on lease.
Name: ____
Location: ______________________________________
Structure: _____________________________________
Floor number and area of Premises:
_________________________________ floor
_________________________________ square meters
_________________________________ *tsubo*

Article 2 Term of Lease

The terms of the lease hereunder shall be _____(____) years, commencing on _____, 200___ and terminating on _______, 200___, and subject to extension for an additional ____(____) year(s) in the event that no notice is made to the contrary or for change of terms and conditions thereof by the Lessor six (6) months prior to the expiration date or by the Lessee _____(____) months prior to the expiration date. In the event of renewal of this Agreement, the Lessee shall pay to the Lessor an amount equal to the revised rental fee of one (1) month as a renewal fee. The same shall apply to all subsequent renewals.

Article 3 Purpose of Use

The Lessee shall use the Premises as ______ and not for any other purposes.

Article 4 Rental and Other Fees

A. The rental fee shall be yen ______ per month and shall be included with the related imposed consumption tax of yen _______. The management and maintenance fee shall be yen ______ and shall be included with the related imposed consumption tax of yen _______. The Lessee shall pay the rental fee, the management and maintenance fee, and related imposed consumption taxes for any one month by the ______ day of the previous month by bank transfer to the bank account designated by the Lessor.

   The amount charged for rent and management and maintenance fees for any period less than one (1) month shall be calculated per diem.

B. The Lessee shall pay, in addition to the rental and management and maintenance fees, the cost of ______, which shall be paid to the Lessor in the same manner as defined in the foregoing item.

Article 5 Revision of Fee

Revision of the rental fee and the management and maintenance fee may be made at any time during the term of the lease, whenever deemed necessary due to fluctuation of prices and/or rent market, change in economic circumstances, increase or decrease in the taxes and public charges, or an unbalance in rental fees for comparable Premises in neighboring buildings, upon consultation between the Lessor and the Lessee.

Exhibit 6-1 (continued)

Article 6 Deposit Money

A. The Lessee shall deposit the sum of yen _____ as Deposit Money upon signing this agreement. The Deposit Money shall bear no interest.

B. In the event of Agreement termination, whether due to cancellation or other reasons, after complete redelivery of the Premises by the Lessee, the Deposit Money shall be appropriated to settle any and all obligations of the Lessee to the Lessor. Any amount of the Deposit Money that remains shall be refunded by the Lessor to the Lessee.

C. A depreciation fee of yen _____ shall be deducted from the Deposit Money when the Deposit Money is refunded.

Article 7 Offsetting Deposit Money

A. In the event the Lessee should default in the payment of rental fee or otherwise fail to perform any of its obligations herein, the Lessor may appropriate the Deposit Money without prior notice. The Lessee may not assert or claim that the rental fee or any other obligation incurred herein be offset with the Deposit Money during the term in which the Agreement is in effect.

B. In the event the Lessor appropriates the Deposit Money as described in the preceding paragraph, the Lessee shall make up the shortage in the Deposit Money within seven (7) days of notification by the Lessor that such appropriation has been so made.

Article 8 Assignments of Deposit Money Prohibited

The Lessee shall not assign or transfer, put pledge, or otherwise dispose of its claim to the Deposit Money hereunder.

Article 9 Prohibitions

The Lessee may not perform the following actions.

A. Assign or transfer its own leasing right to the Premises or sublease the Premises to a third party without the approval of the Lessor.

B. Permit a third party to share the Premises or display name plates other than the Lessee's own.

C. Endanger, make unsanitary, or otherwise cause inconvenience or annoyance to the neighborhood, destroy or damage the building, or undertake any action that may result in such damages during the Lessee's occupation of the Premises.

Article 10 Liability for Damages

A. The Lessee shall be liable to the Lessor for any damage caused by malicious intent or negligence of the Lessee, its agent, or employees.

B. The Lessee shall be liable for any damage caused third parties due to malicious intent or negligence on the part of the Lessee, its agent, or employees. The Lessee shall ensure settlement of all such matters in a manner that causes no inconvenience to the Lessor.

C. The Lessor shall not be liable for any damages suffered by the Lessee due to fire, earthquake, flood, theft, or any other unforeseen, accidental cause. This provision does

Exhibit 6-1 (continued)

not apply to damages resulting from malicious intent or negligence on part of the Lessor, its agent, or employees.

Article 11 Alterations

Any alterations to the Premises, including remodeling or installation of facilities, which result in changes to the original state of the Premises, shall be conducted only with the prior consent of and subject to the instructions of the Lessor, and at the expense of Lessee.

Article 12 Repair

A. The Lessor shall be obligated to conduct repair work related to the maintenance and security of the main structure of the building (roofs, exterior wall, and structural wall) and facilities installed by the Lessor, as required.

B. Other work, such as repairs and repainting, that is not described in the previous paragraph shall, in principle, be conducted by the Lessee at the Lessee's expense.

C. Whenever repairs on the Premises become necessary, the Lessee shall notify the Lessor without delay and shall carry out the repair work only with the prior consent of and subject to the instructions of the Lessor, even when such repairs are conducted at the Lessee's expense.

Article 13 Inspection of Premises

The Lessor, its agent or employee may, after first notifying the Lessee, enter the Premises and take such measures as may be necessary for the inspection, repair, or the prevention of fire or theft in respect to the building, the fixtures, or facilities thereof. In emergencies the Lessor may enter the Premises without prior notification although the Lessor shall notify the Lessee promptly after such entries are made.

Article 14 Right of Claim for Purchase of Fixtures

When redelivering the Premises to the Lessor, the Lessee shall not make any claim, no matter what the nature or name, against the Lessor for repayment of expenses incurred by the Lessee for fixtures or facilities in the Premises, or compensation for the Lessee's moving or evacuating the Premises at the request of Lessor. Nor shall the Lessee make any claim against the Lessor for purchase of fixtures or facilities previously installed in the Premises at the Lessee's own expense.

Article 15 Termination

When either party wishes to terminate the Agreement during the period in which it is effective, either may do so. However, the Lessor shall notify the Lessee in writing six (6) months prior to the date of same while the Lessee shall notify the Lessor in writing ______(_____) months prior to the date of same. However, the Lessee may terminate the Agreement immediately by paying ________________(_______) month's rental fee.

Article 16 Cancellation of the Agreement

The Lessor may cancel the Agreement without any notice, if the Lessee has:

A. Failed to pay the rental or management and maintenance fee for two (2) consecutive months or more;

B. Received seizure, provisional seizure, provisional disposition; applied for company arrangement, reorganization, composition, bankruptcy, or special liquidation; or has been subjected to suspension of business with a bank;

C. Violated the provisions of Articles 3 or 9;

D. Allowed Specified Gangs or members of the same to use the Premises;

E. Otherwise acted in violation of the provisions herein.

Article 17 Restoration

Upon redelivery of the Premises on completion of the Agreement:

A. The Lessee shall redeliver the Premises after first restoring the Premises to its original condition by removing, at the Lessee's own expense, fixtures, and facilities previously installed in the Premises by the Lessee as well as other of the Lessee's property contained within the Premises. Prior to redelivery, the Lessee, at its own expense, shall repair any damage suffered by the Premises and attached facilities resulting from actions conducted by the Lessee. In the event the Lessee fails to restore promptly the Premises to its original condition, the Lessor reserves the right to take the above measure at the expense of Lessee.

B. The Lessee shall, at the request of the Lessor, remove any property of the Lessor previously installed by the Lessor at the request of the Lessee at the expense of the Lessee and deliver it to the Lessor.

C. The Lessor reserves the right to dispose at its own discretion any property left by the Lessee within the Premises after redelivery of the Premises.

D. In the event the Lessee fails to redeliver the Premises to the Lessor upon termination of the Agreement, the Lessee shall pay the Lessor a penalty equaling twice the amount of the rental fee. This fee shall be calculated for the period commencing from the day immediately subsequent to the date of the termination of the Agreement until the day of complete redelivery.

Article 18 Consumption Tax

Any invoice issued by the Lessor to the Lessee, including those issued for rent and any other liabilities arising from this Agreement as well as attached agreements, shall include all consumption tax imposed upon such payments, shall include all consumption tax imposed upon such payments, and Lessee shall bear the cost of same.

Article 19 Consent in Writing

All applications submitted by the Lessee to the Lessor shall be in writing.

Article 20 Building Regulations

The Lessee shall observe building regulations as well as those regulations issued by the Lessor concerning building management.

Article 21 Notification

In the event changes occur in the name of the Lessee registered at the time of signing during the period in which the Agreement is in effect, or if any important changes occur in the Lessee's organization or business, such as mergers, changes in the purposes of business, the Lessee shall immediately notify the Lessor of same.

Exhibit 6-1 (continued)

Article 22 Joint Surety

The joint surety bears jointly with the Lessee all obligations owed the Lessor by the Lessee under the Agreement.

Article 23 Notary Deed

The Agreement may be written as a notary deed, with the cost thereof being equally shared by the Lessor and the Lessee.

Note: The Notary Deed has a power to do forcible execution of a monetary obligation without the judgment from the court to do the forcible execution. It might save time and money to make the Notary Deed, in case there is a possibility of discord between the parties to the deed in the future.

Article 24 Jurisdiction

Any dispute arising from this Agreement between the Lessor and the Lessee shall be settled at the regional court that exercises jurisdiction over the district in which the Lessor is located.

Article 25 Supplementary Provision

Any matter not covered herein or any misunderstandings concerning the interpretation of the provisions contained herein shall be conferred upon and solved by and between the Lessor and the Lessee in good faith in accordance with relevant laws, ordinances, and customs.

IN WITNESS HEREOF, THIS AGREEMENT has been prepared in duplicate of which the Lessor and the Lessee shall retain one (1) copy each.

Date:

Lessor:

Lessee:

Joint Surety:

Attested by: Sanko Estate Co., Ltd.
International Sales Department
Head Office: Ginza Sanwa Bldg.
4-6-1 Ginza, Chuo-ku
Tokyo 104-0061 Japan
Tel: 81-03-3564-8051
Fax: 81-03-3564-8031

Source: Sanko Estate Co., Ltd. Reprinted with permission.

The ideal time for building redevelopment or renovation is a recession, when ample vacant office building space in the immediate vicinity may be under the control of the landlord.

Special Office Building Terms Found in the Japanese Market

Exhibit 6-2 outlines the meaning of some special office building lease terms that are found in the Japanese market. These special terms relate to (1) floor space, (2) deposit money, (3) rent payment, (4) maintenance fee, (5) repair fees, (6) cohabitation and subleasing, (7) restoration to the original condition, (8) length of the lease, (9) cancellation of the lease contract, (10) depreciation fee, (11) renewal fee, (12) liability for building construction costs, and (13) payment of the real estate agent's commission.

CHANGES IN LEASING

Property owners who view the existing leases as generally favoring tenants now think that the "tide is turning." They think the pendulum is swinging back toward the building owner position so that the lease is more balanced between the lessee and the lessor. For example, shopping center leases are being influenced by Western-style lease provisions. Since Japanese landlords want to attract strong international retailers, including strong U.S. retailers, they are tending to move toward longer leases with percentage-of-sales clauses rather than flat square meter rents whose lease terms run only three or four years. The onerous advance payment of rent for the length of the lease and the payment of key money may weaken with the rising vacancy rates and lower retail sales from the long-term recessionary conditions. From the office building arena, we note that leases may be revised due to the higher vacancy rates even in the "Class A" office properties in the heart of Tokyo. The clauses concerning key money payment and payment in advance of the rent for the entire two years of the office lease may weaken with the coming announced employee cutbacks at most of Japan's companies. During the recession without employee reductions, companies have experienced less need for as much office space as they currently have. In company restructuring for profitability, the downsizing of the company has meant fewer employees and less demand for industrial, commercial, and residential building space. Company housing for employees is being reduced as housing for most Japanese people is being provided by private companies and the government.

MARKETING JAPANESE REAL ESTATE

Japan has vast networks for the marketing of real property interests to (1) Japanese retail customers, (2) foreign retail customers, (3) Japanese institutional and government customers, (4) Japanese wholesale customers such as publicly

Exhibit 6-2
Important Office Building Leasing Terms

1. Floor Space (*Menseki*). Space in Japan is usually expressed in square meters (m^2), though the term *tsubo* is also common (1 *tsubo* = 3.305785 m^2 or about 35.58 square feet). Floor space is usually measured from wall center to wall center. However, prospective lessees should be careful when comparing offices as rental contracts usually differentiate between two types of space. One type refers only to the space occupied exclusively by the tenant (*senyo menseki*), while the other refers to both exclusive tenant space and common space (*kyoyo menseki*) such as halls, restrooms, and foyers.

2. Deposit Money (*Hosho-kin* or *Shikikin*). Before tenants can assume occupancy of any rental accommodation in Japan, they are required to pay the building owner a non-interest-bearing deposit. This gives the new tenant credibility while the owner generates a financial reserve out of which any tenant-incurred losses are paid. The owner will return the deposit after "the delivery by the lessee of the leased premises to the lessor." Most rental contracts stipulate that the deposit money will be raised in proportion to a property's rent when the rent itself is increased.

3. Rent (*Chin-ryo*). As soon as a tenant delivers belongings or begins office remodeling, rent payments must begin. Rent is usually paid for the coming month on the last day—or by the 25th day—of the month preceding it. In theory, rents can be raised if dramatic changes in economic circumstances occur, and often contracts contain such a warning. In practice, however, rents are not increased until the rental contracts fall due for renewal.

4. Maintenance Fee (*Kyoeki-hi*). In addition to rent, tenants are usually asked to pay a monthly building maintenance fee. This fee covers the cost of utilities expenses for common space such as lobbies, halls, and restrooms, as well as the costs of building maintenance and security services. Items covered by the fee usually vary from building to building, so prospective tenants should confirm in advance whether the fee covers cleaning and air conditioning and/or heating costs.

5. Repair Fees (*Shuzen-hi*). Whether it is the property owner or the tenant who pays for building repairs varies from building to building. The property owner is obliged to pay for structural repairs to the building, such as those in common areas, and repairs to equipment and machinery. The tenant is usually asked to pay for office repairs such as repainting or papering of ceilings, walls, and floors and other areas; replacing or repairing fixtures, blinds, glass, lighting, switches or electrical outlets; and repairs of tenant-installed partitions, fixtures, and special-use equipment. For any others, review the contract.

6. Cohabitation and Subleasing (*Dokyo Tentai*). Japanese lease contracts prohibit both cohabitation and subleasing. Tenancy is generally restricted to those whose names appear on the lease contract. Often, though, these rules are waived for a tenant's affiliated companies. The building owner's flexibility on the issue should be first determined when the lease is being negotiated.

7. Restoration to Original Condition (*Genjo-kaifuku*). Unlike in other countries, when a tenant in Japan terminates a lease contract and prepares to vacate, all premises must be restored to their condition at the time that the contract commenced. This restoration is

Exhibit 6-2 (continued)

at the tenant's expense and usually includes—at a minimum—repairs to all walls, floors, and ceilings and the removal of any fixtures installed by the tenant.

8. Lease Terms (*Keiyaku Kikan*). Lease terms in Japan are mostly for two years but are automatically renewed for an additional two years unless either party wishes to terminate the contract. In contrast with European and North American practices, where tenants must generally pay rent for as long as the lease is in effect, tenants in Japan can usually leave leased space before the contract expires. So long as ample written notice of cancellation is given, tenants can leave without paying for the entire contract period.

9. Notice of Cancellation (*Kaiyaku Yokoku*). Cancelling a contract prior to expiry usually carries no penalty for lessees in Japan as long as the lessor is notified beforehand and within the time period specified in the contract (usually three to six months). Recently, however, some landlords have demanded penalty payments.

10. Depreciation Fee (*Shokyaku-hi*). Owners of small- and medium-sized buildings often demand that tenants pay a depreciation fee. This is deducted as a percentage from the deposit (usually 10% to 20%) when the contract ends, and the deposit minus the fee is then returned to the lessee. The term "depreciation fee" is used here, but there is no direct relationship between the fee and building depreciation.

11. Renewal Fee (*Koshin-ryo*). Most office leases stipulate a two-year contract period, and rental contracts can be renewed upon expiry. It is common for owners of small- and medium-sized buildings to demand a renewal fee when rental contracts are renewed, and this fee is usually one month's rent at the rate stipulated in the new rental contract.

12. Construction Involving Building Structure (*Kutai-ni-kakawaru Koji*). Construction work like that below may affect the building's structure, the property value or other tenants. Such work requires the building owner's express approval. It must be done by contractors the owner designates or approves of, and the tenant bears all construction costs. Some examples:

    - Construction altering the building structure (where pillars, beams, and/or ceilings are affected, or where a room partition is extended to the ceiling)
    - Changes in air-conditioning and security systems
    - Installation of heavy machines or structures
    - Changes in electric equipment where the whole building's power supply system could be affected

13. Commission (*Chukai Tesu-ryo*). In Japan, at the time of contracting for new space, it is the tenant and not the landlord who pays the introducer, the agent, a fee equal to one month's rent. This practice gives the tenant important advantages by ensuring that the agent represents the tenant only while diligently maintaining the tenant's position and acting in the tenant's best interests in all negotiations.

Source: Sanko Estate Co., Ltd. Reprinted with permission.

listed and privately held real estate companies and venture capital customers, (5) foreign institutional customers, and (6) foreign wholesale customers such as publicly listed and privately held real estate companies and investment funds. The majority of the real estate marketing branch offices are maintained by large marketing subsidiaries of publicly listed real estate companies. Small and medium-sized real estate companies also maintain branch office networks that reach the far corners of the multiple-island nation.

Real estate marketing offices may be found in the subterranean shopping levels of major office buildings, in street-level storefront locations in commercial districts and in residential neighborhoods, on upper floors of high-rise office buildings, and in other similar locations that meet the needs of retail and wholesale customers. The wholesale real estate marketing offices, for example, tend to be located in high-rise office buildings in the central three wards of Tokyo, where representatives of large domestic and foreign investment funds and institutions tend to do business. Real estate sales offices that attempt to reach wealthy domestic and foreign customers may be located on upper floors of prestigious high-rise office buildings in Tokyo areas such as Shinjuku. Real estate investment bankers are also located in such center-city prestigious areas. The retail offices are located in areas that can easily reach large volumes of retail real estate customers. The retail offices are located near the center city and suburban offices of many employees and near the homes of many employees who may wish to transact business in the evenings and on the weekends.

The commissions of the real estate agents are usually paid by the customer if office space is being rented with the assistance of a real estate agent who makes the introductions. These real estate agents must be licensed. The license exams are given once a year by the Japan Real Estate Companies Association. Since the passing rate of the national exam is relatively low, many prospective real estate agents must take the license exam more than once in order to eventually pass it. The license covers a multiyear period and then must be renewed. To earn a commission from marketing real property, the agent must be licensed. Many large, medium, and small companies employ many licensed agents for their office operations, which may range widely across Japan or may engage in business in only a limited area, perhaps in only one city, such as Tokyo.

Real estate ads giving information about the availability of real estate marketing services and space availability are found in (1) English-language newspapers such as the *Japan Times*, (2) building-front signs, (3) company advertising brochures and flyers that are distributed in public places, and (4) business-oriented magazines, as well as other distribution channels. To supplement the print media usage, personal contacts are made by real estate agents to persuade prospects to use the services of their companies and to suggest various alternatives that might meet the needs of the prospective customer.

Consultation services are offered by diversified, publicly listed real estate companies for fees from clients for services rendered. The consulting service may recommend joint-venture partners for the acquisition of major properties and may recommend appropriate offering prices that should be made for specific buildings following valuations by the diversified real estate company. Of course, there may be conflicts of interest when the services of major diversified real estate companies are utilized. At present, there is a large lawsuit in progress that was brought by a foreign prospective acquirer of a substantial partial interest in a major office building of Tokyo. The consulting major Japanese real estate company suggested to the client a higher offering price than the seller of the office building was inclined to accept. When the consulting company saw that the prestigious office building could be bought for a far lower price, the consulting company acquired the property interest as the client sought to purchase the same property at the suggested higher price.

Japanese and foreign marketing representatives are anxiously seeking to list primary and secondary Japanese and foreign properties that are being disposed of by bankrupt companies and companies that are restructuring and seek to pay down their enormous debt before bankruptcy is faced. For example, Sumitomo Realty & Development Company, a real estate subsidiary of the major Sumitomo diversified trading company, is currently attempting to sell at advantageous prices major properties abroad and in Tokyo, its headquarters city. The company has recently announced in a News Digest article in the *Financial Times* that it plans to withdraw from its overseas operations and wishes to sell the Tischman Building in New York, the Hotel Nikko in Sydney, and its landmark high-rise building in Tokyo's Shinjuku district as the company reduces its debt by approximately $2 billion by the end of the 1999 fiscal year. Many international real estate marketing companies, including Japanese real estate investment banking firms and major foreign and Japanese real estate brokerage companies, will bid for the contract.

The Use of the Internet and Electronic Mail in Marketing Property

The use of the Internet and electronic mail has exploded in Japan along with the use of cellular phones. The presence of electronic mail for use by Japanese real estate marketing personnel permits economical communication worldwide. The marketing of real property interests within Japan and outside Japan is stimulated by the use of this electronic communication method. The high rate of usage of computer systems in Japan permits the adoption of electronic mail by company marketing people from the top echelon to the bottom echelon of a real estate marketing company. Young people of Japan have particularly adopted this new method of communication.

On a worldwide scale, Japan ranks first in the top 10 non-U.S. countries in Internet traffic. Larger businesses in Japan particularly use a Web site in their marketing and other operations. The percentage of large business usage of a Web site in Japan is approximately equal to that of Canada. The percentage of large business usage of a Web site is the highest in the United States; Japan and Canada compete for second place. The percentage of Japanese medium-sized business usage of a Web site ranks behind that of the United States, Italy, the United Kingdom, and Canada; Japan's medium-sized businesses rank fifth in Web site usage. In looking at small-sized business usage of a Web site, Canadian small businesses rank first; Japan's small business usage ranks behind Canada, the United States, Germany, Italy, and the United Kingdom, according to British Telecom and IDC. Therefore, there is ample opportunity for Japanese real estate marketing by small-, medium-, and large-sized companies that are quite adept at Internet usage.

At present, Hong Kong property companies are quickly developing Web-based commerce in cyberspace. The young heirs to the large property companies, in particular, are expanding the profitability of the companies by adding higher-margin services and products over the Web. This is an Asian trend that the large property companies of Japan will be watching closely. Since marketing of property and property services as well as other products and services may be enhanced through use of this marketing medium, property companies worldwide will be exploring opportunities in cyberspace. During the recession in Japan, time may be available or will be found to expand the real estate business in this medium.

CHAPTER SUMMARY

In Japan's recent recession, lease terms came under examination for possible change. Changes in leases are reflections of long-term changes in the leasing environment. Since land and buildings are often leased in Japan, the chapter examines the current lease conditions and lease terms that tenants are offered.

The chapter started with the question: Do leases favor the lessor or the lessee? The importance of ground leases is associated with the current government leasing of land to increase government revenues. The leasing circumstances and terms of shopping centers in various locations included discussion of non-interest-earning key money, advance payment of rent, the ways rents are quoted in Japan, security deposits, common area maintenance charges, the usual length of shopping center leases, and the length of required notice for vacation of the premises. The terms and leasing conventions also related to lines of business permitted on the premises, the usable space associated with the shopping center storeroom, and the general terms of the commission of the marketing person. Tenant tenure rights may be changing from past patterns.

Office building leases are similar to, and different from, Western-style office building leases. The Japanese lease may have two-year terms, require rent payment in advance with a non-interest-bearing key money deposit, and require advance payment of the security deposit. The special significance of a Notary Deed is pointed out in Article 23 of the sample lease. Some explanation of special office building terms is given immediately after the sample lease. Because tenant tenure rights of the past have hampered office building renovation and redevelopment, the court system is tending to favor somewhat landlord rights in this era of reform, restructuring, and redevelopment. Other leasing changes also are appearing in the marketplace.

The numerous real estate marketing networks in Japan permit marketing people to reach foreign retail and wholesale customers and Japanese retail, wholesale, and government customers.The major publicly listed property companies particularly maintain large national marketing networks. The small and medium-sized property companies also have branch office networks across Japan. The branch marketing offices are located near the various customer groups in a variety of high- and low-traffic locations across Japan, including in subterranean shopping levels of major office buildings, on upper floors of high-rise office buildings, and in street-level storefront locations of commercial districts.

Real estate agents must be licensed to collect commissions for property sales and leasing. The license exams are given once a year by the Japan Real Estate Companies Association. The license covers a multiyear period and then must be renewed.

Real estate ads appear in a variety of print media in the English and Japanese languages to market real property to foreign and domestic prospects. Personal marketing supplements marketing through the print media.

Consultation about property questions may be sought from various Japanese sources, including major property companies and international accounting and law firms. Conflicts of interest have resulted recently in lawsuits brought by consulting clients against consulting sources.

Marketing representatives are anxiously trying to list primary and secondary properties that are linked to defaulted loans and restructuring companies so that sales may be made to domestic and foreign clients who are interested in acquisitions during the relatively low-price era. Some of the marketing contacts are being made through the World Wide Web and through use of electronic mail, which reaches potential clients around the world. Business usage of Web sites in Japan ranks second in world terms along with Canada behind the leader, the United States. All sizes of Japanese businesses are actively using the Web for marketing and other functions.

REFERENCES

"Big Prospects for On-Line Sales." *Focus Japan*, 26:4 (May 1999), pp. 3–5.

Dempster, James. "Have You Done Your Homework on Japan?" *Target Marketing*, 22:10 (October 1999), pp. 172–180.

Hargreaves, Deborah. "Europe's Internet Shopping Could Get Caught Up in a Legal Tangle." *Financial Times*, November 1, 1999, p. 3.

Hines, M. A. *Global Corporate Real Estate Management*. Westport, CT: Quorum Books, 1990.

———. *Guide to International Real Estate Investment*. Westport, CT: Quorum Books, 1988.

———. *Guide to Real Estate License Exam Preparation.* New York: Harcourt Brace Jovanovich, 1985.

———. *International Income Property Investment.* Scottsdale, AZ: International Real Estate Institute, 1985.

———. *Investing in International Real Estate.* Westport, CT: Quorum Books, 2000.

———. *Investing in Japanese Real Estate.* Westport, CT: Quorum Books, 1987.

———. *Marketing Real Estate Internationally.* Westport, CT: Quorum Books, 1988.

Hiro, Sachiko. "Hotel Okura Opts to Protect Service in Tough Times." *Japan Times*, November 1, 1999, p. 17.

"Important Terms." *Tokyo Office Market Report 1999.* Tokyo: Sanko Estate Co., p. 17.

Nusbaum, Alexandra. "Convenience Retailing: Japan Stores Group in Internet Alliance." *Financial Times*, January 13, 2000, p. 16.

Nusbaum, Alexandra, and Naoko Makamae. "Store Wars in Cyberspace." *Financial Times*, February 8, 2000, p. 18.

Rahman, Bayan. "Real Estate: Sumitomo Property Up for Sale." *Financial Times*, December 15, 1999, p. 28.

———. "Sony's Online Sales Push in Japan Could Threaten Retail Distribution." *Financial Times*, February 2, 2000, p. 12.

"Sample Lease Agreement." *Tokyo Office Market Report 1999.* Tokyo: Sanko Estate Co., pp. 18–19.

7

Land Development and Construction

Construction cranes for various land development projects and construction jobs penetrate the skyline of every urban area even in the midst of one of the deepest economic recessions that Japan has ever experienced in its long history. Huge office building projects are advertised as construction commences for the early phases of the plans, while economic indicators show little chance for an economic upturn. This is the situation during a major recession. The reader can imagine the ongoing development projects during economically prosperous periods in Japan.

Most Japanese citizens look forward to the next economic boom that will presage more public and private land development and redevelopment. At present, traffic snarls and congestion are partly due to the improvement of existing major roadways as part of the government stimulus of the economy with public works spending. As the economy returns to prosperity, additional roadway construction will be needed because more personal and business vehicles will be purchased with the new prosperity and driven on the existing roads, which are already filled to capacity. Since the subways already are accommodating traffic that is said to represent 200 percent of capacity, the need for new subway construction and for redevelopment of the existing subways is felt every day by most citizens. But the average citizen who rides the trains and/or subways to and from work dreads the inconvenience of the needed rail renovations and extensions. Public and private land development comes at a high personal and business price in the highly congested urban areas of Japan. The examples from the development of urban transportation infrastructure illustrate the complexity of Japanese land development.

In this chapter we review some chief characteristics associated with the development, redevelopment, and construction of golf courses, shopping centers, office buildings, hotels, and other important land uses. Some general observations about Japanese commercial land development need to be viewed before more specific information about the various types of land development is reviewed.

A BRIEF HISTORY OF JAPANESE LAND DEVELOPMENT

Japan represents a rather old civilization. Its development from an agrarian to a commercial and industrial economy more or less parallels that of Western Europe. Much older civilizations are found in China and the Middle East. The United States, in contrast, is a newly developed country. Feudalism was a part of the development of Japan, other parts of Asia, and Europe, but it was never a part of the history of development of the United States.

Because Japan is a nation of a small group of islands and is highly mountainous, it shares common land development problems with other island nations such as Taiwan, the Philippines, Indonesia, and the United Kingdom. Due to the initiative of its people and the cooperation of the government, its citizens, and its businesses, a thriving industrialized economy—ranked second in the free world—must exist in limited space. Japan does not want to buy all of its foodstuffs from abroad, fearing possible trade embargoes in future wars. It needs the reserve food supplies in the event of an emergency. Its terrain and limited space do not permit more than a limited amount of production of its needed food supplies. The meat that its people are learning to enjoy is generally imported from Australia and South America. Japan produces from its paddy fields large harvests of rice, but China, its next-door neighbor, is a reliable source of rice. What can be procured from China, Russia, Canada, and other countries is imported. Since certain Japanese foodstuffs are based on the soybean, soybeans are imported.

Nuclear power plants are important to Japan, which lacks coal reserves for the fueling of fossil fuel–fed traditional power plants. Hydroelectric power is available from mountain and coastline water supplies. Since refineries often operate in the countries from which Japan imports most of its oil, Japan does not need to use a large portion of its land for oil and gas exploration and refining. Supertankers can usually bring refined oil products to Japan from Brunei, Indonesia, Iran, and Alaska.

Heavy industry has absorbed large amounts of the Japanese island acreage. Since competition from South Korea, Taiwan, and Hong Kong is eliminating the need for heavy industrial production, some industrial land is being vacated for new land uses. There is plenty of habitable space for residential and commercial development, but the majority of the Japanese people want to live and work in the densely populated industrial and commercial corridor from Tokyo to Kobe in the south-central part of the island grouping.

A HIERARCHY OF LAND DEVELOPMENT AREAS

Due to the salary and wage differentials and the density of employment sources, most Japanese residents wish to work in Tokyo. Ranked second are the employment opportunities and salary and wage levels of Nagoya and Osaka. Kyoto and Kobe may be ranked third by such criteria. The farther away the site is from Tokyo, generally the less desirable it is for employment and other reasons. The island of Hokkaido, the northernmost large island, is mountainous and relatively cool year-round. The island of Kyushu, the southernmost large island, is mountainous and not favored for habitation due to its long distance from the cultural, employment, government, and educational center of Tokyo. The west coast of Japan tends to have extreme weather—very hot in the summer and very cold in the winter—as compared with the rather moderate climate of the east coast of Japan. Therefore, the population and business tend to be located on the east coast of the central large island.

Land development normally follows the transportation corridors. The Kobe–Tokyo corridor is well served by public and private railroad companies. The parts of Japan with less-developed transportation networks, including rail, are the northern and southern sectors of the country. The commuting traffic in the Kobe–Tokyo corridor keeps the rail systems well financed.

The Japanese have developed land in many other countries for numerous reasons. One is the scarcity of development land at home. Another reason is the economic dependence on foreign trade and permanent Japanese business development in numerous foreign countries. A third reason is the opportunity for attractive investment yields from overseas land development. For these reasons and perhaps others, one of the large Japanese trading companies has had land developments in Japan in numerous locations and outside Japan in numerous countries, including Hong Kong, Brazil, Singapore, the United States, Nepal, and Saudi Arabia. Land development abroad may or may not be a part of the trading company's business of trading in commodities and services. The foreign land development may be a profit center on its own.

Japan continues to develop its foreign trade and foreign investments. It continues to invest in Asia, where the country has many vested interests. The reduced value of the U.S. dollar and the euro prompts more investment in the United States and Europe. The threat of foreign import restrictions in some product areas also prompts Japan to retain its substantial trade surplus with the United States and Europe by building manufacturing plants in the United States and Europe.

ACHIEVEMENTS FROM PUBLIC–PRIVATE COOPERATION

The industrial economy of Japan was built on the close cooperation between the government and the business community. The trading companies have been encouraged to grow and prosper as they fulfilled the objectives set for them cooperatively by the government and the companies themselves. The trading companies were permitted to diversify widely. Most of the dozen trading companies included at least one city bank, major industrial companies, wholesale and retail companies, and service firms of various types. The overlapping board membership within the trading group and across trading groups permitted the financing of worthwhile enterprises. A wide knowledge of the plans of many national companies permitted better business planning for less risk of success. The government and related trade associations assisted the companies in accomplishing the national goals. Today the horizontal (*kinyu*), vertical (*sangyo*), and distribution *keiretsu* are breaking up. Perhaps new types of *keiretsu* are forming as business is restructuring. Business consolidations are prompting new business forms.

DEVELOPMENT OF INFRASTRUCTURE

As the cooperative objectives of the government and business have promoted foreign trade, the infrastructure of Japan has been ignored to some extent. The development of the domestic economy and its infrastructure has long been placed in a secondary position in the business hierarchy.

The planned infrastructure is gradually being implemented. It is a long way off before the traffic congestion is eliminated, the sewerage problems are brought under control, and the neighborhood environments are created for healthy, safe, and unpolluted living. The problems of infrastructure involve more than 1,600 urban places in Japan. Urban development projects involving land readjustment, new town development, industrial estate development, urban redevelopment, and residential block development involve perhaps 800 urban places.

SPECIALIZED DISTRICTS OF TOKYO

On reclaimed land the Ginza, with its retail and entertainment emphasis, was built. The headquarters stores of many of the major department stores of Japan are located within the Ginza district. Ample surface and underground transportation media facilitate the movement of people in and out of this famous commercial district. Since the Ginza is a major shopping district for the Tokyo metropolitan area, suburbanite families often visit the Ginza on weekends, their free days each week. Food is purchased along with other merchandise and services.

The Marunouchi district surrounds the main Tokyo rail terminal. Mid- and high-rise office buildings in the Marunouchi district house many of the principal financial institutions and Japanese and multinational company headquarters. Some retail space underground serves the daytime needs of the office employees in the district. Many office buildings have one or two below-surface retail levels in the high-rise structures. Auxiliary rail and bus lines serve the area so that it can be reached easily from many directions.

After a swamp was drained and filled, the new Shinjuku commercial district was filled with high-rise office buildings and international-class hotels. This district is found on the west side of the Imperial Palace grounds on the opposite side from the Ginza. This district also has underground rail service, but, like the other districts, it has congested traffic on the surface streets.

In the central business district of Tokyo is found the government district. In addition to the grounds of the Imperial Palace, which houses Emperor Hirohito and his family, the central government office buildings house the various ministries to the south of the palace grounds. In the same general district are found the various foreign embassies. The government complex represents the capital of Japan.

CURRENT DEVELOPMENT AREAS

Japanese real estate development is currently taking place in Japan and abroad, but overseas development has been reduced significantly as Japan's recession continues. Let us note a few of the more important development projects and their locations.

With the divestiture of the assets of the Japan National Railway, real estate developers are vying for the land and air rights that have become available for acquisition at the many terminals and stations of the Japan National Railway Company. These are extremely valuable commercial and residential sites. A large portion of the Japanese population uses the rail system as its primary mode of transportation. The high accessibility of transportation and consumer markets at these stations prompts high values for the recently released rail company land.

Abandoned military reservations have also become areas of new development. Such large tracts give ample space for new town development. Abandoned warehouse and shipping areas such as part of Yokohama's waterfront have recently become available for urban redevelopment. Office, retail, and cultural space is being developed in this area along an estimated 10-year development plan. Abandoned industrial areas are also being redeveloped with residential, retail, and recreational space, including marinas. The Japanese people enjoy spectator and active water-related sports.

The building of the Osaka International Airport offshore was a gigantic public–private project that continues to attract additional industry and commerce to the Osaka metropolitan area. It may alleviate some of the current traffic at the Narita International Airport, which serves Tokyo from its Chiba location east of Tokyo. The international airport development will prompt many other forms of development that are complementary to the new transportation hub.

ARCHITECTURE

The architecture of commercial buildings tends to be traditional as a reflection of the social system of Japan. Generally, the architectural designs for shopping centers, retail stores, apartment buildings, and office buildings tend to be tried-and-true designs that have worked well in the past in Japan and foreign companies. Building owners as a whole are not adventurous when they select their architects. For example, a new shopping center on the Yokohama waterfront reflects architecture that denotes a New England village; the multibuilding, two-story shopping center displays facades of the wood frame waterfront structures that remind one of the traditional New England style of U.S. building. That is not to say, though, that Japan does not have futuristic and very modern building designs. Many buildings, for example, in the Tokyo metropolitan area, reflect the architecture of leading world designers. As well as displaying advanced designs, these spectacular buildings—principally office buildings—reflect advanced earthquake-resistant structural features.

CONSTRUCTION COSTS IN GENERAL

The relatively high-cost construction of Japan has previously been de-emphasized due to the even higher cost of the land beneath high-quality, high-rise commercial buildings. Today, as the center-city land prices declined 70 percent or more during the recession of the 1990s and early 2000, the relative position of construction cost in the total development scheme may assume a more prominent role. As the price of land assumes a lesser percentage of the total development cost of a high-rise office building, for example, the construction cost of the improvements will assume a larger percentage of total cost.

As capitalism sets into the Japanese business scheme more thoroughly and as optimization of shareholder value becomes the focus of the companies, competition in the construction sector may bring down Japanese construction costs from relatively high levels to more reasonable levels. For example, competition among architects for project contracts is relatively weak, for construction companies usually give architectural services as part of their services that are included in the bid for the project work. If architects competed for the specialized architectural work, the resulting prices might be deflated. Since many building materials must be imported, the cost of construction must include the cost of transporting needed construction materials to the Japanese site. The traditional distribution system of Japan may also add unnecessary costs to the construction budget. With the gradual breakup of the *keiretsu* as the lead banks of different *keiretsu* merge in the new millennium, this may lead to restructuring of the *keiretsu* and more competitive relations among companies associated with building construction. The traditional distribution system may change as the *keiretsu* change.

LAND RECLAMATION

Land continues to be reclaimed from the sea. The reclaimed land may provide new sites for commercial land development. Recently, sites for factory outlet shopping centers have developed from reclaimed land from Tokyo Bay, for example. Office complexes in Chiba Prefecture have been developed on land reclaimed from Tokyo Bay.

GOLF COURSE DEVELOPMENT AND RELATED FACTORS

The enthusiasm for the game of golf in Japan remains high. It's a game that is played by businessmen, the actively employed, and the retired. But many aspire to play golf after they save enough for a golf club membership, the proper clothing and equipment, golf lessons from the right golf pros and other instructors, and the transportation cost from home or office to the distant golf course location. In the meantime, many practice their golf swings and keep their muscles in good shape for playing an 18-hole golf course at the multilevel golf driving range that is located in most residential neighborhoods, no matter what the Japanese city. Of course, there are far more Japanese citizens who aspire to play golf with golf club memberships than there are Japanese citizens who actually play golf. Then there are the Japanese who buy golf clothing and equipment for gifts for family members and friends who never get around to playing golf or using their gifts at golf driving ranges.

The families of the golfers are greatly affected by the playing of golf by certain family members. The non-golf players of the family have less family money available for other possible expenditures such as rental or purchase of apartments for young adults and senior citizens of the multigeneration family. Saving for retirement and for new, more spacious family homes may suffer as the golf expenses continually take funds. The playing of golf by family members takes time away from family group activities; the weekend is prime time for the employed golfer.

According to *Golf Digest* (Japan) magazine, there were over 2,000 golf courses in Japan in the fall of 1994. From October 1993 to October 1994 Japanese golf courses increased in number by 103, an increase of 5 percent. The increase from 1992 to 1993 was 12 percent; 205 golf courses were added to the inventory as the long-term Japanese recession set in. The decreasing increase from 1993 to 1994 is not surprising. But, from this pattern, we would expect golf course development and construction to continue slowly through the recession of the 1990s and early 2000s. Historically, a backlog of golf club membership applications has always assured a market for new golf courses. Using a conservative 2 percent rate of increase a year, we would expect the number of golf courses in Japan to approximate 2,200 to 2,300 at the beginning of the new millennium.

Where are Japan's golf courses? Of the five prefectures that house the most golf courses, three are in the Kanto region, in which Tokyo lies. Hokkaido Prefecture on Japan's northernmost island has more than 160 golf courses. Golf courses in the second ranking prefecture for golf courses, Hyogo, surround its prefecture capital, Kobe; this prefecture houses approximately 150 golf courses, which would be in easy proximity in the Kinki region to Kyoto, Nara, and Osaka, which are major urban places in the south-central part of Japan. Chiba, the third ranked prefecture for golf course locations, lies to the east of Tokyo; this prefecture houses approximately 140 golf courses. The fourth and fifth ranked prefectures for golf courses, Tochigi and Ibaraki, lie on the Kanto plain to the north and northeast of Tokyo Prefecture; there are approximately 250 golf courses in these prefectures. To the south and west of highly populated Yokohama lies Shizuoka Prefecture, in which 85 or more golf courses are located. Prefectures to the west, southwest, and northwest of Tokyo—Nagano, Gifu, Gunma, and Saitama—contain nearly 400 golf courses to cater to the demand from the highly populated Tokyo metropolitan area. The top 10 golf-course prefectures represent roughly 800 golf courses in total surrounding the Tokyo metropolitan area. These are only the top 10 prefectures of the total 47 prefectures that house golf courses in Japan. The prefecture with the lowest number of golf courses is Shimane, which has seven. This prefecture lies on the west coast, where the weather is less attractive, and to the west of Hiroshima and Nagasaki, which are very populous cities. Most of the golf course areas can be reached by train as well as by car.

Recently, Mitsukoshi Department Store finished the acquisition of land near the Narita International Airport for the Yachimata Country Club, whose land acquisition started in 1988. The cost of the land was $420 million, an amount nearly equal to the annual sales of the Mitsukoshi store in Tokyo's Ginza district. The decision about the development of the golf course comes at a time when major Japanese department stores are losing market share to specialty fashion retail stores and when major department store sales are lower due to the recession since 1992. The development of the golf course would require borrowing more than 10 billion yen (approximately $100 million) when Mitsukoshi Department Store already bears a large amount of debt. In 1998 one analyst stated that the Mitsukoshi group had lost money for seven years straight.

Characteristics of the Japanese golf equipment and clothing market reflect golf course and golf driving range importance to the Japanese society and the sectors of the society that are more directly associated with golf. The main consumer segment centers on men above the age of 25. The 30–44 age bracket of men represented one-third of golf equipment purchases; the 25–29 age group represented only 20 percent of golf equipment ownership. Imported equipment, which makes up about 30 percent of the market, attracts purchase by men over the age of 40. Specialty stores sell the most golf equipment, followed by department stores in a very distant second place. Women in the 25–29 age bracket tend to buy the most golf equipment, followed by women in the 30–34 age bracket. The criteria for golf equipment purchase focus on quality and then move to design, price, and brand name or maker in second to fourth place in the ranking from surveys.

Golf equipment imports approximated $640 million in 1998; this total was down by about 10 percent from the previous year. As the Japanese economy moved into a recession in 1991, imported golf equipment sales fell precipitously to the $450 million level. This total dropped by about $350 million by 1994 and then increased in 1995 to earlier levels. This sales pickup may be due to the increased overseas production of Japanese golf equipment manufacturers. There has also been an increase in imports of golf club shafts and heads from Taiwan and China for use in producing finished golf clubs in Japan. Most of the finished goods are imported from the United States, Taiwan, and China. The United States represents professional-caliber, name-brand golf clubs or popular brands with high brand awareness levels. The United States is the leading exporter of golf balls to Japan; 50 percent of the market for imported golf balls is associated with the United States. The other leading import origins are Malaysia and Taiwan. Since Japanese golf ball manufacturers are now located in Malaysia, imports from that country have increased.

Looking to golf clothing, men over the age of 25 make up the primary market; women—who represent only a very small part of the total golf clothing market—in the 25–34 age bracket buy the most golf clothing in the female sector. As with golf equipment, golf wear is purchased mainly in specialty stores; the distribution channel in a distant second place is the department store. The top-ranked criteria for Japanese purchase of golf wear are design, followed by quality, price, and brand/maker, in rank order from high to low. Around 25 percent of golf wear is imported.

RETAIL DEVELOPMENT IN GENERAL

Japan is a nation of shopkeepers! Yes, this comment is true to some extent. Japan has a lot of small retail businesses, just as other parts of Asia and Europe are filled with small shopkeepers.

Japanese shopping complexes are currently found in five basic locations: (1) central business districts of urban areas, (2) the community urban centers within major metropolitan areas, (3) railroad stations, (4) storefront building locations in smaller towns and neighborhoods within large urban communities of metropolitan areas, and (5) suburban locations. The majority of retail development is located in concentrated retail districts and at railway stations. The top ranked Japanese retail district, for example, is the Ginza district in Tokyo. Each of the major cities of Japan has secondary business districts outside its primary or central business district. Retail development is found in these commercial districts as well as near the train stations throughout Japan. The stations are so congested with people in the early morning and in the evenings with commuting traffic that the retailers simply have to be located in these markets. In the last 10 years shopping centers have been developed in suburban waterfront and other suburban areas of Japanese cities.

Foreign and domestic chain stores and superstores have been growing even more rapidly than department stores in Japan. While the department stores are gradually losing their share of retail market sales, chain stores and superstores are absorbing the department stores' lost sales.

SHOPPING CENTER DEVELOPMENT

Over 2,550 shopping centers are open for business in Japan, according to the Japan Council of Shopping Centers (JCSC), headquartered in Tokyo. In 1964 Japanese shopping centers numbered only 46. The rapid pace of Japanese shopping center development and construction took place in the latter 1970s, early 1980s, and the 1990s. Of the total of 2,658 centers in existence in 1999, 1,087 were developed between 1990 and 1999.

Average Center Size, Average Number of Tenants per Center, and Average Amount of Tenant Space Leased

In 1967 the average center size approximated 72,000 square feet; about 23 years later, the average center size was more than 205 times that size, about 200,000 square feet (see Exhibits 7-1–7-3). Since the mid-1990s, the average center size has been 160,000 square feet or larger. As the recession set in in 1991, the average center size was 110,000 square feet; the average center size increased through the decade of the 1990s as the recession continued. One reason for this enlargement of the average Japanese center was the introduction of factory outlet malls to serve the recession-weary population.

The Japan Council of Shopping Centers, Tokyo

In 1973 the Japan Council of Shopping Centers was established as a nonprofit trade association by its 180 original members to serve the shopping center industry. The association developed from a study team that was organized by businessmen who sought to advance the development of Japanese shopping centers. The study team at that time was chaired by Yoshio Matsushita, who was the director of the shopping center development division of the Daiei Company. (During the 1970s the Daiei Company became Japan's largest retail company.) At the initial meeting of the JCSC, Yoshio Matsushita was elected executive vice president, and Hideo Edo of Mitsui Fudosan was elected president.

The JCSC membership included retailers, developers, and related organizations. In the early years of the council, the number of retail and related company members far exceeded the number of members who were developers. As the years passed, the number of developer members began to significantly exceed the number of retail and related company members. The membership fees differ by member category; the fees for developers and related companies may be much higher than the membership fees for retail members.

The Japan Council of Shopping Centers is informally associated with the International Council of Shopping Centers of the United States, whose head-

Exhibit 7-1

Annual Context of Shopping Centers, 1971-1999: Increased Number of Shopping Centers by Year, Average Center Size in Square Meters, and Anchors (Numbers and Average Store Size in Square Meters)

Year	Increased Number of Shopping Centers by Year	Average Center Size in Square Meters	Anchors: Numbers	Average Size in Square Meters
Before & 1970	210	10,150.69	121	4.530.47
71	43	10,773.17	42	4,671.17
72	51	11,283.54	40	5,577.70
73	70	12,605.94	77	6,145.65
74	56	11,443.19	49	6,354.44
75	47	10,392.15	47	5,049.43
76	79	10,094.85	81	4,717.38
77	71	12,664.82	72	5,519.75
78	87	13,284.73	80	5,663.03
79	91	11,561.67	86	5,508.41
80	90	10,077.15	77	5,234.76
81	93	12,251.55	90	6,081.80
82	86	10,421.05	79	5,245.99
83	67	9,818.88	64	5,000.01
84	61	9,990.26	61	4,575.71
85	66	10,838.07	58	5,095.02
86	68	10,724.45	59	5,289.45
87	75	11,288.72	73	5,311.68
88	73	13,019.71	66	7,902.35
89	87	12,002.83	72	6,011.20
90	82	12,867.12	80	5,683.37
91	81	11,149.71	82	5,085.23
92	111	12,732.90	123	5,694.90
93	145	13,734.28	142	6,206.81
94	124	13,613.35	134	6,593.16
95	112	13,713.16	138	6,253.33
96	106	16,928.14	111	8,571.67
97	113	17,043.00	121	10,059.00
98	108	16,395.10	114	8,630.79
99	105	19,857.26	116	9,240,38
Total	2,658	13,370.20	2,556	6,271.87

Note: The increased number of shopping centers by year indicates the results of the newly opened centers minus the closed-out centers during the year.

Source: Japan Council of Shopping Centers, Tokyo, 2000. Reprinted with permission.

Exhibit 7-2
Shopping Center Tenant Characteristies: Tenants (Total Numbers, Numbers per Center, Average Size of Tenant Zone in Square Meters, and Average Size of a Tenant in Square Meters)

Year	Tenants: Numbers	Number of Tenants per one Center	Average Tenant Zone Size in Square Meters	Average Tenant Size in Square Meters
Before & 1970	14,013	67	4,816.92	75.87
71	2,074	48	4,111.09	89.67
72	2,396	47	4,090.45	88.75
73	3,149	45	3,746.54	87.34
74	2,313	41	3,625.48	91.88
75	2,076	44	3,333.38	79.26
76	3,326	42	3,508.24	84.90
77	3,390	48	4,482.89	97.85
78	4,486	52	4,164.08	81.16
79	3,966	44	3,643.10	86.46
80	4,084	45	3,540.16	81.37
81	3,923	42	3,561.90	86.20
82	3,551	41	3,141.02	76.78
83	2,269	34	2,913.91	87.54
84	2,318	38	3,282.17	88.71
85	2,782	42	3,606.72	86.58
86	2,768	41	3,762.85	94.93
87	3,245	43	3,407.14	81.05
88	3,125	43	3,625.46	85.20
89	4,205	48	4,380.17	93.35
90	3,382	41	4,657.52	113.77
91	2,797	35	3,448.66	99.17
92	4,209	38	3,577.13	93.98
93	5,745	40	4,809.91	122.51
94	4,596	37	3,625.00	99.61
95	4,440	40	3,971.35	102.22
96	4,545	43	5,670.35	133.11
97	4,753	42	5,742.00	136.51
98	4,205	39	5,633.86	143.18
99	4,783	46	7,255.00	159,27
Total	116,914	44	4,246.02	96.49

Source: Japan Council of Shopping Centers, Tokyo, 2000. Reprinted with permission.

Exhibit 7-3
Shopping Center Profile of Japan

	As of 1999 Survey
Total Number of Shopping Centers	2,658
Total Number of Tenants	116,914
Retail Tenants	87,360
Food Tenants	18,355
Service Tenants	11,199
Average Number of Tenants per Center	44
Total Leasable Area	35,538,006 square meters
Average Size of Center	13,370 square meters
Average Size of Anchor Stores	6,272 square meters
Average Space for Tenant Areas	4,246 square meters
	As of 1998 Survey
Total Shopping Center Sales	25,108,300 million yen
Average Sales per Center	9,589 million yen
Percent of Total Retail Sales	17.33
Average Sales per Tenant	87,661 thousand yen
Retail Tenants	90,329 thousand yen
Food Tenants	81,178 thousand yen
Service Tenants	72,865 thousand yen
Average Sales per Square Meter	3,253 thousand yen
Anchor Store	3,216 thousand yen
Ordinary Tenants	3,282 thousand yen

Source: Japan Council of Shopping Centers, Tokyo, 2000. Reprinted with permission.

quarters office is located in New York. In the year 2000, the JCSC celebrates its eighteenth anniversary. As well as holding an annual convention, the JCSC holds monthly meetings, lobbies for legislation that is favorable to shopping centers, and provides seminar training in marketing, management, and other areas of operation for prospective and current employees. Shopping center study tours in the United States, Europe, and other global regions are arranged for members and their employees to allow them exposure to advanced shopping center methods and practices in other countries. Self-study correspondence courses are offered to members. A monthly magazine and textbooks are published for the Japanese-speaking and -reading members. The various educational events that are sponsored by the JCSC have moved from the development focus to the marketing and management focus just as the educational events of the International Council of Shopping Centers have as the industry matures.

The Types of Centers and the Nature of the Shopping Center Developers

Centers that are planned and developed as integrated goods and service centers "under one roof" by a single development group are generally classified by JCSC as convenience and fashion centers. They probably could be categorized as superregional, regional, specialty, power, neighborhood, and community centers, as multiple centers fit into each such category with the continued development of Japanese shopping centers.

Traditionally, Japanese shopping centers have been developed primarily by department stores and their affiliated real estate companies and by real estate development companies that were not affiliated with retailer companies. Earlier statistics offered by the Japan Council of Shopping Centers split the categories of developers into (1) retailers, (2) non-retailers, and (3) private–public partnerships. The retailers that have been particularly associated with shopping center development include Daiei, Jusco, Mitsukoshi, and Takashimaya. The non-retailers that have particularly been absorbed in Japanese shopping center development include Mitsubishi Estate Co., Mitsui Fudosan, and Mori Building Company. The recently built factory outlet malls have involved private–public partnerships in which a governmental unit may have leased the land for 10 to 20 years to the private developer for the development of the mall. A summary description of a new 1.1 million-square-foot regional center, Himeji River City Shopping Center, with one department store, may be viewed in Exhibit 7-4. A descriptive summary of the new 2.3 million-square-foot regional mall Canal City Hakata Shopping Center, with one department store, in Fukuoka—a major city in southwestern Japan on Kyushu Island—may be viewed in Exhibit 7-5.

Some Trends in Retailing and Large-Scale Retail Stores in Particular

The number of large-scale retail stores generally leveled off during the 1990s at approximately 17,500 to 18,000. Large-scale retail stores are assumed to have 500 square meters or more space. Five hundred square meters is approximately 5,000 square feet. Together, these 18,000 large-scale retail stores utilize about 44 million square meters or 440 million square feet of space. As the recession of the 1990s occurred, the total square footage of these large-scale retail stores leveled off by the mid-1990s at roughly 44 million square meters.

By the end of the 1990s, the sales of department stores were suffering a little from the Japanese recession overall, but the traditional pattern of a quarterly peak during the third quarter of every year remained in place. The third quarter runs from October through December. The Christmas trade brings in more sales than any other quarter of the fiscal year for the department store. Among the top 10 retailers of Japan we find, in order of sales volume from highest to lowest,

Exhibit 7-4
Himeji River City Shopping Center Fact Sheet

Location:	520 Hosoe, Harima-ku, Hijemi-shi, Hyogo-ken 672-8064
Total Development Land Area:	26.6 acres
Architectural Design:	Five-level, climate-controlled, enclosed retail environment
Leasable Area:	50,161 square meters
Building Area:	107,610 square meters
Major Department Stores:	Jusco, Toys "R" Us, Japan
Number of Shops and Services:	148
Automobile Parking Spaces:	3,200
Bicycle Parking Spaces:	2,000
Other Facilities:	The Space, sports club; Space Lanes, bowling lanes; Plid's, entertainment centers
Owner:	Shikishima Boseki Co.
Developer:	Jusco Co.
General Contractor:	Takenaka Komuten Co.
Population of Total Trading Area:	1.1 million
Hours of Operation:	10:00 A.M.–8:00 P.M., anchor stores 10:00 A.M.–8:00 P.M., other stores 10:00 A.M.–10:00 P.M., restaurants
Annual Sales Volume:	38,500 million yen
Number of Visiting Customers:	10,000 weekdays, 30,000 weekends
Features:	The largest shopping center in Western Japan in 1993

Source: Japan Council of Shopping Centers, Tokyo, 2000. Reprinted with permission.

Mitsukoshi, Takashimaya, Seibu, and Daimaru. The volatility of quarterly change in department store sales increased as the new millennium approached. On average, about 20 percent of a department store's products are food products; about half of the merchandise amounts to clothing; and the remaining 30 percent includes houshold goods, home furnishings, furniture, sundries, accessories, and other products.

While the department store sales volume declined a little over the decade of the 1990s, supermarket sales rose somewhat over the same period. The volatility in their sales increased with the recessionary conditions, also. The supermarket companies that are normally listed among the top 10 retailers, from highest sales to lowest, are Daiei, Ito-Yokado, Seiyu, Nichii, and Uny.

Exhibit 7-5
Canal City Hakata Shopping Center Fact Sheet

Location:	217-30 Sumiyosi, Hakata-ku, Fukuoka-shi, Fukuoka 812-0018
Total Development Land Area:	8.6 acres
Architectural Design:	13 levels above ground, 2 levels underground building complex with canal
Leasable Area:	78,257 square meters
Building Area:	234,460 square meters
Major Department Stores:	Daiei Department Store (MEGA Vandle)
Number of Shops and Services:	133
Automobile Parking Spaces:	1,300
Other Facilities:	Fukuoka Washington Hotel, Fukuoka City Theater, Grand Hyatt Fukuoka, Business Center building, amusement specialty stores
Owner:	Fukuoka Jisho Co.
Developer:	F. J. Toshi Kaihatsu Co.
General Contractor:	Zenitaka-gumi, Shimizu Construction Co.; Ohbayashi-gumi, Fujita & Co.
Population of Total Trading Area:	2.12 million
Hours of Operation:	10:00 A.M.–8:00 P.M.
Annual Sales Volume:	50,000 million yen
Number of Visiting Customers:	5,000–6,000 weekdays, 100,000 weekends
Features:	Leading entertainment

Source: Japan Council of Shopping Centers, Tokyo, 2000. Reprinted with permission.

Government Restrictions

Government restrictions have been associated with retail store development, mergers and consolidations, and retail operating and leasing conditions. The restrictions have been associated more specifically with retail company size, store location, store opening hours, lease terms, and other chain and non-chain store operations in general. As retail companies and stores grew in size by the early 1970s, the small retailers asked the government to protect them against "unfair" competition from the large retailers and the large retail operations of shopping centers. As early as 1954 the government imposed limitations on store size and location. Generally, the federal, prefectural, and local governments resisted store and shopping center development involving selling space of 3,000 square meters or 32,258 square feet or more in the 10 biggest cities and store and shopping center development involving selling space of 1,500 square meters or 16,129 square feet or more in other shopping districts through an approval process that involves government, retail business, community, and professional representatives. The development, redevelopment, or expansion of a store building or center of any substantial size is dependent on the approval of the diversified membership of the approval organizations. Federal and local approvals are both required before the development, redevelopment, or construction may move forward. These regulations come from the 1977 amendment of the law concerning the Adjustment of Retail Business Operations in Large-Scale Retail Stores, passed by the Diet in 1954, the law on Special Measures for the Adjustment of Retail Business, passed in 1974, and other newly established state and local government regulations and rules. The enforcement of the approval process rests with the Ministry of International Trade and Industry (MITI). Smaller shopping centers and retail stores that are not subject to federal government approval may be subject to approval of prefectural and local governments.

In 1973 the Japanese government stepped into the private sector to regulate store hours. Isetan, one of the major department store/chain store operations, was affected by these store hour regulations, for example. In 1979 the government tightened curbs on chain store operations as the superstores were constructed in many city and suburban areas and competed effectively with existing small and large retailers. Since the retailing scene is filled with chain store operations, these restrictions were felt by the expanding sector of the retail distribution system.

Then in 1981 the government imposed obstacles to further mergers and consolidations among retail organizations, especially those with sales of more than $2 billion a year. The Japan Fair Trade Commission particularly focused its attention on the competitive aspects of the continuing merger and consolidation policy of the large Daiei retail company. The Daiei Company sought growth, until that time, from retail mergers and consolidations within the Japanese retail community. With the restrictions now on Japanese retail growth by this means, the Daiei organization looked abroad for new store locations, new store acquisitions, and new retailing partners for joint ventures.

These government restrictions on retailing growth of the 1970s and early 1980s have been compared by analysts to the European retailing growth restrictions imposed about the same time. Generally, the same government rationale underlies the trade restrictions in Western Europe and in Japan. These restrictions were brought about by the voting public among the numerous small retailers that felt the effective competition from chain store growth, including the growth of superstores or hypermarkets. The small retailers appealed to the federal, regional, prefectural, and local governments for protection against the "unfair" competition coming from the urban and suburban expansion of the growing and profitable chain store companies. Such limitations on store and center establishment, redevelopment, and expansion improve the profit position of existing retail stores and centers whose competition is limited by the government.

As the Japanese developers and retailers observed no retailing and shopping center development and redevelopment restrictions from the government in other market- and non-market-oriented economies of Asia and the United States, Japanese chain and department store retailers sought overseas markets in these two areas for expansion. These large-scale chain and department stores, including the superstores, entered the centralized, controlled, and socialistic economies such as the PRC as the Chinese and similar governments permitted good investment opportunities. The large Japanese retailers sought locations in growing economies where operating and locational restrictions were not present to impede their store growth.

The Large-Scale Retailing Law, which once greatly restricted the development of large-scale retail stores and shopping centers, has been revised in recent years. This change is part of the economic reform that has been encouraged by the international business community; this law greatly restricted the entry of foreign retailers and foreign land developers as well as the development plans of domestic retailers and of developers and their associated large-scale retail companies in the proposed project. Today public sentiment and the government, as represented by the revised Large-Scale Retailing Law, are more in favor of new, major land developments that may bring lower prices of desired consumer goods and services and more diverse retail offerings from new retail market entrants that may be based overseas.

The Entrance of Foreign Retailers

After McDonald's and Tiffany found success in their retail operations in Japan, the United States, the United Kingdom, and other foreign retailers ventured into this market. Toys "R" Us from the United States has located in a variety of positions in Japan. From the United Kingdom, Paul Smith, Boots, and Pizza Express have established themselves in Japan. While Boots established a joint venture with Mitsubishi, Pizza Express funded its entry costs with its own money. Virgin Cinemas has been particularly successful in Canal City Hakata Shopping Center in Fukuoka (Exhibit 7-5). This mixed-use complex is said to be one of the leading entertainment centers in Japan.

Shopping Center Lease Relationships

At this point in the shopping center development review, we want to look at the effect of the commercial code on landlord–tenant relations, some general leasing relationships, and some management and operational relationships.

The Effect of the Commercial Code of Japan on Lease Relationships

The commercial code, rather than the common law, is used in Japan for contracts and land development work. Generally, negotiation and reconciliation are used extensively before any lawsuit is considered in the case of a dispute. Japan is not a litigious society as the United States is.

Landlord–tenant law is a part of this general civil code legal system. Eviction of a shopping center tenant is rarely possible. Replacement of one retail tenant for another usually involves landlord discussion and negotiation with a tenant so that they mutually agree to the desired vacation of the storeroom premises. Negotiation and reconciliation are also used when the tenant does not agree to the landlord's suggested percentage rent, the base square footage rent terms, or the common area maintenance terms.

Some General Leasing Relationships

The tenants of both convenience-and fashion-oriented shopping centers tend to face good prospects for fixed or minimum guaranteed rents plus overage or percentage rent clauses. The rents of fashion-oriented centers generally exceed those of convenience-oriented centers in terms of average rent and the range of rents from the highest level to the lowest level. The storeroom square footage rent is, on average, the highest in underground malls; second highest in railway station retail complexes; third highest in underpass locations where the road or railway is above the retail space, which is located at ground level; and fourth highest in multiuse complexes. The rents of fashion-oriented centers tend to be highest for centers in major city central business district locations and second highest for centers in small city central business district locations. The larger the city, the higher the storeroom rent, whether the retail tenant is located in a fashion-oriented center or a convenience-oriented center. The tenant rent for space in an anchorless shopping center may exceed the rent in a center with at least one anchor if the center is a fashion-oriented center; the tenant rent for space in an anchorless shopping center may *not* exceed the rent in a center with at least one anchor if the center is a convenience center.

Storeroom square footage rents are, on average, higher the larger the shopping center. The rents for tenants of both fashion- and convenience-oriented centers tend to be higher the larger the center, but the relationship holds even more so for tenants of convenience-oriented centers. The retail tenant usually pays higher square footage rents than the food and service tenants of the same center, but the service tenants of a convenience-oriented center may pay higher square footage rents than the food or retail tenants. In a fashion-oriented center, the food tenant tends to pay higher rent than the service tenant; the reverse tends to be true in a convenience-oriented center. Tenant rents of fashion-oriented centers tend to be significantly higher than tenant rents of convenience-oriented centers.

Tenant rents in centers developed by non-retailers tend to be higher than tenant rents in centers developed by retailers and private–public partnerships; this relationship tends to hold true if the non-retailing organization is a real estate company.

The tenant of a shopping center pays, on average, more key money the larger the urban area of Japan. But tenants of convenience centers in the suburbs may pay more key money than tenants of convenience centers located in cities, in the distant outskirts of cities, and in rural areas. Tenants of fashion-oriented centers may pay far more key money to non-retail developers than to private–public partnership developers. But tenants of convenience-oriented centers may pay more key money per square foot to retail developers than to other types of convenience center developers. Regular storeroom tenant deposits may be higher when the shopping center is developed by a non-retail company than when the center is developed by retail companies or private–public partnerships. Higher regular deposit money may be required for tenants on the street level than for tenants located on higher levels and on the basement level of the shopping center. The higher the level of the tenant location, the lower the regular deposit on a square footage basis. In a fashion-oriented center, the level of the regular deposit for the tenant located on the basement level may be close to the level of the regular deposit for the tenant on the street level. The landlord may return the regular deposit to the tenant after 10 years of tenant occupancy; the reimbursement of the regular deposit may be spread over the next five to 15 years. When the tenant vacates the storeroom, which is usually at the end of the extended lease, the deposit is totally returned to the tenant by the landlord.

The costs for security, maintenance, regular and seasonal advertising, and heating and cooling must be borne by the center management and/or the center tenants. Rarely does the center landlord assume the costs of mall management. The common area maintenance expense per square foot is usually much higher for the tenant who occupies space in a fashion-oriented center than for the tenant in a convenience-oriented center. Common area maintenance expense per square foot tends to run significantly higher for tenants in centers developed by real estate companies than in centers developed by retailers and cooperatives. Retail tenants tend to pay higher common area maintenance expenses per square foot than food and service tenants in the same shopping center.

Generally, the storeroom lease permits tenants to use hallway space to display some of their goods and to store inventory that is awaiting use or disposal. For example, the refuse from the current operation of a restaurant in a high-rise office building may be permitted to extend out into an office building corridor as the tenant awaits trash pickup by a contracted service. In a shopping center, tenants may place their goods for sale a foot or two out into the shopping center hallway from the front finished exterior wall of the storeroom.

Some Management and Operational Relationships

The management of shopping centers is aided by computer data storage and analysis. For example, daily sales are reported by each tenant and stored on the computer for later analysis. In past years, JCSC has sampled shopping center data and published it for the membership to allow JCSC members to compare their center performances with industry averages.

HOTEL AND INN DEVELOPMENT

According to a White Paper on Tourism that was prepared by the Office of the Prime Minister from materials from the Environmental Health Bureau of the Ministry of Health and Welfare and the Tourism Department of the Transport Policy Bureau of the Ministry of Transport, the number of inns in Japan (approximately 2,000 inns) in the late 1990s was double the number of hotels in Japan (approximately 1,000 hotels). Even though Japan had many fewer hotels than inns, the number of hotel guest rooms (approximately 190,000 hotel guest rooms) far exceeded the total number of inn guest rooms (approximately 120,000 inn guest rooms). The inns, on average, contained 95 guest rooms, while hotels, on average, accommodated 120 guest rooms. The hotels attract, in general, a higher-paying clientele that is associated with business and tourism and provide a more complete set of services than the inns. The inns are often found in resort and recreational areas in the mountains and along the coastlines where particularly attractive weather conditions and associated recreational facilities attract tourists.

The domestic and foreign business traveling clientele is split among several categories of business hotels, but the high-priced hotels with more business services attract more of the foreign business clientele. The deluxe major city hotels, for example, attract foreign travelers due to their multilingual services at their reservation, concierge, and business center desks.

According to the previously mentioned White Paper on Tourism in the late 1990s, the *keihanshin* hotels maintained the highest occupancy rate of the three major types of registered hotels through most of the period from 1983 through 1997. This occupancy rate, which fluctuated a little between about 70 percent and about 80 percent, compared favorably with the lower occupancy rates of the *keihin* and national major registered hotels. The national major registered hotels maintained occupancy rates between 70 and 75 percent during the period analyzed; these hotels had the lowest occupancy rates during the period.

OFFICE BUILDING DEVELOPMENT

As we move from hotels and inns, let us review some office building demand and supply factors and the changing characteristics of Japanese office buildings.

Some Office Building Demand and Supply Factors

Increasing office space demand is encouraged by (1) the increase in employment in computer software development and telecommunications development, (2) the decline in Japanese office rents, which encourages more office space usage, (3) the increasing amount of office space per Japanese employee, and (4) the increasing number of office workers in Japanese cities such as Tokyo. The demand for office space is also encouraged by the two-year office building leases rather than longer leases like those in the United States and the United Kingdom and tenant tenure that gives tenant security as long as the contract rent terms are met. Increase in the supply of office space is discouraged by (1) the stringent underwriting requirements of Japanese banks for new loans associated with office space expansion, (2) the increasing office building vacancy rates, (3) the threatened unemployment on the horizon that is derived from numerous company announcements of large impending labor cutbacks, (4) the currently high unemployment rate (about 4.5%), (5) the declining office rents, which reduce the potential income and cash flow from the office building investment, (6) the continuing taxation of Japanese capital gains at the same rate as ordinary business taxable income, and (7) the relatively high bankruptcy rate. Office building development is encouraged by the rapidly declining commercial land prices but discouraged by the high construction cost associated with building structures that are "earthquake-proof." Office building development is discouraged by the high cost of land that is attractively located near established mass transit stations and the lack of developed lots for new office structures.

Characteristics of the Office Market

Office space in Japan is a very important component of the total Japanese real estate market. But the Tokyo office building market is a special part of the total market. The existing stock of Greater Tokyo office space continued to climb from 1980 through 1997, according to research into the price of fixed assets of the Japan Ministry of Home Affairs. In this research, the Greater Tokyo area for which data were collected includes the city of Tokyo and Kanagawa, Chiba, and Saitama Prefectures. In 1980 the total office stock approached 8,000 hectares; in 1997, in comparison, the stock was close to 20,000 hectares. The office floor area in the city of Tokyo made up more than half of these totals. Looking to essentially the same period trend for the 23 wards of Tokyo, we observe a higher increase in the office stock from the beginning to the end of the period: in 1975 office floor area comprised roughly 2,500 hectares, but by 1997 it comprised a little more than 7,500 hectares—a tripling of the office floor area in a little more than 20 years. For the Greater Tokyo area, the total office floor area slightly surpassed a doubling of space over the period 1980 to 1997, a 17-year period. Most of the increase in office space within the 23 wards of the city of Tokyo is associated with the 20 wards, excluding the three central wards. There was only a small gain in office floor space in the central three wards compared to the gain in the other 20 wards.

During the "bubble" real estate period from the mid-1980s to the early 1990s, office building starts added a lot of floor space in the Greater Tokyo area. The office building starts in the city of Tokyo added more floor space than did those in Kanagawa, Chiba, and Saitama Prefectures. Within the city of Tokyo, the office building starts of the 20 wards outside the three central wards of the city added more floor space than those in the inner wards. The peak in late 1989 and early 1990 absorbed more than 500 hectares of land. The building starts slid quickly down in the early 1990s and stabilized with smaller additions to office floor space (roughly 155 hectares a year) in the last half of the 1990s. In the latter period, vacancy rates of large-scale office buildings of the greater Tokyo area reached a peak—around 14 percent—in late 1994. As the available office space declined over the last half of the 1990s, the space available in the three central wards fell to 2,800,000 square meters from about 8,500,000 square meters available in 1993.

As the office vacancy rates declined during the last half of the 1990s, the index of offered rent for new tenants, which is based on the data of the Commercial Property Research Institute, fell significantly. By the fall of 1999 the office vacancy rate of Tokyo, for example, had fallen to 6 percent from a 1994 peak of 9.8 percent, according to the Tokyo Metropolitan Government and Ikoma Data Service System. According to the Ikoma Data Service, Tokyo office market rents at the end of 1992 were, on average, over 28 million yen per *tsubo* (one *tsubo* equals 3.3 square meters). This translates to about 8.6 million yen per square meter or $86,000 per square meter or $8,600 per square foot. In contrast, in the 1980s office land per square foot in central Tokyo was said to be worth approximately $25,000 per square foot. But, due to the decline in Tokyo office rents, the average rent was about 15 million yen per *tsubo* or 4.5 million yen per square meter or $4,500 per square foot. This is between one-fifth and one-sixth of the rent a few years earlier as the recession set in. The older the office building, the higher the amount of vacant space, according to a Miki Office Report. In this report, new buildings were defined as those built within 12 months of the survey date. The smaller the scale of the building, the higher the vacancy rate, generally speaking. At least, the large-scale buildings from late 1990 to the fall of 1999 exhibited the lowest vacancy rates in comparison with small- and medium-sized office buildings. Large-scale buildings were defined to contain more than 100 *tsubo* per floor; medium-sized buildings had 50 to 99 *tsubo* per floor; and small-scale buildings had less than 50 *tsubo* per floor.

Japan Building Owners & Managers Association (Japan B.O.M.A.) analyzes office buildings from a sample of over 3,000 office buildings from diverse locations across Japan from data contributed by close to 2,000 Japan B.O.M.A. members in most of Japan's prefectures. About one-fourth of the office building sample contained less than 3,000 square meters of space (Exhibit 7-6). At the

Exhibit 7-6
Analysis by Size

( ) : %

	Under 3,000m²	3,000m²~ 5,000m²	5,000m²~ 10,000m²	10,000m²~ 20,000m²	20,000m²~ 50,000m²	50,000m² and Over	Total Number of Bldgs.
All Cities	757 (27)	429 (15)	670 (24)	491 (18)	318 (11)	127 (5)	2,792 (100)
Sapporo	23 (20)	19 (17)	33 (29)	27 (24)	11 (10)		113 (100)
Aomori	15 (75)	2 (10)	3 (15)				20 (100)
Morioka	3 (27)	2 (18)	3 (27)	2 (18)	1 (10)		11 (100)
Sendai	12 (19)	9 (14)	19 (30)	18 (29)	5 (8)		63 (100)
Niigata	9 (43)	1 (5)	7 (33)	4 (19)			21 (100)
Ibaraki	10 (44)	4 (17)	6 (26)	2 (9)	1 (4)		23 (100)
Saitama	18 (50)	3 (9)	8 (23)	3 (9)	3 (9)		35 (100)
Chiba	13 (20)	12 (18)	19 (29)	11 (16)	7 (10)	5 (7)	67 (100)
Tokyo	399 (31)	213 (17)	290 (23)	176 (14)	132 (10)	70 (5)	1,280 (100)
Kanagawa	29 (31)	25 (27)	15 (16)	9 (10)	11 (12)	4 (4)	93 (100)
Nagoya	26 (16)	21 (13)	37 (23)	36 (22)	35 (21)	9 (5)	164 (100)
Gifu	32 (54)	4 (7)	13 (22)	7 (12)	3 (5)		59 (100)
Toyama	4 (20)	2 (10)	3 (15)	8 (40)	3 (15)		20 (100)
Kanazawa	5 (26)	4 (21)	5 (26)	2 (11)	2 (11)	1 (5)	19 (100)
Fukui	8 (41)	2 (11)	6 (32)	2 (11)	1 (5)		19 (100)
Kyoto	10 (28)	2 (6)	8 (23)	8 (23)	5 (14)	2 (6)	35 (100)
Osaka	51 (14)	44 (12)	85 (24)	99 (27)	52 (15)	27 (8)	358 (100)
Hyogo	31 (26)	19 (16)	35 (30)	17 (15)	12 (10)	3 (3)	117 (100)
Nara	20 (70)	5 (17)	1 (3)	3 (10)			29 (100)
Okayama	4 (17)	5 (21)	6 (24)	4 (17)	5 (21)		24 (100)
Chugoku	16 (20)	11 (14)	27 (33)	19 (23)	7 (9)	1 (1)	81 (100)
Shikoku	7 (20)	3 (9)	15 (43)	6 (17)	4 (11)		35 (100)
Tokushima	2 (18)	4 (37)	1 (9)	3 (27)		1 (9)	11 (100)
Kyushu	10 (11)	13 (14)	25 (26)	25 (26)	18 (19)	4 (4)	95 (100)

Source: Japan Building Owners & Managers Association (B.O.M.A.), "Extracts from Annual Survey on Japan B.O.M.A. Member Buildings, 1997" (Tokoyo: B.O.M.A.). Reprinted with permission.

same time, less than 5 percent of the sample buildings contained 50,000 square meters (roughly 500,000 square feet) or more; more than half of these large office buildings were located in Tokyo. The second most highly represented group of office buildings was the group with 5,000 to 10,000 square meters of office space or 50,000 to 100,000 square feet. When we consider the height of Japanese office buildings from the most recent B.O.M.A. Japan-wide sample research, we note that the category with about 40 percent of the office buildings was the eight- to nine-story building category (Exhibit 7-7). The second ranking height category was that of the six- to seven-story buildings; this category accounted for 20 percent of the sample. About 2.5 percent of the sample buildings had more than 20 floors and were located mainly in Tokyo and Osaka.

Let us turn to the findings of the latest B.O.M.A. sample office building research as they concern the use of the office building total floor space. The area of the average office building devoted to office use was 40 percent of the total office building space (Exhibit 7-8). About 1.5 percent of the total space was devoted to warehouse space; about 1 percent to conference room space; about 6 percent to parking space; about 12 percent to retail stores; and about 8 percent to building owner use.

The latest B.O.M.A. survey research shows that Japanese office rents range from under 2,000 yen per square meter per month to 15,000 yen per square meter per month (roughly \$2 per square foot per month to about \$15 per square foot per month) (Exhibit 7-9). The majority of the office rents fall in categories between \$3 per square foot per month and \$5.5 per square foot per month. Thirty-six office buildings in the B.O.M.A. national sample were associated with rent of \$15 per square foot per month or more. The average rent for the national sample was over \$6 per square foot per month. The definition used for "substantial monthly rent" was monthly rent plus the monthly allocation of 10 percent deposit money plus lease loan times 10 percent minus the average rate of the lease loan. The formula for substantial monthly rent is monthly rent + (deposit money 10% + lease loan × [10% − average rate of lease loan]) × 1/12.

International office rent comparisons in mid-1999 show that the office rent in the three central wards of the city of Tokyo ranked at the top of the worldwide sample in either Japanese yen, the local currency, or U.S. dollars per square foot or per square meter. Moscow and Beijing were not included in the CB Richard Ellis international comparative analysis. The central Tokyo office rent in local terms was quoted at 39,000 yen per *tsubo* per month or U.S.\$131.36 per square foot per annum.

When the average vacant space was examined more closely, some strategic relationships were observed. The percent of vacant rentable office space was over 4 percent. The vacant retail store space amounted to a little over 1 percent of the total retail space (Exhibit 7-10). Of the warehouse space of the average office building, 3.5 percent was vacant. Therefore, from the nationwide office building sample we may note that the vacancy rates are relatively low in U.S.

Exhibit 7-7
Analysis by Height

( ) : %

	Under 5 Stories	6 ~ 7 Stories	8 ~ 9 Stories	10~11 Stories	12~15 Stories	16~20 Stories	Above 21 Stories	Total	The Highest Stories
All Cities	373 (13)	529 (20)	1,185 (43)	371 (13)	200 (7)	64 (2)	68 (2)	2,790 (100)	70
Sapporo	7 (6)	32 (28)	56 (50)	11 (10)	5 (4)	2 (2)		113 (100)	20
Aomori	9 (45)	8 (40)	3 (15)					20 (100)	9
Morioka	3 (27)	3 (27)	4 (37)	1 (9)				11 (100)	10
Sendai	2 (3)	13 (21)	39 (61)	5 (8)	3 (5)	1 (2)		63 (100)	20
Niigata	7 (32)	5 (24)	6 (29)	2 (10)	1 (5)			21 (100)	13
Ibaraki	4 (17)	5 (22)	10 (44)	3 (13)		1 (4)		23 (100)	19
Saitama	11 (31)	14 (40)	9 (26)		1 (3)			35 (100)	14
Chiba	14 (21)	19 (29)	21 (32)	6 (9)	3 (4)	1 (1)	3 (4)	67 (100)	29
Tokyo	143 (11)	225 (18)	576 (45)	197 (15)	77 (6)	22 (2)	40 (3)	1,280 (100)	60
Kanagawa	18 (20)	20 (22)	40 (43)	10 (11)	1 (1)	2 (2)	1 (1)	92 (100)	70
Nagoya	14 (9)	20 (12)	71 (43)	27 (16)	19 (12)	10 (6)	3 (2)	164 (100)	26
Gifu	36 (61)	9 (15)	10 (17)	3 (5)	1 (2)			59 (100)	14
Toyama	3 (15)	7 (35)	4 (20)	4 (20)	2 (10)			20 (100)	14
Kanazawa	5 (26)	3 (16)	8 (42)		1 (5)	2 (11)		19 (100)	18
Fukui	8 (43)	5 (26)	4 (21)	1 (5)	1 (5)			19 (100)	12
Kyoto	3 (9)	6 (17)	19 (54)	5 (14)	2 (6)			35 (100)	13
Osaka	25 (7)	58 (16)	155 (43)	47 (13)	45 (13)	13 (4)	15 (4)	358 (100)	39
Hyogo	20 (17)	22 (19)	40 (34)	19 (16)	9 (8)	2 (2)	5 (4)	117 (100)	32
Nara	19 (66)	10 (34)						29 (100)	7
Okayama	2 (8)	6 (25)	12 (50)	1 (4)	3 (13)			24 (100)	14
Chugoku	9 (11)	13 (16)	35 (43)	11 (14)	9 (11)	4 (5)		81 (100)	20
Shikoku	1 (3)	5 (14)	20 (57)	4 (11)	3 (9)	2 (6)		35 (100)	16
Tokushima	4 (37)	3 (27)	2 (18)	2 (18)				11 (100)	11
Kyushu	6 (6)	18 (19)	41 (44)	12 (13)	14 (15)	2 (2)	1 (1)	94 (100)	21

Source: Japan Building Owners & Managers Association (B.O.M.A.), ''Extracts from Annual Survey on Japan B.O.M.A. Member Buildings, 1997'' (Tokoyo: B.O.M.A.). Reprinted with permission.

Exhibit 7-8

Analysis by Use of Floor Space (square meters)

	Number of Bldgs.	Rentable Area							Used by Owner m²	(Common Use) Total (A) m²	A/B %	Grand Total (B) m²
		Rentable to Tenant										
		Office m²	Store m²	Ware House m²	Conference Room m²	Parking m²	Miscellaneous m²	Total m²				
All Cities	2,106	10,914,104	2,957,148	337,262	249,229	1,512,622	975,859	16,946,224	1,913,525	(6,351,293) 18,859,749	75	25,211,042
Sapporo	102	361,430	75,100	6,272	11,938	41,182	27,948	523,870	57,829	(218,934) 581,699	73	800,633
Aomori	20	20,314	3,511	1,482	1,010	3,082	835	30,234	5,856	(14,151) 36,090	72	50,241
Morioka	10	22,305	16,363	1,242	3,268	876	13,218	57,272	1,839	(31,395) 59,111	65	90,506
Sendai	44	144,600	49,341	3,688	3,865	23,640	28,440	253,574	45,484	(79,877) 299,058	79	378,935
Niigata	21	45,369	17,699	1,962	1,114	993	9,703	76,840	12,229	(32,600) 89,069	73	121,669
Ibaraki	19	57,007	6,929	147	6,983	2,791	258	74,115	5,480	(36,009) 79,595	69	115,604
Saitama	33	63,905	36,155	2,821	3,614	7,690	1,706	115,891	8,657	(69,484) 124,548	64	194,032
Chiba	50	167,398	237,828	5,642	4,225	29,435	33,420	477,948	52,079	(166,216) 530,027	76	696,243
Tokyo	792	5,102,232	622,532	156,187	47,752	627,929	229,539	6,786,171	718,506	(2,409,712) 7,504,677	76	9,914,389
Kanagawa	66	169,230	305,474	5,283	3,030	67,398	8,161	558,576	44,562	(146,513) 603,138	80	749,651
Nagoya	146	871,294	341,129	22,935	23,916	156,358	122,898	1,538,530	146,253	(622,112) 1,684,783	73	2,306,895
Gifu	37	47,604	53,589	1,692	9,488	3,628	22,050	138,051	104,153	(40,783) 242,204	86	282,987
Toyama	18	50,584	9,722	2,986	8,091	1,751	6,904	80,038	74,700	(33,698) 154,738	82	188,436
Kanazawa	18	43,765	51,173	1,682	899	11,567	6,404	115,490	10,542	(57,913) 126,032	69	183,945
Fukui	10	15,391	6,429	331	7,781	3,484	5,943	39,359	18,979	(22,599) 58,338	72	80,937
Kyoto	32	147,684	25,023	2,146	10,006	16,764	17,622	219,245	16,710	(94,028) 235,955	72	329,983
Osaka	337	2,285,295	621,090	86,860	44,171	340,793	267,772	3,645,981	276,953	(1,391,788) 3,922,934	74	5,314,722
Hyogo	98	354,259	83,058	8,417	13,360	37,896	29,916	526,906	32,481	(233,974) 559,387	71	793,361
Nara	29	24,955	29,429	1,379	712	3,275	4,062	63,812	2,543	(15,150) 66,355	81	81,505
Okayama	23	61,210	53,236	1,509	9,537	2,077	19,724	147,293	63,773	(57,054) 211,066	79	268,120
Chugoku	73	257,568	80,861	6,531	6,518	49,039	44,478	444,995	129,555	(168,406) 574,550	77	742,956
Shikoku	35	128,172	42,415	2,777	4,272	12,929	9,972	200,537	14,248	(60,408) 214,785	78	275,193
Tokushima	11	16,082	43,848	3,744	3,915	2,403	11,953	81,945	4,883	(39,447) 86,828	69	126,275
Kyushu	82	456,451	145,214	9,547	19,764	65,642	52,933	749,551	65,231	(309,042) 814,782	73	1,123,824

Source: Japan Building Owners & Managers Association (B.O.M.A.), "Extracts from Annual Survey on Japan B.O.M.A. Member Buildings, 1997" (Tokoyo: B.O.M.A.). Reprinted with permission.

Exhibit 7-9
Substantial Monthly Rent of Standard Office Space

Cities \ 100Yen/m² Month	Under 20	20 ~ 25	25 ~ 30	30 ~ 35	35 ~ 40	40 ~ 45	45 ~ 50	50 ~ 55	55 ~ 60	60 ~ 65	65 ~ 70	70 ~ 75	75 ~ 80	80 ~ 85	85 ~ 90	90 ~ 95	95 ~ 100	100 ~ 105	105 ~ 110	110 ~ 115	115 ~ 120	120 ~ 125	125 ~ 130	130 ~ 135	135 ~ 140	140 ~ 145	145 ~ 150	150 and Over	Total	Average Yen/m² month
All Cities	8	18	48	65	62	69	59	54	46	27	29	17	22	21	15	13	2	4	5	2	2	3	3	3	2	1	1	36	637	6,177
Sapporo	2	3	3	6	2	5	4	1		1		1																	28	3,729
Aomori		1		2																									3	2,912
Morioka			1																										1	2,790
Sendai		1	5	6	4	1	4			3					1	1													26	4,268
Niigata	1	1	1		2	1																							6	3,119
Ibaraki			1	2			1		1																				5	3,880
Saitama					1	3																							4	4,102
Chiba				1	3	1	1		1					1															8	4,561
Tokyo	1	2	1	9	9	9	12	21	13	13	20	12	18	14	11	10	2	3	4	2	1	3	1	3	2	1	1	36	234	9,143
Kanagawa		2		5	2	1	2	1	2	3	1																		19	4,491
Nagoya		2	5	10	8	11	6	7	5	3	1		1	1					1										61	4,501
Gifu					1																								1	3,680
Toyama			1		1																								2	3,049
Kanazawa	1						1	1																					3	3,891
Fukui																														
Kyoto		1	2			1	2	2	2																				10	4,268
Osaka	1	2	4	7	12	13	10	5	17	4	6	4	3	5	3	2		1			1		2						102	5,525
Hyogo			2	1	10	6	3	8	3		1																		34	4,518
Nara		1	5	1	1				1																				9	3,271
Okayama		1	2	1		3	2																						9	3,677
Chugoku			2	6	1	5	7																						21	3,939
Shikoku	1		2	2	2	1																							8	3,178
Tokushima			1																										1	2,990
Kyushu	1	1	10	6	3	8	4	8	1																				42	3,870

Note: Substantial rent is calculated by the following: Substantial monthly rent = monthly rent + (deposit money 10% + lease loan × [10% − avg. rate of lease loan]) × 1/12.

Source: Japan Building Owners & Managers Association (B.O.M.A.), "Extracts from Annual Survey on Japan B.O.M.A. Member Buildings, 1997" (Tokoyo: B.O.M.A.). Reprinted with permission.

Exhibit 7-10
Vacancy Rate Analysis by Use of Floor Space

	Total Area	Rentable Area	Rentable Area other than Owner's use			Office			Store			Warehouse		
			Space (A)	Vacant Space (B)	B/A	Space	Vacant Space	Vacancy Rate	Space	Vacant Space	Vacancy Rate	Space	Vacant Space	Vacancy Rate
	m²	m²	m²	m²	%	m²	m²	%	m²	m²	%	m²	m²	%
All Cities	24,706,968	18,420,388	13,793,340	515,710	3.7	10,692,815	470,893	4.4	2,769,736	33,195	1.2	330,789	11,622	3.5
Sapporo	777,576	573,109	454,518	18,964	4.2	375,374	17,701	4.7	72,841	1,089	1.5	6,303	174	2.8
Aomori	50,241	36,090	25,307	2,953	11.7	20,314	2,888	14.2	3,511			1,482	65	4.4
Morioka	90,506	59,111	39,910	55	0.1	22,305	55	0.2	16,363			1,242		
Sendai	489,484	374,310	258,710	15,927	6.2	200,053	15,094	7.5	54,401	79	0.1	4,256	754	17.7
Niigata	121,669	89,069	65,030	4,151	6.4	45,369	3,403	7.5	17,699	650	3.7	1,962	98	5.0
Ibaraki	117,890	81,714	66,269	2,157	3.3	59,124	1,776	3.0	6,998	381	5.4	147		
Saitama	232,215	160,152	136,513	1,643	1.2	61,838	1,112	1.8	71,960	480	0.7	2,715	51	1.9
Chiba	563,192	434,248	314,354	16,004	5.1	120,548	14,758	12.2	190,718	756	0.4	3,088	490	15.9
Tokyo	9,220,370	6,958,930	5,467,582	209,005	3.8	4,770,495	201,776	4.2	548,404	5,509	1.0	148,683	1,720	1.2
Kanagawa	1,048,653	789,704	521,369	14,069	2.7	252,278	12,281	4.9	257,752	1,551	0.6	11,339	237	2.1
Nagoya	2,244,821	1,647,219	1,232,787	33,215	2.7	869,836	28,474	3.3	340,364	3,375	1.0	22,587	1,366	6.0
Gifu	275,223	234,172	105,412	1,026	1.0	50,735	609	1.2	53,444	390	0.7	1,233	27	2.2
Toyama	185,055	153,093	61,087	2,027	3.3	48,803	1,934	4.0	9,375	93	1.0	2,909		
Kanazawa	183,007	125,378	96,348	5,126	5.3	43,493	2,577	5.9	51,173	2,442	4.8	1,682	107	6.4
Fukui	73,871	52,463	21,211	870	4.1	15,816	492	3.1	5,064	378	7.5	331		
Kyoto	308,346	220,209	160,674	7,609	4.7	134,829	7,440	5.5	23,919	121	0.5	1,926	48	2.5
Osaka	5,265,058	3,885,915	2,922,125	117,203	4.0	2,250,910	107,113	4.8	585,068	5,191	0.9	86,147	4,899	5.7
Hyogo	805,319	564,443	455,240	22,118	4.9	365,783	20,356	5.6	81,947	1,259	1.5	7,510	503	6.7
Nara	80,555	65,484	55,314	3,715	6.7	24,796	2,801	11.3	29,139	914	3.1	1,379		
Okayama	268,120	211,066	115,955	2,306	2.0	61,210	700	1.1	53,236	1,606	3.0	1,509		
Chugoku	728,845	554,302	361,228	8,897	2.5	274,475	8,524	3.1	80,661	303	0.4	6,092	70	1.1
Shikoku	272,342	212,795	171,399	682	0.4	126,207	581	0.5	42,415	86	0.2	2,777	15	0.5
Tokushima	126,275	86,828	63,674	1,433	2.3	16,082	1,047	6.5	43,848	362	0.8	3,744	24	0.6
Kyushu	1,178,335	850,584	621,324	24,555	4.0	482,142	17,401	3.6	129,436	6,180	4.8	9,746	974	10.0

Source: Japan Building Owners & Managers Association (B.O.M.A.), ''Extracts from Annual Survey on Japan B.O.M.A. Member Buildings, 1997'' (Tokoyo: B.O.M.A.). Reprinted with permission.

terms; that the retail store space is almost fully occupied, on average, during Japan's recession era; and that the greatest vacancy rates are experienced in office and warehouse space within the total office building. In the last half of the 1980s, all parts of most office buildings in Japan were essentially totally rented since the vacancy rates on average and for the office and the retail space were less than 2 percent at any time. The vacancy rates that have been disturbing to Japanese real estate market participants have occurred since the recession started in 1992; the office vacancy rates within the office building sample rose to a peak in 1994 and then declined (Exhibit 7-11). The vacancy rate for the retail space of the average office building stayed less than 2 percent even when a peak vacancy rate was reached in 1995.

Office space per worker comparisons across the world show that rentable office space per worker in Tokyo is significantly less than that of Frankfurt, Paris, or New York and very close to that of London. Comparisons of gross office space per worker in terms of square meters show that the 1997 Tokyo gross office space per worker is significantly less than that for London. In Tokyo the office space per worker has been rising on a square meters per worker basis since the early 1970s. In 1995 there was a sizable average increase in office worker space; a decline in office space per worker in Tokyo took place in 1996; and then an upsurge of office space per worker occurred in 1997, the last year for which B.O.M.A. office research findings are available (Exhibit 7-12). A national survey of per capita office floor area in Japan that excluded the B.O.M.A. data shows even more improvement in per capita space since 1978; there was steady improvement in worker space through the sample period 1978 through 1997.

The 1997 survey of Japan B.O.M.A. member buildings shows some interesting highlights about office building service charges for the common space and for tenant space. Exhibit 7-13 shows that the tenant service charges for the common space of an office building generally are included in the monthly service charge, not charged by an individual fee nor included in the monthly rent. But the way the service charges for the tenant space are handled depends on the type of tenant space charge. Quite often air conditioning, heating, ventilation, and window cleaning are included in the monthly service charge. But electricity, water, gas, and floor cleaning are quite often charged through an individual tenant fee.

Japan B.O.M.A. is a federation of 24 associations of building owners and managers that has 1,859 corporate members who manage 31,985 buildings. Tokyo B.O.M.A. has approximately 450 corporate members who manage roughly 1,300 office buildings.

HOUSING DEVELOPMENT AND VARIOUS HOUSING CHARACTERISTICS

Since housing development is a strategic form of land development in every country, let us review some housing development, spatial, price, and price-

Exhibit 7-11
Trend of Vacancy Rate (1985–1997)

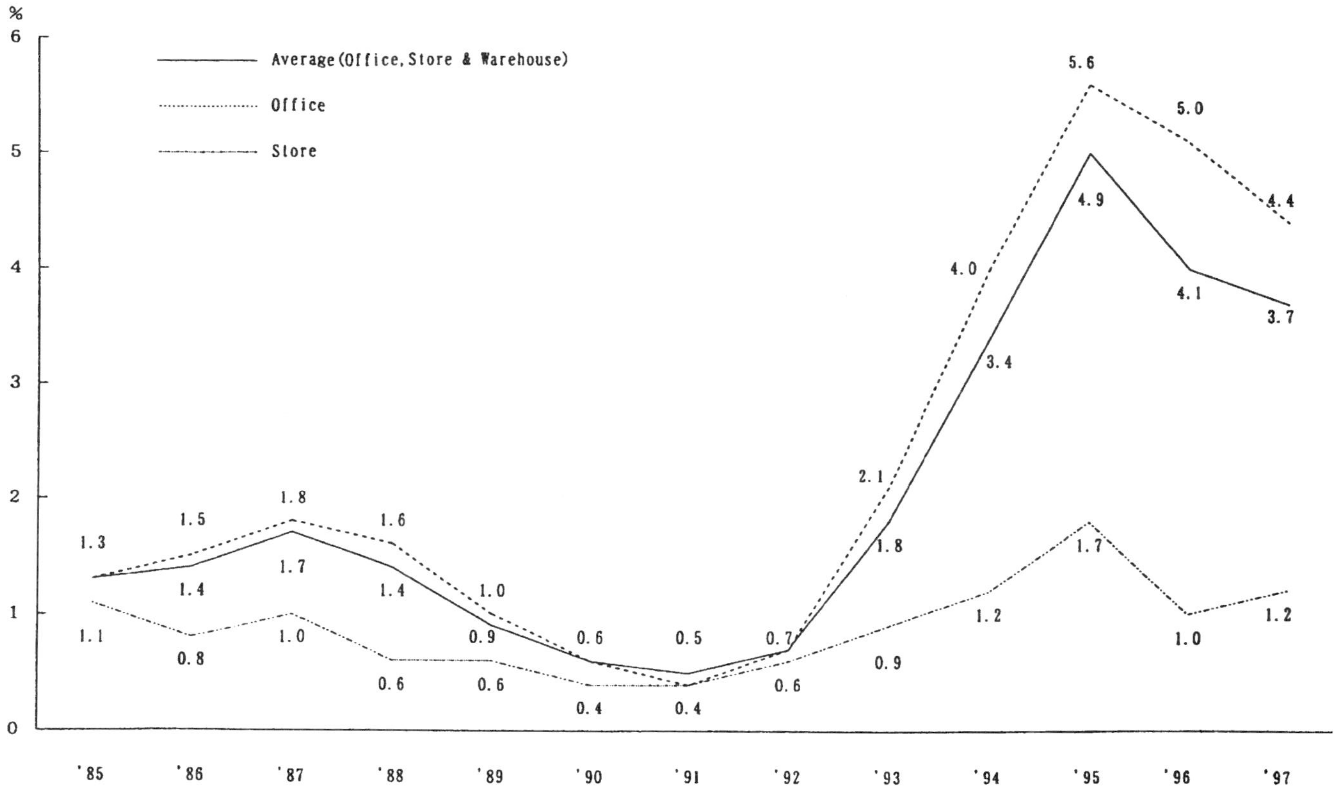

Source: Japan Building Owners & Managers Association (B.O.M.A.), ''Extracts from Annual Survey on Japan B.O.M.A. Member Buildings, 1997'' (Tokoyo: B.O.M.A.). Reprinted with permission.

Exhibit 7-12
Average Square Meters per Person

	Number of buildings	Number of Occupants	Avg. Sq. M. Per Person-Total Area	Ave. Sq. M. Per Person-Rentable Area
All Cities	1,931	967,826	24.0 m²	17.7 m²
Sapporo	90	32,240	22.6	16.3
Aomori	20	1,682	28.1	19.7
Morioka	10	3,306	27.4	17.9
Sendai	41	13,253	24.7	18.9
Niigata	21	4,491	26.2	18.9
Ibaraki	19	4,667	24.2	16.5
Saitama	31	7,833	23.8	15.0
Chiba`	42	18,011	28.8	21.0
Tokyo	696	382,880	23.3	17.5
Kanagawa	61	23,810	29.7	23.8
Nagoya	145	94,683	23.5	17.0
Gifu	32	6,685	38.5	32.5
Toyama	17	5,623	30.8	24.9
Kanazawa	17	5,092	34.8	23.4
Fukui	9	1,997	37.6	26.3
Kyoto	29	10,316	29.2	20.4
Osaka	324	218,319	23.3	17.0
Hyogo	87	31,508	22.8	15.8
Nara	22	2,113	28.3	22.0
Okayama	23	8,060	33.0	25.9
Chugoku	71	26,753	23.9	18.8
Shikoku	35	12,689	21.6	16.8
Tokushima	9	2,492	43.4	29.2
Kyushu	80	49,323	21.5	15.5

Source: Japan Building Owners & Managers Association (B.O.M.A.), ''Extracts from Annual Survey on Japan B.O.M.A. Member Buildings, 1997'' (Tokoyo: B.O.M.A.). Reprinted with permission.

Exhibit 7-13
Some Data about Service Charges

( ) : %

		Included in Monthly Service Charge	Charged by Individual Fee	Included in Monthly Rent	Number of Buildings
S.C. for Common Space	Cleaning	1,671 (92)	27 (1)	132 (7)	1,830 (100)
	Night Watch	1,564 (87)	14 (1)	211 (12)	1,789 (100)
	Elevator	1,596 (89)	23 (1)	176 (10)	1,795 (100)
	Repairs & Maintenance	1,621 (89)	10 (1)	190 (10)	1,821 (100)
	Supplies	1,594 (88)	57 (3)	160 (9)	1,811 (100)
	Electricity	1,579 (86)	139 (8)	112 (6)	1,830 (100)
	Water	1,463 (80)	249 (14)	105 (6)	1,817 (100)
	Gas	1,073 (77)	219 (16)	94 (7)	1,386 (100)
S.C. for Tenant Space	Air Conditioning	935 (56)	681 (40)	69 (4)	1,685 (100)
	Heating	955 (56)	690 (40)	74 (4)	1,719 (100)
	Ventilating	963 (62)	492 (32)	85 (6)	1,540 (100)
	Electricity	51 (3)	1,720 (95)	32 (2)	1,803 (100)
	Water	197 (14)	1,139 (83)	41 (3)	1,377 (100)
	Gas	161 (20)	623 (75)	39 (5)	823 (100)
	Window Cleaning	1,007 (68)	330 (22)	144 (10)	1,481 (100)
	Floor Cleaning	175 (21)	616 (74)	26 (3)	817 (100)

Source: Japan Building Owners & Managers Association (B.O.M.A.), ''Extracts from Annual Survey on Japan B.O.M.A. Member Buildings, 1997'' (Tokoyo: B.O.M.A.). Reprinted with permission.

income features of the Japanese market and comparative features from the United States and leading European countries.

Housing Development

Housing development must accommodate the growing diversity of residents of Japan. The indigenous population is very homogeneous in terms of race, religion, and family and household size. Even though most Japanese people consider themselves "middle-income," there is a rather wide disparity in income per capita and per household. Diversity of the population increased when Japan permitted entry of various types of foreigners who would provide labor in areas of scarcity as unemployment rates became very low and as people became affluent. The population became more diverse as Philippine, Taiwanese, Korean, and other Asian nationals were permitted immigration to provide unskilled labor that was quite scarce. The changes in the population have continued with the permanent and temporary immigration of more affluent, skilled workers in financial services, computer software and hardware, and telecommunications. At present, housing development must accommodate a more diverse population in Japan than was true in earlier decades. The new millennium promises even more population changes that will impact housing development further.

The basic challenges of Japanese housing development are associated with scarce and expensive land zoned for housing, generally expensive housing production due to earthquake- and fire-resistant building codes, and the density of development in locations relatively convenient to numerous workplaces. More and more Japanese residents are attracted to the major cities, which offer higher levels of employment, higher incomes, ample opportunities for leisure-time activities, educational opportunities, and cultural attractions by way of museums, shrines, and other land improvements.

Housing Supply and Demand

As the total number of households has increased since the 1960s, the number of dwellings has also increased in even greater magnitude. The latest national housing survey shows that the number of vacant dwellings has increased in this process of change. As one example, we note that the number of condominiums in inventory in the late 1990s had increased with the slowdown in condominium demand during the uncharacteristically long recession. But, with the general affluence of the population, the number of dwellings per household was steadily increasing; by 1993, the number of dwellings per household reached 1.12.

The rate of owner-occupied households had gradually fallen to a little less than 60 percent. In the Greater Tokyo area, the rate of homeownership has been rather steady over recent decades at approximately 50 percent.

In comparison, the homeownership rate of the United States is approximately 65 percent; the rate in the United Kingdom, 66 percent; the rate in Germany,

38 percent; and the rate in France, 53 percent. Most major cities in whatever country usually have lower homeownership rates than smaller cities and towns; we just mentioned this relationship for Japan as a whole versus the Greater Tokyo area.

The older the persons occupying a dwelling unit, the more chance there is for homeownership rather than rental. Seventy percent of persons 50 years old or older tend to own their own dwelling units, which include attached and detached single-family units and low-, mid-, and high-rise condos.

As housing starts fell to 1.3 million units per year in the late 1990s, the development of new residential lots declined to approximately 10,500 hectares a year. Consumer expectations during the 1990s recession reduced the number of built-to-suit houses by landowners. The annual development of housing units for sale held steady around 350,000 units a year. Approximately 25,000 corporate housing units continued to be provided for employees each year. Roughly 500,000 to 600,000 housing units for rent continued to be provided annually by the developers, according to the Japan Ministry of Construction.

As to the location of housing from the workplace, the national average published by the Japan Ministry of Construction shows that about 12 percent of workers have no commuting time and that a little more than one-third of all Japanese workers commute one way up to 30 minutes. About one-third commute from 30 to 120 minutes; two-thirds of this group commute one way from 30 to 60 minutes. The one-way commuting time of over 17 percent of workers was unknown or not covered by the survey. In the Greater Tokyo area, half of the workers covered commute one way more than 30 minutes; close to 25 percent commute one way 30 to 120 minutes. In contrast, more than half of the workers in the Greater Nagoya area commute one way less than 30 minutes; this commuting group drops to 40 percent in the Greater Osaka area. But the longest commuting times are experienced by workers in the Greater Tokyo area.

The Comparative Price of Residential Land and Trends

Tokyo led the way in the price of residential land (525,400 yen) in 1997; Fukuoka exhibited the lowest price of residential land (165,800 yen) that year, according to the Japan National Land Agency. At 200 yen to the U.S. dollar, the Tokyo residential land would have cost approximately $2,600, and Fukuoka residential land would have cost approximately $830. As consumer prices in general rose steadily from the early 1980s to the mid-1990s, urban residential land prices hit a peak in 1991; residential land prices in the six largest Japanese cities hit a peak a little earlier, in 1990.

Cost of a Home, the Cost–Income Relationship, and Home Floor Area

In 1996 the average Japanese home would cost, at 125 yen to the U.S. dollar, approximately $370,000. In the Greater Tokyo area, this average home cost, in the same year, $430,000. By paying this amount, one would purchase, on average, a 930-square-foot home. In Tokyo payment of the average price was associated with a home of 900 square feet on average. The average price per square foot in Japan on a nationwide basis ran close to $40,000 per square foot. In the Greater Tokyo area, the average price per square foot of a home ran to $48,000.

In the same year, 1996, we have some international comparisons on an indexed basis, as compiled by the Japan National Land Agency and the Japanese Association of Real Estate Appraisal. If we set the cost of a detached house in Tokyo at 100.0, we could conclude that the indexed cost for the same detached home in New York would be approximately 25 and in Paris, 22. If the price of a condominium home in Tokyo were indexed at 100, the price of a condominium home in New York would be approximately 130 and the price of a condominium home in Paris, 120.

In Japan the size of built-to-suit houses by landowners rose from 1,000 square feet in the early 1970s to roughly 1,400 square feet in the late 1990s. Housing for sale is usually more spacious than housing for rent in Japan and in most other countries. We can compare the 650-square-foot housing unit for sale in the early 1970s in Japan to the 925-square-foot housing unit for sale in the late 1990s. The square footage of housing for rent has been quite stable over the last three decades; the narrow range has fluctuated from about 480 square feet to 550 square feet on average.

In 1998 an international comparison of housing floor area per unit showed a figure of 1,500 square feet for the United States as a whole, 920 square feet for the United Kingdom as a whole, 930 square feet for Germany, 950 square feet for France, and 920 square feet for Japan as a whole. In terms of housing floor area per person, the international comparative range is considerable: the United States, about 600 square feet per person versus roughly 310 square feet per person in Japan, according to the Japan Ministry of Construction. While the square footage of housing space per person in Japan has remained about the same since 1993, the square footage of housing space per person in the United States, the United Kingdom, Germany, and France has increased significantly. For example, the square footage per person of housing space in the United Kingdom, Germany, and France in the early 1990s was reported by the Japan Ministry of Construction to be approximately 380 square feet.

The ratio of home price to yearly income fluctuated widely during the two decades of the 1980s and 1990s. In the middle of the 1980s the ratio of the average price of a condominium to the average yearly income of the purchaser approximated four. By the end of that decade, in 1990, this price–income relationship had reached eight, or the average condominium cost eight times the annual income of the average buyer. The ratio fell to a little less than five by 1995 and then rose to a little over five in the last half of the decade of the 1990s. In a related comparison, we may note that the average condominium floor area rose as the price–income ratio rose in the latter 1980s. As the price–

income ratio declined, the average floor area declined. The price–income ratio continued to decline as the average floor area started to increase during the first half of the 1990s. By the latter half of the 1990s, the floor area on average had risen to about 700 square feet, and the price–income ratio had stabilized at five.

Residential Investment in Total

In Japan the nominal gross residential investment reached a peak of 30 trillion yen in 1996. If we use an exchange rate of 125 yen to the U.S. dollar for 1996, this yen amount translates to roughly $240 billion. Even though the yen value reached a peak at this time, the percent of nominal Japan GNP was rather low in terms of trends at 6 percent. The portion of the nominal Japan GNP represented by private nominal residential investment was even lower at approximately 5.6 percent. Therefore, public sector investment in housing represented about 0.4 percent of the GNP of Japan or approximately $16 billion.

The Status of Condominium Sales and Inventory

Developers supplied about 180,000 units to the housing-for-sale Japanese market in 1994, 1995, and 1996. In 1997 approximately only 150,000 units were supplied to the overall Japanese market. This supply was related to the favorable housing loan finance provided to individuals by public and private financial institutions in the years 1994 through 1996. Another reason for the development of so many condominium units was the favorable tax treatment given mortgage interest during these years. When these favorable financing and tax conditions ended in the latter part of the decade, sales of condominiums dropped off and left a higher than normal inventory of vacant, for-sale units. Housing consumers have also become conservative in their spending due to the continued announcements of impending layoffs of company employees during the early part of the first decade of the twenty-first century. Due to unsatisfactory profit conditions, companies are restructuring with government encouragement so that adequate profitability will be attained for future operations. As a result, roughly 10 percent of the condominium units supplied to the market were unsold by the beginning of the new millennium.

Sales of used condominiums in the Greater Tokyo area have been rather stable in terms of contracts concluded during the last half of the 1990s. But the average price paid for resale condominiums has fallen from approximately $250,000 to approximately $220,000. Approximately 2,000 resale condominiums are continuing to be sold each month. In comparison, resale detached houses sell in lower volume, and the prices have been fluctuating more widely. Perhaps 1,200 contracts for resale detached houses are concluded each month in the Greater Tokyo area. In comparison with another related area, we may note that signed apartment leases increased in volume in the latter part of the 1990s. Average monthly rents, though, have declined from roughly $320 to $280 as we use 100 yen to the U.S. dollar and 10 square feet to one square meter as our conversion frame of reference. Average rents leveled off at $280 per square foot at the end of 1996.

The Leaders in Condominium Sales and Housing Construction Companies

Let us consider the leaders in condominium sales and housing construction. The top two condominium developers in terms of condominium sales volume are Daikyo and Dia Kensetsu. Mitsui Fudosan and Towa Real Estate Development tend to tie for third place in the latter part of the 1990s. Other leading condominium developers include Marubeni Corporation, Anabuki Construction Co., Nomura Real Estate Development Co., and Recruit Cosmos.

The housing construction companies who have recently sold the most housing units are Sekisui House and Daiwa House Industry. These companies also appear to be the most profitable of the top housing construction companies. Other housing construction companies with large businesses include Sekisui Chemical, Sumitomo Forestry, Asahi Chemical Industry, Misawa Homes, National House Industrial, and Mitsui Home Company.

REFERENCES

Abrahams, Paul and Gillian Tett. "The Circle Is Broken." *Financial Times*, November 9, 1999, p. 18.

Daimon, Sayuri. "Hilton Execs Looking to Expand Presence in Japan." *Japan Times Weekly International Edition*, 38:17 (April 27–May 3, 1998), p. 13.

"Factory Outlet Malls: New Retail Centers Boom Despite Slump." *Focus Japan*, 26:6 (July/August 1999), pp. 3–5.

Hines, M. A. *Guide to International Real Estate Investment*. Westport, CT: Quorum Books, 1988.

———. *International Income Property Investment*. Scottsdale, AZ: International Real Estate Institute, 1985.

———. *Investing in Japanese Real Estate*. Westport, CT: Quorum Books, 1987.

———. *Japanese Shopping Centers: Financial and Investment Features*. With Ikunoshin Yoshida, Japan Council of Shopping Centers, Tokyo. Scottsdale, AZ: International Real Estate Institute, 1985.

———. *Shopping Center Development and Investment* (Japanese language edition), 2nd ed. Tokyo: Toyo Keizai Shimpo Sha, 1990.

Inoki, Linda. "Citadel of Dreams for Young Ladies of Japan." *Financial Times*, February 5/6, 2000, p. xxx.

Japan Marketing Data 1995. Tokyo: Media Information, 1995.

Japan Marketing Data '95/'96. Tokyo: Media Information, 1996.

Japanese Consumer Handbook 1991: A Businessman's Guide to the Japanese Consumer Market. Tokyo: Japan External Trade Relations Organization, 1991.

Landers, Peter. "Crumbling Pillars." *Far Eastern Economic Review* 161:26 (June 25, 1998), pp. 58–60.

Miller, Theresa. "Securitization Frontierland." *Best's Review* (Property/Casualty), 100:3 (July 1999), pp. 55–56.

Nakamae, Naoko, and Bayan Ragman. "British Retailers Try to Make It Big in Japan." *Financial Times*, December 30/31, 1999, p. 14.

"Strategic Location for Distribution." *Focus Japan*, 25:10 (November 1998), p. 16.

8

Appraising Japanese Real Estate

As real estate is bought, sold, and leased and as it is developed, financed, insured, and taxed in Japan, the real property must be appraised. A large number of real estate appraisers are needed for such ongoing work, which affects all real property in Japan. This chapter covers the Japanese appraisal process, education and licensing, the principal appraisal and appraisal-related professional institutes and associations, and some of the principal differences between U.S. and Japanese office building valuation.

PURPOSES OF REAL ESTATE APPRAISAL IN JAPAN

Common purposes for appraisal reports in Japan are:

- Financing with the use of real estate collateral
- Estate settlement where the deceased was a real property owner
- Property insurance underwriting and the payment of property losses
- Property taxation based on property value
- The use of eminent domain by the government
- The use of the right of preemption by the government
- Depreciation of land improvements for income tax deduction
- Sale or purchase of real property

Since the collapse of the "bubble economy," the appraiser has been faced with the task of evaluating property values that have generally declined. The hypothetical comparison of Exhibit 8-1 shows what the appraiser may face on

Exhibit 8-1
Comparison of Two Valuations of the Same Property in Metropolitan Tokyo

Appraised Values during the Bubble Economy	
Value based on the sales comparison approach:	¥10 million per square meter
Value based on the income capitalization approach (direct capitalization):	¥6 million per square meter (3% capitalization rate)
Appraised Values after the Bubble Economy	
Value based on the sales comparison approach:	¥4 million per square meter
Value based on the income capitalization approach (direct capitalization):	¥3.8 million per square meter (6% capitalization rate)

Source: Yuji Hirota, "New Trends in the Japanese Real Estate Appraisal Industry," *The Appraisal Journal* (October 1999), p. 407, Figure 1. Reprinted with permission from the Appraisal Institute, Chicago.

any one assignment. The use of the sales comparison approach to value an office building may reflect today a decline in value of ¥6 million per square meter. The use of the income capitalization approach to value the same office building might reflect a decline in value of ¥2.2 million per square meter.

THE JAPANESE REAL ESTATE APPRAISAL PROCESS

The Japanese real estate appraisal system is similar to that of the United States. Therefore, Japanese real estate appraisers define the real estate appraisal process in much the same way that the United States does. The process starts with the acceptance of the appraisal assignment and ends with the delivery of the appraisal report (Exhibit 8-2). After the client's need for the report is established and after the necessary appraisal work is planned, the subject property is identified, and data are collected for application of the three basic approaches to the subject property. The three basic appraisal approaches are the cost, market, and income approaches. The indicated values of the subject, using each of the approaches, are correlated to develop a single value for the property. The preparation of the appraisal report includes the certificate of appraised value. When the report is delivered, the remainder of the appraisal fee is due. Part of the appraisal fee may be paid by the client before the valuation is commenced.

The appraisal work involves urban land and buildings, paddy fields, truck farms, forestland, factories and other going concerns, marine vessels, various rights and interests in real estate, ground rents, and rents of improved properties. The appraisal work is accomplished by private real estate appraisers employed by financial institutions, personnel of the Japan Real Estate Institute, and private real estate appraisers employed by non-financial companies.

Exhibit 8-2
The Appraisal Process

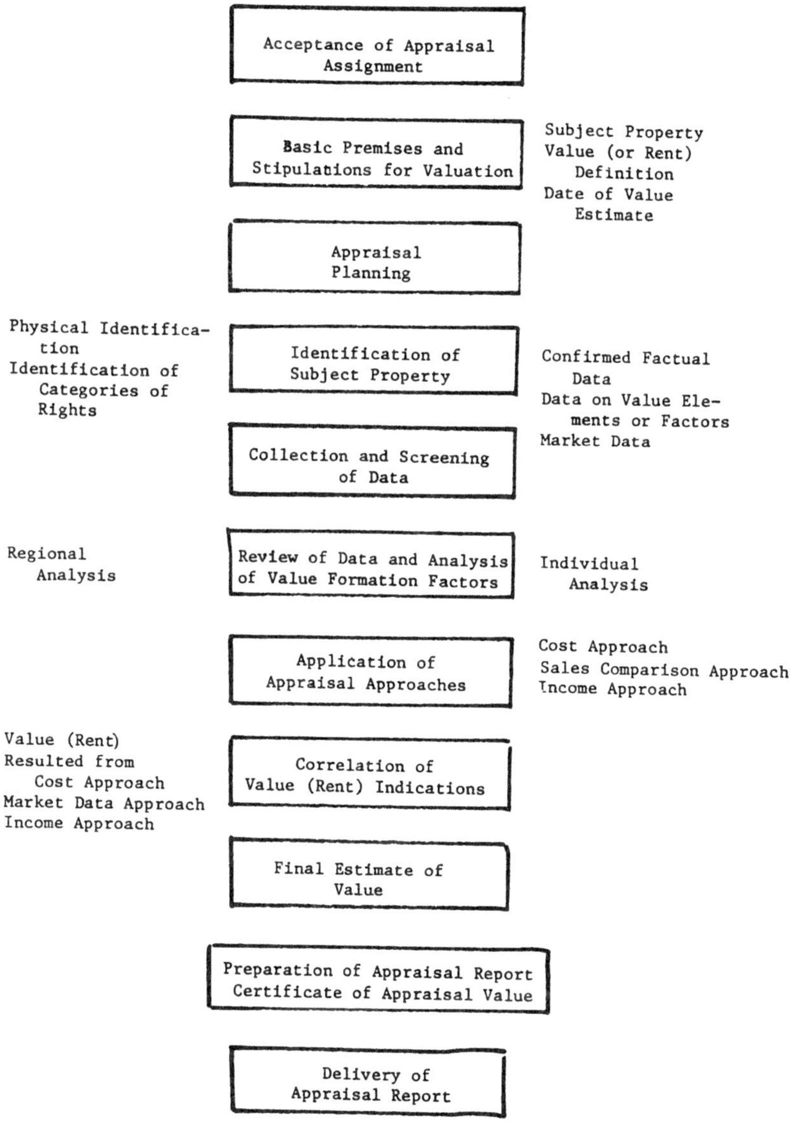

Source: Japan Real Estate Institute. Reprinted with permission.

THE APPRAISAL REPORT CONTENT

The Japanese real estate appraisal report generally has three important sections, whether they are well delineated in the report or not. The first section is general information about the subject property. The second section covers the appraisal analysis and the value conclusions. The third section is the addenda, which contain the supportive tables and maps. The outline for an appraisal report for a hotel in Shinbashi illustrates the basic information covered within a particular style of report presentation (Exhibit 8-3). The Shinbashi hotel appraisal report outline shows that land value is estimated by three methods. The first estimate of land value is based on the published land price compiled by the Japan National Land Agency. (The Land Price Publication Law, revised in August 1983, may be seen in Appendix 8-1.) The second estimate of land value is based on the sales comparison approach. Then the third estimate of land value is based on the land residual approach. The value of the building is estimated through both the cost and the income approaches. The appraisal may include a grid analysis such as that presented in Exhibit 8-4. By means of the grid analysis, the appraiser may let three closely comparable properties reflect the appropriate overall capitalization rate (net operating income divided by the sales price) and gross rent multiplier (sales price divided by the potential gross income) for the subject.

Discounted cash flow analysis is employed. Revenues and expenses are estimated over a selected time period using appropriate growth rates. Rationale is given for the selection of an appropriate discount rate for the discounted cash flow analysis and a terminal capitalization rate for the estimation of selling price or terminal property value.

The concepts of "temporary criterion lot within the subject land" and the "standard price of the temporary criterion lot" have been used in many Japanese real estate appraisals of land. These terms are associated with the use of published land prices from the numerous Japanese properties each year. The appraisal of each parcel has been linked to government-published appraised values for land parcels close to, or within, the subject land parcel.

When buildings and other structures of the subject property are appraised, the cost of construction or purchase of the land improvements after depreciation is taken into consideration. Discounted cash flow income analysis of the income approach is also used to appraise land improvements. The appraised values of the individual components of the subject property—the land, buildings, other structures, machinery, and equipment—are added together to give the client the estimated appraisal value of the total property. The annex of an appraisal report for the valuation of a factory in Tochigi shows the data analysis by factory component (Exhibit 8-5).

Exhibit 8-3
Appraisal Report Content: Hotel in Shinbashi

Letter of Transmittal
Table of Contents

I. INTRODUCTION
Certification of Value
Summary of Important Conclusions

II. PREMISES OF THE APPRAISAL
1. Identification of Subject Property
   (1) Legal Description of Subject Property
   (2) Type of Property Appraised
2. Assumptions of the Appraisal
3. Effective Date of Appraisal
4. Purpose and Function of the Appraisal
5. Conflict of Interest
6. Date of Completion of Appraisal Assignment
7. Property Inspection
8. Confirmation of Lease Contract

III. PRESENTATION OF DATA
1. Socioeconomic Situation of Japan
2. General Outline of Greater Tokyo
3. Land Value Trend
   (1) Land Value Trend in Tokyo
   (2) Land Value Trend in Minato-ku
4. Hotel Market Overview
   (1) Hotel Industry in Japan
   (2) Hotel Market in Tokyo
   (3) Prospect of Hotel in Shinbashi
5. Tax
6. Neighborhood Description
   (1) Neighborhood Boundaries
   (2) Transportation Facilities
   (3) Land Use
   (4) Zoning
   (5) Surrounding Areas
   (6) Summary
7. Site Description
8. Improvement Description
   (1) Building Specifications
   (2) Structural Characteristics
   (3) Conclusion
9. Highest and Best Use
   (1) As if Vacant
   (2) As Improved

Exhibit 8-3 (continued)

IV. ANALYSIS OF DATA AND CONCLUSIONS
1. Valuation Rationale and Methodology
   (1) Premise for Decision of Valuation Approach
   (2) Assumptions of the Appraisal
   (3) General Methods
   (4) Available Methods for This Appraisal
2. Valuation
   (1) Cost Approach
      A. Land Value Estimate
         (A) Sales Comparison Approach
         (B) Income Approach (Land Residual Technique)
         (C) Estimation of Subject Site Value as if Vacant
      B. Building Value Estimate
      C. Subject Property Value Through Cost Approach
   (2) Income Approach (DCF [Discounted Cash Flow] Analysis)
      A. Scenario
      B. Revenues and Expenses
      C. Growth Rates
      D. Terminal Cap Rate and Discount Rate
3. Reconciliation and Final Value Estimate

ADDENDA
1. Indicated Land Value Estimate Based on the Published Land Price Compiled by the National Land Agency
2. Indicated Land Value Estimate Based on the Sales Comparison Approach
3. Land Value Indication by Income Approach (Land Residual Approach)
4. DCF Analysis
5. Summary of Income and Expense Data
6. Competitive Hotel Location Map
7. Location Map
8. Registered Land Map
9. Photographs
10. Building Plan and Floor Plan
11. Qualifications: Takumi Watanabe

Source: Japan Real Estate Institute. Reprinted with permission.

THE EDUCATION AND LICENSING OF REAL ESTATE APPRAISERS

Employers of appraisers, the Japanese Real Estate Institute, and other real estate trade associations educate Japanese appraisers in general. The Japan Real Estate Institute provides education for appraisers seeking licenses as real estate appraisers and assistant real estate appraisers. The Japan Real Estate Institute, which licenses real estate appraisers, is a non-profit organization supervised by

Exhibit 8-4
Office Building Example

Elements of Comparison	Subject	Comparable 1	Comparable 2	Comparable 3
Location	Toranomon	Shinbashi	Ginza	Akasaka
Zoning	Commercial	Commercial	Commercial	Commercial
Site area (square meters)*	500	6,000	2,000	1,800
Floor area ratio (%)**	700	700	700	700
Total floor area (square meters)	3,600	37,000	12,000	3,500
Building use	Office	Office	Office	Office
Date of sale	10/98	2/98	9/98	6/98
Sales price	¥1,800 million (appraised value)	¥40,000 million	¥7,500 million	¥2,900 million
Potential gross income	¥180 million	¥2,300 million	¥600 million	¥260 million
Net operating income	¥106 million	¥1,600 million	¥450 million	¥175 million
Overall capitalization rate = *NOI*/Sales price	5.9%	4.0%	6.0%	6.0%
Gross rent multiplier = Sales price/*PGI*	10.0	17.4	12.5	11.2

* One square meter is equal to 10.764 square feet.

** Maximum floor area ratio provided by zoning regulation; not actual floor area ratio.

NOI = net operating income; *PGI* = potential gross income.

Source: Yuji Hirota, "New Trends in the Japanese Real Estate Appraisal Industry," *The Appraisal Journal* (October 1999), p. 409, Table 1. Reprinted with permission of the Appraisal Institute, Chicago.

the Ministries of Finance, Construction, and Home Affairs and the Japan National Land Agency. Its special, supporting, and regular appraisal members come from the private and public sectors. A series of courses and seminars prepares prospective appraisers for examination, the passage of which precedes appraisal licensing.

The Japanese version of the American Institute of Real Estate Appraisers' text, *The Appraisal of Real Estate*, is used for appraisal education. The first translation was completed in 1969; the second edition was compiled with the assistance of academicians associated with the Massachusetts Institute of Technology.

THE OVERALL ROLE OF THE JAPAN REAL ESTATE INSTITUTE

A non-profit organization, the Japan Real Estate Institute prepares appraisals for clients, educates appraisers for appraisal certification, conducts continuing education seminars for the real estate community, provides consulting services related to real estate for clients, conducts real estate research, publishes mate-

Exhibit 8-5
Appraisal Report Content: Factory in Tochigi (Only the Annex That Summarizes the Details of the Bases on Which the Subject Property Was Appraised)

1. Premises of Appraisal
2. Conditions of Tochigi City
3. Conditions of the Neighboring Area
4. Conditions of the Subject Property
   (1) Land
   (2) Buildings
   (3) Other Structures
   (4) Facilities and Equipment
5. Highest and Best Use of the Subject
6. Analysis of Data and Conclusion
   (1) Land, Buildings, and Other Structures
      (a) Land Value as if Vacant
      (b) Reproduction Cost of Buildings
      (c) Other Structures
      (d) Depreciation
      (e) Value of Buildings and Other Structures
      (f) Integrated Prices of land and Structures
   (2) Facilities and Equipment
   (3) Reconciliation and Final Value Estimate

Source: Japan Real Estate Institute. Reprinted with permission.

rials, and coordinates real estate research undertakings that also involve academic organizations, other research institutes, and specialized real estate trade associations at home and abroad. The consulting services involve the development of land price formation models using computer systems, land redevelopment, housing development, market research, profit-and-loss analysis, and demand analysis. The continuing education seminars cover such topics as estimating the reproduction cost of frame houses and steel and reinforced concrete office buildings. Research studies focus on problems associated with finance, valuation, the economy, law, management, accounting, and other business and economic areas. The studies also cover real estate systems abroad.

The publications of the institute include:

The Japan Real Estate Institute Journal Real Estate Research (quarterly)

Periodical issues of research data including:

Indices of Urban Land Prices in Japan (semiannually)

Indices of Construction Costs of Wooden Houses in Japan (semiannually)

Prices of Paddy Fields and Truck Farms and Rentals of Farm Land (annually)

Prices of Forest and Marginal Land and Standing Timbers (annually)

Commentary of Real Estate Laws and Regulations (annually)
Collection of Real Estate Dockets
Theory of Condemnation Systems
Urban Center Land and Land Price
Tables of Real Estate Terms
Glossary of Real Estate Terms
The Appraisal of Real Estate (book)

The institute has many branch offices located in almost all of the prefectures of Japan. The numerous sustaining members include principal corporations of Japan.

OTHER ORGANIZATIONS ASSOCIATED WITH JAPANESE REAL ESTATE APPRAISAL

The Japan Real Estate Appraisers Association was formed in 1963. Recently, the Academy of Japan Real Estate was formed for the pursuit of real estate research. The two organizations are completely independent. Company moneys including those of banks, financially support the academy, whose members include academicians. Individuals and companies associated with real estate appraisal belong to the Japan Real Estate Appraisers Association.

Membership fees of the Japan Real Estate Appraisers Association vary between individuals and companies and between individuals employed at headquarters or branch company offices. Individual members pay monthly membership fees if they are employed at branch offices and higher monthly membership fees if they are employed at company headquarters. Within the branch of headquarters' offices, the fee assessment depends on the rank of the individual. The highest fees are assessed the highest-ranked appraisers. Appraisal company membership fees are assessed by the company ranking in terms of total asset values. Annual fees are paid by companies and related entities and individuals.

DIFFERENCES BETWEEN U.S. AND JAPANESE APPRAISAL WITH RESPECT TO OFFICE BUILDING VALUATION

There are several differences between U.S. and Japanese appraisal systems with respect to the valuation of office buildings. The Japanese system operates as follows:

1. Measurements are in square meters or *tsubo* (3.3 square meters).
2. Three kinds of deposits may be payable by a prospective tenant in order to acquire quality office space: (a) key money deposit, (b) fee to acquire and occupy the space, and (c) security deposit. Then the rent is usually payable monthly over the two-year

lease, which is subject to rent negotiation and renewal at the end of the two-year period. Often the rent for the space is paid in advance for several months or for the entire lease period of two years.

Interest may be paid by the landlord on the key money deposit at a low interest rate after a grace period of five or six years. The fee to acquire and occupy the space or the sublease privilege is usually not interest-bearing; neither is the security deposit.

The payment of the space acquisition fee may include a business right, including perhaps the previous occupant's equipment. Such a fee may be paid by a food shop, bar, or restaurant. The space acquisition fee may be merged with the key money deposit by a developer, or the space acquisition fee may balance with the key money deposit. If the acquisition fee is relatively high, the key money deposit may be lower than usual.

The office building developer usually collects about 60 to 70 percent of the building construction cost from prospective tenants. The effective rental area of the office building is usually only 60 percent of the total building area. Therefore, the key money deposit may cover only 60 percent of the total construction costs.

3. Commercial tenant tenure is preserved and enforced by the legal system. It is difficult to renovate or rebuild a building because the tenants have a right to do business in the specific space and usually do not want to occupy temporary space while the building is being renovated or demolished and reconstructed.
4. The government requires publication of standard land prices. At the beginning of each year, on January 1, 14,000 places in Japan are selected by the central government for appraisal. Then their appraisals are published by April 1 of that year. Approximately 15,000 parcels are selected by the prefectural governments for appraisal as of July 1. The values are published by October 1 of that year. The real estate appraiser must relate appraised values to the published standard values. Therefore, the appraiser has published standard values for approximately 30,000 parcels nationwide each year from which to base her or his appraisal judgment. The revised Land Price Publication Act may be seen in Appendix 8-1.

CHAPTER SUMMARY

As the long Japanese recession of the 1990s and 2000s continues, real estate appraisal in Japan is gradually changing to fit the need of the real estate marketplace. Instead of concentration on the price appreciation experienced by a real property, the real estate appraiser, in an era of falling real estate values and prices, must concentrate on capitalization of income and market value decline.

The traditional reasons or purposes for real estate appraisals exist in Japan as in other parts of the world. Financing with real property as collateral requires a timely real estate appraisal. Where estates must be settled when the deceased person held real property, appraisals will be sought for all the real properties owned at the time of death. Property insurance underwriting and the payment of property-related losses call for real estate apraisals. The taxation of real property is dependent on property appraisal. When the government uses its right of preemption, an appraisal is required. When depreciation of land improvements is challenged by tax officials, property appraisal is called for. When property is sold or purchased, the prospective seller or buyer may desire a real estate appraisal to establish a listing price or an appropriate bid for the property.

The appraisal process in Japan is similar to that of the appraisal process promulgated by the Appraisal Institute of the United States. The Japanese textbook for appraisal education is based on the U.S. Appraisal Institute book *The Appraisal of Real Estate*. The appraisal system uses three basic approaches to the estimation of value of a subject property—the sales comparison, income, and cost approaches. An illustration of a grid analysis for an income property showed how Japanese appraisers pursue the income and sales comparison approaches. A brief illustration utilizing the sales comparison and income approaches to an office building valuation showed a hypothetical value before and after the "bubble era" in Japan. The appraisal report outline for a hotel in the Shinbashi district of Tokyo shows that the government-published land prices remain a part of the real estate appraisal process. A copy of the 1983 revised Land Price Publication Law is found in Appendix 8-1. A copy of a lengthy 1998 office building valuation by the Japan Real Estate Institute is located in Appendix 8-2.

The content of a Japanese real estate appraisal is split into three main sections, but a five-part appraisal report may contain these three important areas. Outlines for both hotel and factory appraisal reports illustrate the main sections of typical appraisal reports.

Education and licensing are associated with the Japan Real Estate Institute and the Japan Real Estate Appraisers Association. The Academy of Real Estate was recently established to include many real estate market participants, including academicians. The Japan Real Estate Institute plays an important role in Japanese real estate appraisal and consulting; the institute publishes many periodicals and books and maintains important real estate cost and price indexes.

Differences and similarities exist between U.S. and Japanese real estate appraisal practices and methodologies. Some of the differences with respect to office building valuations were pointed out.

Appendix 8-1. The Land Price Publication Law, Revised August 1983

CONTENTS

CHAPTER I. GENERAL PROVISIONS

(Purposes)

Article 1. The purposes of this Law are, by selecting representative lands in cities and their environs or other areas and publishing their fair prices, to set up standards concerning the sale prices of lands at large, to conduce to fixing of reasonable amounts of compensation money for lands to be used for public benefiting projects and thereby to contribute to establishment of fair land prices.

(Obligation on the Part of Person Performing Transactions in Land)

Article 1–2. Any person who performs transactions in lands in cities and their environs or other areas shall endeavor to perform each transaction taking as the standards the published prices of the representative lands which are deemed to be of approximately same use value with the land which is the object of the transaction.

CHAPTER II. PROCEDURE FOR PUBLISHING PRICES OF REPRESENTATIVE LANDS

(Decision of Prices of Representative Lands)

Article 2. The Land Appraisal Committee shall annually request two or more licensed real estate appraisers or licensed assistant real estate appraisers to appraise the representative lands designated by the pertinent Ordinance to be issued later within the city planning areas (means the city planning areas defined in Article 4, paragraph 2, of the City Planning Law [Law No. 100 of 1968]), shall examine the results of the appraisal, make necessary adjustments, and decide the fair prices per unit area of the designated lands as the fixed basic day and shall publish the prices, in accordance with the provisions of the pertinent Ordinance to be issued later.

''Fair price'' in the preceding paragraph means the price* of a land at which it is considered to be usually sold and bought in free transaction (except selling and buying of agricultural land, mowing or grazing land, or woodland [except selling and buying of such for using it not as agricultural land, mowing or grazing land, or woodland but for some other purpose]) (*in case there are on the land any buildings or other assets fixed to the land, or in case there exist on the land superficies or other rights which restrict the use of or the profits from the land, the price at which it is considered to be sold and bought in normal business transaction on the supposed condition that there are no such fixed assets or rights).

(Selection of Representative Lands)

Article 3. As the representative land mentioned in paragraph 1 of the preceding Article shall be selected by the Land Appraisal Committee, in accordance with the provisions of the pertinent Ordinance to be issued later, such a block of land within an area in which all the lands are deemed to be of approximately equal use value in the light of the natural and social conditions as in considered to be representative in respect of the actual condition of land use, environment, etc.

(Standards of Appraisal of Representative Lands)

Article 4. In appraising the representative land under the provision of Article 2, paragraph 1, the licensed real estate appraisers or licensed assistant real estate appraisers shall, in accordance with the provisions of the pertinent Ordinance to be issued later, conduct the appraisal taking into consideration its assumed price computed on the basis of the transaction prices of similar neighboring lands and the assumed expenses necessary for developing the land to give it utility equal to that of similar neighboring lands.

(Submitting of Written Appraisal)

Article 5. The licensed real estate appraisers or licensed assistant real estate appraisers who have appraised the representative lands under the provision of Article 2, paragraph 1, shall submit to the Land Appraisal Committee a written appraisal of them which states the matters fixed by the pertinent Ordinance to be issued later as well as their appraised prices.

(Publication of Prices of Representative Lands, etc.)

Article 6. When the Land Appraisal Committee has decided the fair prices per unit area of the representative lands under the provision of Article 2, paragraph 1, it shall without delay publish the matters enumerated below for each of the lands in the Official Gazette:

(1) County, city, ward, town, or village; section; and number of lot where the representative land is located;

(2) Price of the representative land per unit area and the basic day of the price appraisal;

(3) Acreage of the representative land and shape thereof;

(4) Actual situation of use of the representative land and lands in the vicinity thereof;

(5) Other matters fixed by the pertinent Ordinance to be issued later.

(Sending of Documents, etc., Stating Matters Published to Organs Concerned and Opening Them to Public Inspection)

Article 7. When the Land Appraisal Committee has published the required matters under the provision of the preceding Article, it shall without delay send the heads of the cities, towns, and villages concerned (heads of the special wards concerned for the special ward area of the metropolitan prefecture of Tokyo and heads of the wards concerned for the designated cities under Article 252–19, paragraph 1, of the Local Autonomy Law (Law No. 67 of 1947); the same (in the following paragraph) documents stating the matters concerning the representative lands within the prefecture to which the cities, towns, and villages belong out of the matters published and maps denoting the locations of the representative lands concerned.

The heads of the cities, towns, and villages concerned shall offer the documents and maps referred to in the preceding paragraph for public inspection at the offices of the respective cities, towns, and villages, in accordance with the provisions of the pertinent Cabinet Order to be issued later.

CHAPTER III. EFFECT OF PUBLISHED PRICES

(Standards for Appraisal of Land by Licensed Real Estate Appraiser or Licensed Assistant Real Estate Appraiser)

Article 8. When a licensed real estate appraiser or licensed assistant real estate appraiser appraises a land within a city planning area defined in Article 2, paragraph 1, he shall take the prices of the representative lands published under the provision of Article 6 (hereinafter referred to as the "published prices") as the standards in judging the fair price of the land in question (means the fair price defined in Article 2, paragraph 2).

(Standards for Estimating Acquisition Price of Land for Use of Public Works)

Article 9. When a person undertaking a project for which lands may be expropriated according to the Land Expropriation Law (Law No. 219 of 1951) or other law, in acquiring a land within a city planning area defined in Article 2, paragraph 1, in order to use it for the project (in acquiring a land and terminating the rights connected therewith in case there exist superficies or other rights which restrict the use of or the profits from the land), fixes the acquisition price of the land in question (in case there exist superficies or other rights which restrict the use of or the profits from the land in question), includes the money needed (or terminating the rights concerned), he shall take the published prices as the standards.

(Standards for Estimating Amount of Compensation Money for Land to Be Expropriated)

Article 10. In estimation under the provision of Article 71 of the Land Expropriation Law of "the appropriate price of a land as of the date of the recognition of the project concerned" within a city planning area defined in Article 2, paragraph 1, referred to in Article 71 of the same Law, the price of the land in question estimated by taking the published prices as the standards shall be considered.

(Meaning of "Take Published Land Prices as Standards")

Article 11. To "take the published land prices as the standards" in the preceding three Articles means, in estimation of the price of the land in question (in case there exist buildings or other fixed assets on the land in question, or in case there exist superficies or other rights which restrict the use of or the profits from the land in question, the price which is considered appropriate on the supposition that there exist on such fixed assets or rights), to compare the land in question with one, two, or more of the representative lands whose use values are considered to be approximately equal to that of the land in question with respect to the various factors affecting the objective value of land such as the location, acreage, environment, etc., and, on the basis of the results of the comparison, to effect balance between the published prices of the representative lands concerned and the price of the land in question.

CHAPTER IV. LAND APPRAISAL COMMITTEE

(Establishment)

Article 12. There shall be established a Land Appraisal Committee (hereinafter referred to as the "Committee") to exercise the powers based on this Law and the Law concerning Appraisal of Real Estate (Law No. 152 of 1963).

(Affairs under the Committee's Jurisdiction)

Article 13. The affairs under the jurisdiction of the Committee shall be as follows:

(1) Affairs concerning publication of land prices;

(2) Affairs concerning examinations for real estate appraisers' licenses;

(3) Investigation and deliberation on important matters related to real estate appraisal in accordance with inquiries from Minister of National Land Agency;

(4) Disposition of other matters that come under the powers of the Committee as provided for by law (including orders based on law).

When the Committee deems it necessary for conducting the affairs under its jurisdiction, it may request the heads of the administrative organs concerned and the local public bodies concerned to submit data, express opinions, give explanations, and extend other necessary cooperation.

(Organization)

Article 14. The Committee shall consist of seven members.

Six of the members shall serve on a part-time basis.

(Members of the Committee)

Article 15. The members of the Committee shall be appointed by the Minister of National Land Agency, with the consent of both Houses, from among persons of learning and experience in matters concerning appraisal of real estate or concerning land legislation.

When the term of office of the members of the Committee expires or a vacancy occurs, if it is not possible to obtain the consent of both Houses owing to adjournment of the National Diet or dissolution of the House of Representatives, the Minister of National Land Agency may, notwithstanding the provision of the preceding paragraph, appoint a member or members from among persons who have the qualifications fixed in the said paragraph.

In case the Minister of National Land Agency has appointed a member or members of the Committee under the provision of the preceding paragraph, he shall obtain ex post facto approval of both Houses at the first Diet session after the appointment.

In this connection, if the Minister of National Land Agency cannot obtain the ex post facto approval of both Houses, he shall immediately dismiss the member or members.

No person falling under either of the following two items can be a member of the Committee:

(1) Person adjudged incompetent or quasi-incompetent or such bankrupt person as has not been reinstated;

(2) Person who has been sentenced to imprisonment without hard labor or a heavier penalty.

The term of office of the members of the Committee shall be three years. However, the term of office of a member who fills vacancy shall be the remainder of the term of his predecessor.

Members of the Committee may be reappointed.

If any member of the Committee comes to fall under either of the items of paragraph 4, he shall lose his post.

When the Minister of National Land Agency deems that any member of the Committee is unable to perform his duties owing to his mental or physical defect or that any member of the Committee has swerved from his official duty or has otherwise committed an act ill befitting a member of the Committee, he may dismiss the member with the consent of both Houses.

(Chairman of the Committee)

Article 16. The Committee shall have a Chairman, who shall be elected by mutual vote of the members.

The Chairman shall preside over the affairs of the Committee and represent the Committee.

In case the Chairman is temporarily unable to perform his duties, a member nominated by him in advance shall act for him.

(Committee Meeting)

Article 17. Meetings of the Committee shall be called by the Chairman.

The Committee shall not hold a meeting or pass a resolution unless the Chairman and three or more of the other members are present.

The proceedings of the Committee shall be decided by majority of the members present, and, in case of a tie, the decision shall be made by the Chairman.

In applying the provision of paragraph 2 when the Chairman is temporarily unable to perform his duties, the member mentioned in paragraph 3 of the preceding Article shall be regarded as Chairman.

(Service Rules of Committee Members)

Article 18. No member of the Committee shall divulge any secret which has come to his knowledge in connection with his duties. The same shall apply even after he retires from his post.

No member of the Committee shall, while in office, be an officer of any political party or other political body or positively engage in any political movement.

The member of the Committee who is in full-time service shall not, while in office, except in case he has obtained the permission of the Minister of National Land Agency, engage in other duties for remuneration, carry on a profit-making enterprise, or perform any service aimed at making a pecuniary profit.

(Salary of Committee Members)

Article 19. The salary of the members of the Committee shall be fixed elsewhere by law.

(Miscellaneous Affairs)

Article 20. The miscellaneous affairs of the Committee shall be conducted by the Land Bureau of the National Land Agency.

(Matters to Be Fixed by Cabinet Order)

Article 21. Necessary matters concerning the Committee not provided for in this Law shall be fixed by Cabinet Order.

CHAPTER V. MISCELLANEOUS PROVISIONS

(Entry into Land)

Article 22. When it is necessary for a member of the Committee or a person ordered or entrusted with the task by the Committee to enter a land occupied by another person to conduct surveying or investigation for the purpose of performing appraisal or deciding the price under the provision of Article 2, paragraph 1, or to select a representative land under the provision of Article 3, he may enter the land occupied by another party insofar as it is necessary.

Any person who intends to make entry into a land occupied by another party under the provision of the preceding paragraph shall notify the occupant of the land to that effect not later than three days before the day on which he intends to make the entry.

Any person who intends to make entry, under the provision of paragraph 1, into such land occupied by another party as has a building on it or is enclosed with a fence, paling, or the like shall previously inform the occupant of the land to that effect at the time of entry.

No entry shall be made into such land as is mentioned in the preceding paragraph before sunrise or after sunset, except in case the consent of the occupant of the land has been obtained.

The occupant of the land shall not, unless there is a justifiable reason, refuse or obstruct the entry under the provision of paragraph 1.

Any person who intends to make entry into a land occupied by another party under the provision of paragraph 1 shall carry with him an identification card indicating his status and, when any of the parties concerned requests it, shall show him the card.

The form of the identification card mentioned in the preceding paragraph shall be fixed by the Prime Minister's Office Ordinance.

(Compensation for Loss Caused in Connection with Entry into Land)

Article 23. In case a loss is caused to another party by entry under the provision of paragraph 1 of the preceding Article, the Minister of National Land Agency shall compensate the person who has sustained the loss for the loss arising under normal conditions from the entry.

With regard to the compensation for loss under the provision of the preceding paragraph, the Minister of National Land Agency and the person who has sustained the loss shall hold negotiations on it.

If no agreement is reached by negotiations held under the provision of the preceding paragraph, the Minister of National Land Agency or the person who has sustained the loss may apply to the Expropriation Committee for the ruling mentioned in Article 94, paragraph 2, of the Land Expropriation Law, in accordance with the provisions of the pertinent Prime Minister's Office Ordinance to be issued later.

(Obligation to Keep a Secret)

Article 24. No licensed real estate appraiser or licensed assistant real estate appraiser who has made appraisal of a representative land under the provision of Article 2, paragraph 1, shall, without a justifiable reason, divulge any secret which has come to his knowledge while making the appraisal.

(Appraisal Order)

Article 25. When the Committee deems it necessary for appraisal under the provision of Article 2, paragraph 1, it may order licensed real estate appraisers or licensed assistant real estate appraisers to make appraisal of representative lands.

Licensed real estate appraisers and licensed assistant real estate appraisers who make appraisal of representative lands in accordance with an order based on the provision of the preceding paragraph shall be paid traveling expenses and remuneration, in accordance with the provisions of the pertinent Prime Minister's Office Ordinance to be issued later.

(Special Rule in Application of Law Concerning Appraisal of Real Estate)

Article 26. With regard to the application of the Law concerning Appraisal of Real Estate to the appraisal of representative lands made by licensed real estate appraisers or licensed assistant real estate appraisers under the provision of Article 2, paragraph 1, of this Law, the said appraisal of representative lands shall not be regarded as the appraisal referred to in the definition given in Article 2, paragraph 2, of the Law Concerning Appraisal of Real Estate.

CHAPTER VI. PENAL PROVISIONS

Article 27. A person falling under either one of the following two items shall be punished with penal servitude not exceeding six months or a fine not exceeding 50,000 yen, or both:

(1) Person who has made false appraisal in making appraisal of representative lands under the provision of Article 2, paragraph 1;

(2) Person who, in contravention of the provision of Article 24, has divulged a secret which has come to his knowledge while making appraisal of representative lands.

Article 28. A person who, in contravention of the provision of Article 22, paragraph 5, has refused or obstructed entry into land under the provision of paragraph 1 of the same Article shall be punished with a fine not exceeding 100,000 yen.

Article 29. In case a person who has been ordered to make appraisal of representative lands under the provision of Article 25, paragraph 1, fails to make the appraisal or fails to submit a written appraisal mentioned in Article 5, without a justifiable reason, he shall be liable to a nonpenal fine not exceeding 10,000 yen.

SUPPLEMENTARY PROVISIONS

(Date of Enforcement)

1. This Law shall be enforced as from July 1, 1969. However, the part involving the obtaining of consent of both Houses in Article 15, paragraph 1, shall be enforced as from the day of its promulgation.

(Special Rules Concerning First Publishing of Land Price)

2. The first publishing of land prices under the provision of Article 6 after the enforcement of this Law shall be done by the day fixed by Ministry of National Land Agency Ordinance to be within a period of ten months reckoning from the day of promulgation of this Law.

(First Appointment of Committee Members)

3. In case adjournment of the National Diet or dissolution of the House of Representatives prevents obtainment of the consent of both Houses for the first appointment of the Committee members after the enforcement of this Law, the provisions of Article 15, paragraphs 2 and 3, shall apply mutatis mutandis.

[4–8 Omitted.]

SUPPLEMENTARY PROVISIONS (OF THE AMENDMENT LAW)

(Date of Enforcement)

1. This Law shall be enforced as from the day of its promulgation.

(Date of First Land Price Publication after Amendment)

2. The first publication of land prices according to provision of Article 6 of the Land Price Publication Law after the enforcement of this Law to amend it shall be made within one year from the day when this Law comes into force.

Source: Japan Real Estate Institute. Reprinted with permission.

Appendix 8-2. Appraisal of XXX Building by Takumi Watanabe, Japan Real Estate Insitute, August 1998

No. K - H 00000

Appraisal of

XXX Building

X y-chome

X-ku, Tokyo

As of :

August x, 1998

Prepared for :

ABC Bank

Prepared by :

Japan Real Estate Institute

August x, 1998

ABC Bank

Subject: XXX Building
X y-chome
X-ku, Tokyo

Dear Mr. ABC Bank :

As you requested, we have inspected the above subject property for the purpose of estimating the market value of the ownership in the property with present tenants. The last date of inspection of the property was July x, 1998, which will be considered the effective date of the value. We have analyzed information pertinent to the formulation of the market value estimate and are reporting the conclusions in this report. Market value is defined in the report. We believe the following report meets the requirements of ABC Bank and Japanese Appraisal Standard authorized by National Land Agency.

Based on our analysis of the property, it is our opinion that the best estimate of the market value of the ownership in the property as of July x 1998, was in order of :

XXX BILLION XXXX HUNDRED MILLION YEN (x,xxx,000,000 Yen)

If you need any additional information or further clarification, please do not hesitate to contact us.

Respectfully submitted,

Takumi WATANABE, Certified Real Estate Appraiser

Table of Contents

ADDENDA

1. Legal Description of Subject Property (Each Unit)
2. Rental Contract of Each Unit
3. Indicated Land Value Estimate Based on Published Land Price
4. Indicated Land Value Estimate Based on the Sales Comparison Approach
5. Sales Comparison Data
6. Building Data
7. Location Map (Neighborhood Map)
8. Registered Land Map (Copy of Official Map)
9. Photographs
10. Building Floor Plan
11. Professional Qualifications

[*Author's Note*: Only Addenda 3 and 4 are included in this book.]

I. INTRODUCTION

CERTIFICATION

We certify that, to the best of our knowledge and belief :

1. The statements of fact contained in this report are true and correct.
2. The reported analyses, opinions, and conclusions are limited only by the reported assumptions and limiting conditions, and are our personal, unbiased professional analyses, opinions, and conclusions.
3. We have no present or prospective interest in the property that is the subject of this report, and we have no personal interest or bias with respect to the parties involved.
4. Our compensation is not contingent upon the direction in value that favors the cause of the client, the attainment of a stipulated result, or the occurrence of a subsequent event.
5. We have made a personal inspection of the property that is the subject of this report.
6. No one provided significant professional assistance to the persons signing this report.
7. Our analyses, opinions and conclusions were developed, and this report has been prepared, in conformity with Japanese Appraisal Standard authorised by National Land Agency.

Takumi WATANABE, CRE

Certified Real Estate Appraiser
Deputy General Manager
Japan Real Estate Institute

SUMMARY OF IMPORTANT CONCLUSIONS

SUBJECT PROPERTY : Office Bldg. known as
XXX Building
X y-chome
X-ku ,Tokyo, JAPAN

SITE : ????.??□ (by land registry book)
Irregular Shape

IMPROVEMENTS : ?????□ (by building registry book)
Steel Reinforced Concrete,
Office, Store, Storage and Parking

AGE OF BUILDING: Built in 1978

OWNER : XYZ Inc.

CLIENT : ABC Bank

EFFECTIVE DATE OF VALUE : July x, 1998

APPRAISAL PURPOSE : To place a mortgage on the subject property

ZONING : Commercial
Floor Area Ratio 595% (700% / 500% combined)

HIGHEST AND BEST USE : As though vacant :
High Rise Store and Office Building
with residence

As improved :
High Rise Store and Office Building
with residence

INTEREST APPRAISED : Ownership of Land and Building
with present tenants
Land : joint ownership
Building : comparted-ownership

ASSETS EXCLUDED : Tenant's improvements and personal properties

VALUE ESTIMATE:

Value indication
Through the cost approach : X,XXX,000,000YEN

Value indication
Through the sales comparison approach : X,XXX,000,000YEN

Value indication
Through the income approach : X,XXX,000,000YEN

Final estimate of defined value :

XXXX BILLION FIVE HUNDRED MILLION YEN

II. PREMISES OF THE APPRAISAL

1. IDENTIFICATION OF SUBJECT PROPERTY

(1) Legal Description of Subject Property

Land : Ownership is shared by subject property units' owner and other units' owners.

Location	Type of Property	Registered Area
X, y-chome, X-Ku, Tokyo	Building site	????.?? sq. m.

Building : The whole condominium project contains 39 units of office / retail / residential units. The subject property of this appraisal is comprised of 31 units(including 1 tower parking unit) out of the total 39units.

No. and Location	Structure and Utility	Total Floor Area
Building located on the above land	11-story building with a basement, steel-reinforced concrete	????? sq. m.

Addendum 1 shows the details of subject property.

(2) Type of Property Appraised

Ownership of land and building with present tenants

Building : Condominium unit ownership

Land : Joint ownership

(3) Owner as of July x, 1998

The registered owner of the subject property is XYZ Inc.

2. PROPERTY INTEREST APPRAISED

The ownership of the land and building with present tenants

3. ASSUMPTIONS OF THE APPRAISAL

This appraisal disregards the value of each tenant improvements and personal properties in the building.

4. PURPOSE AND FUNCTION OF THE APPRAISAL

The purpose of this appraisal is to estimate the market value of the ownership of the real property appraised, assuming it to be offered for sale on the open market. We understand that this appraisal report will be used for placing mortgage on the subject property.

According to *The Appraisal of Real Estate* published by Appraisal Institute, Chicago, Illinois, USA, "Market value" is defined as :

The most probable price which a property should bring in a competitive and open market under all conditions requisite to a fair sale, the buyer and seller each acting prudently and knowledgeably, and assuming the price is not affected by undue stimulus. Implicit in this definition is the consummation of a sale as of a specified date and the passing of title from seller to buyer under conditions whereby :

(1) buyer and seller are typically motivated ;

(2) both parties are well informed or well advised, and acting in what they consider their best interests ;

(3) a reasonable time is allowed for exposure in the open market ;

(4) payment is made in terms of cash or in terms of financial arrangements comparable thereto ; and

(5) the price represents the normal consideration for the property sold unaffected by special or creative financing or sales concessions granted by anyone associated with the sale.

5. MARKETING PERIOD

The reasonable marketing time is an estimate of the amount of time it might take to sell a property interest in real estate at the estimated market value level during the period immediately after the effective date of an appraisal. (ADVISORY OPINION –7 Appraisal Standard Board)

Since we fully incorporated the risk of office market fluctuations and employed realistic figures for the future revenues realizing both the subject property' current levels of contract rents and forecast of office space supply within the next years, we considered that the marketing time will be shorter than that of the average building.

The subject property will require a marketing time of six to nine months.

6. EFFECTIVE DATE OF VALUE

July x, 1998

7. DATE OF COMPLETION OF APPRAISAL ASSIGNMENT

August x, 1998

8. CONFLICT OF INTEREST

The appraisers have neither a conflict of interest concerning rights in the subject property nor a conflict of interest and/or relationship with any party who has a right in the subject property.

9. PROPERTY INSPECTION

(1) Date of Inspection

July x, 1998

(2) Accompanying Witness

Mr. X, AAA Housing Inc. (building maintenance company)

Mr. Y, General Manager Planning & Development Dept. OOOAsset Management Company

(3) References Used for Inspection

Land register book and its attached official map (refer to **Addendum 9**) available in the registry office.

A building plan prepared by K Architecture and Design Office Inc.

Building Survey Report prepared by XYZ Inc.

(4) Results of Inspection

Land : We confirmed that the subject property corresponded with the contents in the data above in terms of location, shape and size.

Building : We confirmed that the subject property corresponded with the contents in the data above in terms of use, structure, materials, shape and size.

(5) Adopted Area for Appraisal

Land : Registered area

Building : Registered area

10. CONFIRMATION OF LEASE CONTRACT

(1) Purpose of Lease Contract

Building lease

(2) References Used for Confirmation

Due diligence package prepared by TTT

Written building lease contract

Written modified building lease contract

Written parking lease contract

Explanation of witness

(3) Contract Parties

Lessee : refer to **Addendum 2** rental contract of each unit

Lessor : XYZ Inc.

III. PRESENTATION OF DATA

1. REGIONAL ANALYSIS

(1) Regional Description

A. X Ward

The city proper of Tokyo is divided into 23 wards. The subject property is located in X Ward, or X-Ku in Japanese. Situated in the center of the 23 ward area, X Ward has an area of 11.64 square kilometers (approximately 4.55 square miles). The Imperial Palace sits in the middle of the ward occupying approximately 12% of the total ward area.

Loops constructed around the Imperial Palace and streets extended toward outer areas form the arteries of X Ward. In the ward, there are four major areas, which are briefly described below.

a) B Area

The subject property is located in the BBB area. This area is composed of retail/office developments along the major corridors and exclusive residential neighborhoods behind them.

b) O Area

The O area creates a prestigious image of the capital city with the concentration of government and business functions.

c) J Area

The JJJ area boasts its abundance of educational/cultural and commercial/industrial traditions.

d) M Area

The M area is characterized with both high-tech electronics retail stores and various types of old wholesalers.

The whole area of X ward is designated as either Mandatory Fire Proof District or Quasi Mandatory Fire Proof District. Approximately 98% of all the buildings in the ward have met the fire proof standards. In the case of emergency evacuation, large-scale parks and wide street are advantageous to X Ward compared with other parts of Tokyo.

X Ward has a daytime population of approximately one million, which includes people who work in the ward. On the other hand, the number of residents in 1997 was only 40,000. It was common for residential land use to be replaced by business land use. Many former residents moved outside the ward by taking advantage of property appreciation that occurred in the past. The population was approximately 120,000 in 1960.

(2) Land Value

Since 1970, the National Land Agency reports its nationwide land value survey every year.
The 1998 survey covered 30,600 sites. Each site is chosen at a location which is deemed to be typical in the neighborhood. 2,352 licensed appraisers participated in the latest survey.
The market value of each location as at January 1 is estimated and is published as a value per square meter. The results of the survey are utilized in property transactions, condemnations, assessment for tax purposes, etc.

Exhibit 1 represents the land value indexes base on the national land value survey. The base year for the index is 1983. According to the indexes, land value both in the 23 ward area and in X Ward declined for the last seven years. More specifically, the commercial land value index for the 23 ward area was 93.9 in 1998, 7.6 points decrease from the previous year. The 1998 value represents a 72.9% decrease from its peak recorded in 1991. The figures for X Ward is very similar to those of the 23 ward area. Namely, the latest index reported was 86.3, which means a decline of 2.6 points from the 1997 figure and a 79.5% drop from the peak level.

Exhibit 1. Cumulative Change (Official Land Price)

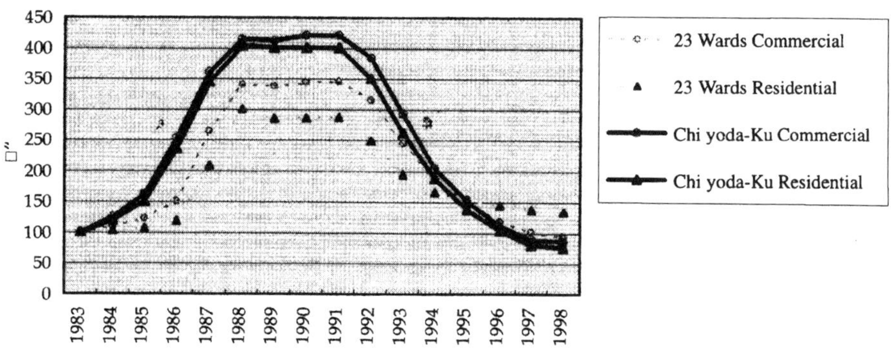

Exhibit 2 shows year-over-year changes in the land value survey results for the 23 ward area and X Ward. The declining rates are decreasing constantly for the last few years.

Exhibit 2. Rate of Land Value Change (Official Land Prices)

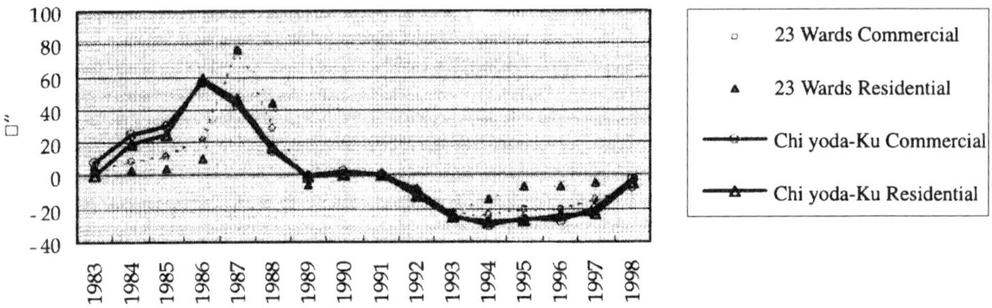

Exhibit 3. Cumulative Land Price Change & Relative Economic Indicators

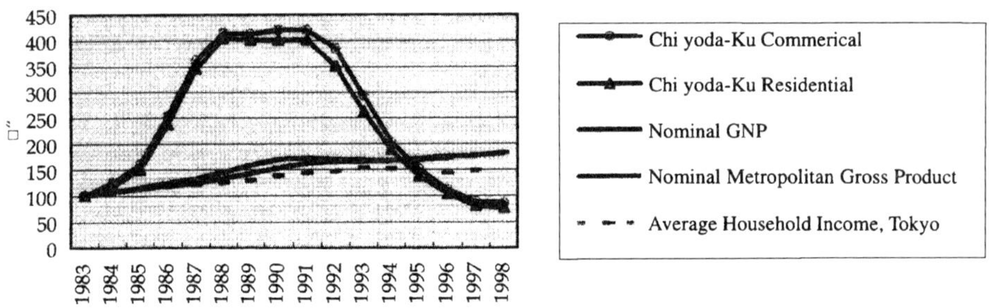

Exhibit 3 compares the land value indexes for the 23 ward area and X Ward with the rates of economic growth. The land values, both commercial and residential, lagged behind the economic growth rates measured as the Japanese GDP and the gross prefectural products of Tokyo since 1995.

Exhibit 4 is a graph showing the relationship between year-over-year value change and land value in 1998 in X Ward. The pattern illustrates that the less expensive the land is, the more the land value declined. In other words, the values of land at prime locations have increased in 1998 for the first time in the past seven years. As a matter of fact, 20 locations in Chiyoda, Chuo, Minato, and Shinjuku Wards witnessed value increases in the latest land value survey.

Exhibit 4. Land Price Level and Annual Change (X-Ku, Commercial)

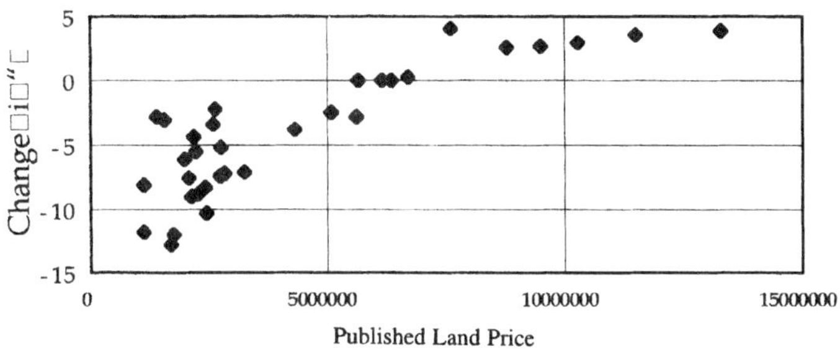

In summary, land value is still sagging in the 23 ward as a whole. However, some prime locations saw a reversal of the prolonged declining trend. Incidentally, the index for a survey site, Chiyoda 5-32, located near the subject property recorded a marginal decline of 0.9 points in 1998.

(3) Office Market

The inventory of office space in X Ward has been constantly increasing to date.
The total floor area of office space in the ward reached 13,893,000 square meters (approximately 140 million square feet) in 1997. The 23 ward area also experienced an increasing trend of office inventory. The total office space in the area amounted to 76,189,000 square meters (approximately 820 million square feet) in 1997. The annual increasing rates of office inventory in the 23 ward area changed over time: around 3% until 1986; from around 6% to 7%+ during the period between 1987 and 1995; and around 4% after 1996. Although they were smaller, the rates of change in X Ward varied in the same way as those of he 23 ward area.

In terms of new office construction, X Ward recorded 62 office building starts with a total floor area of 398,437 square meters (approximately 4.29 million square feet) in 1996. In that year, there were 219 building starts altogether in the ward. The total starts can be broken down as follows (number of buildings in parentheses) :

Exhibit 5. Floor Area of Offices (Existing Stock)

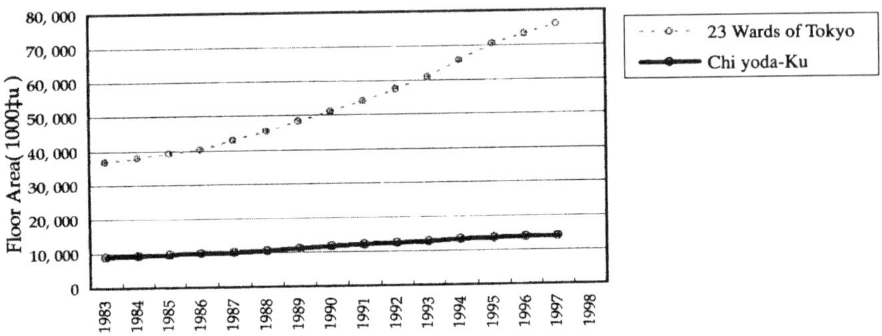

Construction Starts : Structure

Structure	Total Floor Area (square meters)	The number of Buildings
Steel Reinforced Concrete	272,050	45
Steel Concrete	41,105	32
Steel	475,283	129
Others	952	13
Total	789,390	219

Construction Starts : Use

Use	Total Floor Area (square meters)	The number of Buildings
Residential	70,158	52
Mixed-Use	84,814	36
Office	398,437	62
Others	235,981	69
Total	789,390	219

Construction Starts : Total Floor Area

Total Floor Area	Total Floor Area (square meters)	The number of Buildings
Under 2,999 square meters	90,507	188
3,000-9,999 square meters	110,583	19
Over 10,000 square meters	588,300	12
Total	789,390	219

The projects which broke ground in X Ward in 1996 contributed largely to an 18.2 percent increase over the 1995 building starts in the 23 ward area.

Exhibit 6. Total Floor Area of Office Starts (Flow)

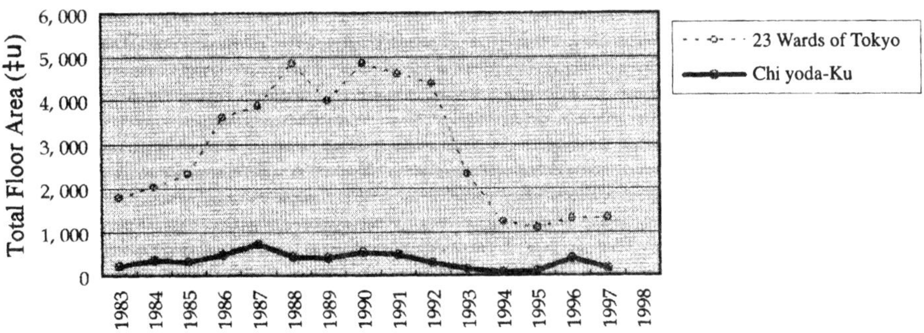

Many large-scale office building projects are currently under construction in the pipeline in downtown Tokyo. Some of those planned high-rise buildings are located in X Ward. Their details are presented later in this section.

The following is a brief overview of rent, vacancy, and absorption. Figures were obtained from either through research by the appraiser or from various market reports prepared by major commercial brokerage firms such as Ikoma, Miki, and Sanko:

- 23 Ward Area

As shown below, the average asking rent in the 23 ward area did not change significantly during the period between March and July of this year, while the vacancy rate in the area increased 0.1 percentage points, mainly due to more vacancies in downtown Class A buildings with a total floor area of more than 33,000 square meters (approximately 356,000 square feet).

	March 1998	July 1998
Average Asking Monthly Rent (Yen per 3.3 sq.m)	15,390	15,360 19,080–25,310 for office with 3,300 sq.m or more in 5 central wards of Tokyo
Average deposit (Yen per 3.3 sq.m)	184,700	182,200
Vacancy Rate (%)	4.6	4.7

- Chiyoda Chuo, Minato, Shinjuku, and Shibuya Wards

In the central five wards of Chiyoda, Chuo, Minato, Shinjuku, and Shibuya, the average vacancy rate exceeded 4% for the first time in the last ten months. It hovered around the mid- to high 3% level before. Due to the recession, increasing is the number of tenants who were forced to cut back space or to vacate the premises. The five ward area is witnessing vacancies even in some of formerly fully leased office buildings. The vacant space in existing large-scale buildings increased approximately 33,000 square meters (approximately 356,000 square feet) over the 1997 level. However, newest buildings, less than one year old and under construction, are enjoying successful occupancy or pre-leasing.

- X Ward

In X Ward, 1,774 buildings with 235,768 square meters (approximately 2.54 million square feet) total floor area were under construction or available for rent in May 1998. The supply of office space increased 8.6%, or 62,000 square meters (approximately 670,000 square feet) from the previous month's figure. Currently, 23 buildings are under construction with a total floor area of 330,000 square meters (approximately 3.6 million square feet), which constitutes 42.3% of the total available space. The latest construction figure is 62,000 square meters (approximately 670,000 square feet), or 23% more than the April level.

- A District in X Ward

The subject property is located in Y District in X Ward. The district saw a rental rate decrease as well as a vacancy rate increase of 1.1 percentage points during the period between March and July of this year as shown below:

	March 1998	July 1998
Average Asking Monthly Rent (Yen per 3.3 sq.m)	15,890	15,320
Average deposit (Yen per 3.3 sq.m)	186,800	174,600
Vacancy Rate (%)	3.3	4.4

- B District

The following is a summary of some of rental data found in the B district, where the subject is situated.

Rental Data in Neighborhood Area

ID #	#1	#2	#3	#4
Location	Ooo 1 chome	Ooo 3 chome	Ooo 4 chome	Ooo 4 chome
Necessary time to nearest station On foot	3 minutes to Subway I Station	5 minutes to JR Y Station	4 minutes to JR Y Station	3 minutes to JR Y Station
Structure	SRC 8F	SRC 14F	SRC 9F	SRC 10F
Bldg. Age	1 YEAR	15 YEAR	N/A	10 YEAR
Floor	2F	2F	2F	5F
Contract area (Sq. m)	99.40	70	45	31.04
Date of contract	June, 1998	November, 1997	November, 1997	August, 1997
Actual rent including interest of deposit	4,841(Yen/sq.m)	4,538(Yen/sq.m)	5,556(Yen/sq.m)	4,226(Yen/sq.m)

Listing Data

ID #	#1	#2	#3
Location	Ooo 4chome	Ooo 6come	Ooo 4-chome
Necessary time to nearest station on foot	4 minutes to JR Y Station	3 minutes to JR Y Station	3 minutes to JR Y Station
Structure	S 11F	SRC 8F	SRC 9F
Floor	4,5,7,10F	N/A	2F

Bldg. Age	10 YEAR	11 YEAR	9 YEAR
Area (sq.m)	2,500 – 15,000	880	430
Date of listing	07/1998	07/1998	07/1998
Rent	8,000 (Yen/sq.m)	6,000 (Yen/sq.m)	6,971(Yen/sq.m)

As mentioned above table, rental data in neighborhood area are considerably small size compared with subject property. On the other hand, although listing data are similar size to subject property, these data are still on list. As a result, we can not directly use these data to estimate tenant rent of subject property in income approach. (refer to Income Approach)

In summary, due to the teetering demand for office space and a possible glut of office buildings in the near future, there is a concern of further increases in office vacancy rate in central Tokyo including X Ward. The conditions of the Japanese economy is still deteriorating because of the lingering slump of domestic demand. The crisis of financial institutions is accelerating the economy to the danger of collapse. The economic instability adversely affects the health of business entities and this, in turn, reduces demand for office space, especially office buildings of inferior quality and small floor areas. On the supply side of office space, an increase in office supply is expected in 1998. On top of that, new projects presently planned will add further space to the existing mass.

	Tokyo Metropolitan (23 Wards)	X Ward B District
Vacancy Ratio (March, 1998)	4.6%	3.3% 3.0%(December, 1997)
Average offering rent (March, 1998)	15,390(Yen/3.3 sq.m) 4,655 (Yen/ sq.m)	15,890(Yen/3.3 sq.m) 4,807 (Yen/ sq.m)
Average Deposit (March, 1998)	184,700(Yen/3.3 sq.m) 55,872(Yen/sq.m)	186,800(Yen/3.3 sq.m) 5,651 (Yen/ sq.m)

Source : Ooo Data Service

(4) Major Properties under Construction and Prospects for New Development

According to *Building Construction Statistical Yearbook*, The Journal of Land Institute, Development Project Information, below is the breakdown of office space that will be produced by the following major buildings.

Main large-scale buildings to be completed in X Ward before long

Location	Structure	Use	Site Area (sq.m)	Bldg. Area (sq.m)	Height	Total Floor Area (sq.m)	Completion
N 1-17 X-Ku	S/SRC	Hotel Office	2,600	1,800	16F 63M	17,000	1998
H 2-2 X-Ku	S/SRC	Hotel Office	3,600	2,800	15F 65M	20,600	1998
N 3-3 X-Ku	S/SRC	Office Residential	4,700	2,500	17F 80M	39,000	1998
K 4-4 X-Ku	S/SRC	Store Office	6,500	2,400	21F 92M	55,000	1999
N 2-8 X-Ku	SRC	Residential	3,300	1,600	25F 96M	27,000	1999
I 3-22 X-Ku	S/SRC	Office	8,600	4,000	23F 99M	47,000	1999
H 2-11 X-Ku	S/SRC	Office	6,800	4,500	23F 109M	42,000	1999
H 2-4 X-Ku	S□SRC	Office	5,700	2,600	15F 77M	34,000	1999

H	S/SRC	Office	7,500	3,900	22F	42,000	1999
2-2-1 X-Ku					90M		
N 2-72 X-Ku	S/SRC	Office	15,000	6,000	44F 194M	200,000	2000
M X-Ku	N/A	Office	N/A	N/A	N/A	120,000	2001
Ji X-Ku	SRC	Office	14,000	8,100	23F	126,000	2001
Y X-Ku	N/A	Office	N/A	N/A	N/A	92,000	2001
M X-Ku	N/A	Office	N/A	N/A	N/A	54,000	2001
N X-Ku	N/A	Office	N/A	N/A	N/A	66,000	2001
N X-Ku	SRC	Store Office	6,000	N/A	30F	59,000	2002

DATA SOURCES : Building Construction Statistical Yearbook, The Journal of The Land Institute□ Development Project Information

2. NEIGHBORHOOD ANALYSIS

The main neighborhood factors that have or may be expected to have an effect on the value of the property in the neighborhood, of which the subject property is a part, are as follows:

(1) NEIGHBORHOOD DESCRIPTION

Social, economic, governmental, and environmental forces influence property value in the neighborhood of a subject property which, in turn, directly affect the value of the subject property itself. This section summarizes those forces for the neighborhood to which the subject property belongs.

A. Neighborhood Location

The neighborhood lies in the K district of X Ward, Tokyo and is located northeast of Y Station. From the station, a train takes about ten minutes to the Tokyo Station. As one of commercial corridors along D Street, the neighborhood consists of Section 1 of OOO (North) y-chome on one side and Sections 5 and 6 of Ooo(South) 4-chome on the other. Approximately five minutes' walk to OooStation. The station is shared by several subway/railway lines, including JR Ooo Line, Subway Ooo and Ooo Lines. Subway Ooo Line has a different Ooo Station which is located within a two minutes' walking distance.

B. Size, Shape, and Topography of Standard Site

In the neighborhood, it is our opinion that the following features are deemed to be typical for a hypothetical standard site:

Size: 400 square meters (approximately 4,300 square feet) more or less:

Shape: Square; and

Topography: Level.

C. Land Use and Future Anticipation

The typical land use in the neighborhood is retail/office building development. The area is fully developed with mid- to high-rise commercial properties. The shops along Ooo Street in the neighborhood enjoys heavy pedestrian and auto traffic thanks to good access and proximity to the railway/subway stations. Judging from the stability of land use, we anticipate that the neighborhood will maintain the status quo as a highly developed commercial area in the foreseeable future.

D. Zoning Regulations for Standard Site

The zoning regulations applicable to the standard site in the neighborhood can be summarized as follows:

-- Commercial Zone;

-- Mandatory Fire Proof District;

-- Maximum Lot Coverage 80% (100% for buildings with fire proof design);

-- Maximum Floor Area Ratio 700%; and

-- Class 2 Special District for Educational/Research Institutions.

3. SITE DATA

(1) Site Description

A. Size, Shape, and Topography

The subject site is located at the center of the neighborhood. The site has an area of Ooo square meters (approximately 20,000 square feet or roughly half an acre).

The shape is irregular with two small rectangular areas extended to the directions of northeast and northwest from the main portion of the site. The southeast side of the site, approximately 31 meter (102 foot) long, has frontage onto Ooo Street.

The street is a 27 meter (89 foot) wide trunk road fully improved with street lights, sidewalks, concrete curbs and so on. The northeast extra area, approximately 11 meter (36 foot) long, faces onto a 4 meter (13 foot) wide private alley. This alley is a designated road for public use. The northwest side of the other irregular portion, approximately 4 meter (13 foot) long, abuts on a 3.2 meter (10 foot) wide dead-end private alley, which falls upon the category stipulated in Section 42, Paragraph 2 of the Building Standard Act. The owner of a site which faces on this type of narrow road must dedicate his/her land to the municipality for road widening. The above-mentioned area includes the necessary dedication of approximately 4 square meters (43 square feet).

B. Service and Access

All services requisite for intensive urban development are available, including natural gas, electricity, water, sanitary and storm sewers, telephone, garbage collection, and fire and police protection. Access to the subject site is from Ooo Street and also from two alleys.

C. Environmental Assessments

With respect to environmental assessments, relevant investigations of the site were not available. It has therefore been assumed that there are no environmental problems or contamination that would affect the valuation contained herein.

D. Zoning

The overall property is zoned Commercial, Mandatory Fire Proof District, and Class 2 Special District for Educational/Research Institutions. Allowed is a maximum lot coverage of 80% (100% for buildings with fire proof design). These regulations are the same as those mentioned in the Neighborhood section for the standard site. However, the subject site has a smaller Floor Area Ratio (FAR) than the one for the standard site. This is because 700% FAR is applicable only to the area within 30 meters (98 feet) from the closer border of Ooo Street on each side of the road. Beyond the

30 meter limit, the FAR is reduced to 500%. Based on our calculation according to the areas included either inside or outside of the limit, the FAR of the subject site was estimated at approximately 595%. In addition, another major modification to the typical zoning regulations has to be considered. Due to the clause included as Section 8 in the X Ward Commercial Property Development Regulation, the developer is required to include a residential component in a commercial project with more than 3,000 square meters (approximately 32,000 square feet) of total floor area.

E. Summary

In summary, the site, while irregular, is good size at roughly half an acre and it is flat with a full complement of services. The site has good frontage onto Ooo Street. Access is further enhanced because the site faces onto two alleys. However, compared with the standard site discussed in the Neighborhood section, the subject site has a smaller FAR. On top of that, if it were vacant and unimproved, the municipal regulation would require residential components be included in a commercial project to be developed on it. In terms of road dedication to the municipality, the subject site includes approximately four square meters (43 square feet) of land for the future public use. Nonetheless, this factor is not considered affecting the value of the subject because of the insignificant amount of the area.

(2) Highest and Best Use

A. Highest and Best Use as Though Vacant

(A) Definition

According to "The Dictionary of Real Estate Appraisal, 3rd edition" published by Appraisal Institute, Chicago, IL, USA, highest and best use may be defined as,

"The reasonably probable and legal use of vacant land or an improved property, which is physically possible, appropriately supported, financially feasible, and that results in the highest value. The four criteria the highest and best use must meet are legal permissibility, physical feasibility, financial feasibility, and maximum profitability."

In other words, to qualify as the highest and best use, both as if vacant and as improved, the use must be:

(i) physically possible;
(ii) legally permissible;
(iii) financially feasible; and
(iv) maximally productive.

This discussion is hypothetical because the subject site has already been improved with the existing building. The purpose of this portion of analysis is to provide the basis for the value estimation of the site. In other words, the land must be valued as vacant and available for development to its highest and best use.

(B) Physically Possible

In our judgement, the site in commercial area has good potential for high rise building for commercial use. The physical features of the site, such as its size, shape, frontage, depth, topography, ground, ingress/egress and presence of utilities, also permit such a use.

With a full complement of services available, the subject site does not have any apparent physical factors which would hinder development. Considering its shape, size, soil, and other physical characteristics, we are of the opinion that the site would be capable of accommodating a building with maximum total floor area which would comply with its F.A.R. of 595%

(C) Legally Permissible

The Commercial zoning allows for office, retail, and entertainment, in addition to residential.

The zoning classification is clearly designed to encourage commercial development. Due to the Educational/Research Institution Special District designation, adult-oriented establishments are not allowed. This fact would help to provide possible better environments for residents.

The present commercial Use Zone permits many uses, such as residence, store, office, hotel, and theater. Any of these uses would be legally permissible. However, we mentioned before, this subject site must have residential component by law.

(D) Economically Feasible

Because of the proximity to the Central Business District, an office use would be financially feasible. Retail facilities such as convenience store, print shop, coffee shop, and restaurant would also be economically possible owing to the heavy pedestrian and automobile traffic on Ooo Street. Furthermore, hotel development might also be reasonable.

Moreover, some of the total floor area must be residential by law, even if residential use is less productive than other uses.

(E) Most Economically Productive

The maximally productive use is most difficult to evaluate, requiring an in-depth analysis of the anticipated values and costs applicable to each alternative use. We have refrained from making this analysis because it would not materially change the type or location of properties which are used to value the land. Suffice it to say that, for a property of the subject's size and location, a combined operation of retail (basement and ground floor) and office (second floor and up) generally produces a greater return to the land than any other alternative uses.

(F) Result

Due to the surrounding land use and zoning, the land as though vacant and available for development, the highest and best use is high rise store and office building with residence, different from standard use of the neighborhood because of site size.

B. Highest and Best Use as Improved

The site is improved with a 11-story retail/office/residential building with a total floor area of ????? square meters, or approximately 123,000 square feet. This is a substantial improvement that has a long expected lifetime ahead. The building is located in a relatively strong market, and it is expected, over time, to be profitable. Thus, the highest and best use of the overall property as developed, is, in our opinion, the existing mix of retail, office, and residential use for the remainder of the property's economic life.

C. Conclusion

The highest and best use of the site as if vacant is for a high-rise retail/office project. The current improvements fit this description. Therefore, the highest and best use of the subject property as improved is its current use as a mixed-use, high-rise retail/office/residential complex.

(3) Specific Features

Comparing the factors composing the standard value in the neighborhood with those composing the value of the subject site, we could find the following specific features that affect the value of the subject property.

Upward Adjustment Factor :

(i) Facing three side on roads

Downward Adjustment Factors:

(i) Residential component requirement by law

(ii) Less Floor Area Ratio

The floor area ratio of the whole area is not 700%. The area beyond 30m the frontage of Ooo Street is 500 %. The weighted mean Floor Area Ratio of total subject site is 595%. This FAR is less than 700% of standard site in neighborhood.

4. BUILDING DATA

(1) Outline of Building

The principal factors which affect the value of the building are outlined below.

Building Name : XXX Building

Age (Date of Construction)	March 0000
Structure & Use	Steel Reinforced concrete, 00-story building with a basement and flat roof. Floor layout : double loaded corridor type Store, Office, Residence, Warehouse and Parking
Size	Total ????? sq. m. 00 units (subject property : 00units)
Materials Used	Foundation : RC pile Structure : steel reinforced concrete Roof : asphalt waterproof sheet Outer Wall : red granite PC panels, ceramic tile cast PC panels and others Inner Wall : heated paint finish panels and others Ceiling : acoustic board plaster board, plywood board Floor : floor tile carpet and others Interior window frames and furnishings : wood, steel, aluminum, stainless steel and others Exterior window frames : aluminum, steel, stainless steel and others
Facilities	Air-conditioning system : air cooling heat pump type air conditioner Electricity : high voltage transformer equipment, self- power generation equipment Fire hydrant with alarm system Smoke sensor, Water sprinklers, Guidance light sign for evacuation Stairs for evacuation Tower parking : space for 00 cars

	Indoor parking : space for 00 cars (two stories parking) Elevators : 17 passengers 1,150 kg 2 units Emergency use 1,150 kg 1 unit
Design and Appeal	Basement : restaurants, stores, office, parking and warehouse 1 F : store(0000), warehouse 2 F – 10F : office, store and warehouse 11F : residence
Exterior site Landscaping	Pavement, garden and flower beds
Grade	Above Average
Present Condition	The building is 00 years old. Condition of maintenance and administration is good because of periodical fix and replacement.

Refer to Addenda 7 and 10:

Addendum 7 shows the details of each unit's materials, condition, and description.

Addendum 10 shows the building floor plan.

(2) Suitability of Building to Site and Surroundings

The subject building is suitable for its site and surroundings.

IV. ANALYSIS OF DATA AND CONCLUSIONS

1. VALUATION APPROACHES

(1) General Methods

The fee simple interest of the land and building could be appraised by three approaches, namely, the Cost Approach, the Sales Comparison Approach and the Income Capitalization Approach.

The Cost Approach --- One of the three traditional appraisal approaches to estimating value. In this approach, an estimated reproduction or replacement cost of the building and land improvements as of the date of appraisal is developed together with an estimate of the losses in value that have taken place due to wear and tear, design and plan deficiencies, or neighborhood influences. To depreciated building cost estimate, entrepreneurial profit and the estimated value of the land, as if it were vacant, based on its highest and best use, are added. The total represents the value indicated by the cost value.

The Sales Comparison Approach --- One of the three traditional appraisal approaches to estimating value. In this approach, the subject property including site and building is directly compared with similar properties that have been sold recently. Data from generally comparable properties are used and comparisons are made to demonstrate a probable price at which the subject property would be sold if offered on the market.

The Income Approach --- One of the three traditional appraisal approaches to estimating value. In this approach, the current rental income to the property is calculated and deductions are made for vacancy and collection loss and expenses. The prospective net operating income of the property is then estimated. To support this estimate, operating statements for the subject property in previous years and for comparable properties are reviewed along with available operating cost estimates. An applicable capitalization method and appropriate capitalization rates are developed and used in computations that lead to an indication of value. In direct capitalization, a single year's income is converted to a value indication using a capitalization rate. In yield capitalization, future cash flows are estimated and discounted to a present value using a discount / yield rate.

(2) Available Method for This Appraisal

2. VALUATION

(1) Cost Approach

In this approach, the value of the subject site is estimated as if it were vacant and available to be put to its highest and best use. Then the value of the present worth of the improvements is added to the land value estimate. In other words, the value through cost approach is value as fee simple interest, that is, the value of land and building without tenants.

(procedure)

(i) The value of the subject site is estimated as if it were vacant and available to be put to its highest and best use.

(ii) Then the value of the present worth of the improvements is added to the land value estimate.

(iii) We can estimate the total value of the building and land (= (i) + (ii)).

A. Land Value Estimate

We estimate the site value through Sales Comparison Approach.

(A) Estimation of Standard Site Value

The standard site in this neighborhood has the following characteristics among other features.

- fronts onto 27 meter (89 foot) wide Ooo Street;
- contains an area of 400 square meters (4,300 square feet); and
- is expected to be used as a site for a high-rise retail/office building.

In order to arrive at the value of the standard site, we compared the following two types of value estimates:

(i) Value Estimate Derived from the Land Value Survey Data
compiled by National Land Agency

□0,000,000 per square meter (Please see **Addendum 3**)

(ii) Value Estimate Derived from the Sales Comparison Approach

□0,000,000 per square meter□□0,000,000 per square meter

(Please see **Addendum 4**)

We estimated the value of the standard site at □?????,000 per square meter after carefully examining the value indicated by each comparable land sale in the Sales Comparison Approach and using the value from the Land Value Survey Data as a benchmark figure.

(B) Estimation of Subject Site Value

The comparison between the subject site and the standard site revealed that the former possesses the following factors which affect its value:

(i) Zoning characteristics

- the subject contains an area with reduced F.A.R.
- a development project on the subject must include a residential component

(ii) Physical characteristics

- the subject fronts onto two alleys as well as Ooo Street

We assigned -13% to the F.A.R. factor, -4% to the residential component factor, and +2% to the alley factor, respectively, as value adjustment rates. More efficient utilization possibility and better income potential of the subject site were taken into consideration in the process of judging the rates. The total value adjustment rate of the subject is calculated as follows:

(Zoning Characteristics) × (Physical Characteristics)

= (100%—13%—4%) × (100%□2%)

= 83% × 102%

= 85% (rounded)

Multiplying the value adjustment rate of 85% by the indicated value of the standard site, which is □0,000,000 per square meter, we calculated the value of the subject site per square meter as □0,000,000.

(Value of Standard Site)×(Value Adjustment Rate)

= □0,000,000 per square meter×85%

= □0,000,000 per square meter (rounded)

Then, by applying the land value of □0,000,000 per square meter to its site area, we estimated the value of the subject site by the Sales Comparison Approach at ??? BILLION FIVE HUNDRED AND ????? MILLION YEN (?,???,000,000 YEN), as the subject site value assuming the site vacant.

(Land Value per Square Meter)×(Site Area)

= □0,000,000 per square meter×????.?? square meters

= □?,???,000,000 (rounded)

B. Building Value Estimate

(A) General

The value of the improvements is based on the current cost of reproducing the improvements less any accrued depreciation. The traditional cost estimating methods are (i) the comparative – unit method, (ii) the unit – in – place method, and (iii) the quantity survey method. The quantity survey method produces a cost estimate based on a detailed inventory of the labor, materials, and equipment used in the subject improvements. The comparative – unit and the unit – in – place methods provide less detail, but they are the bases for the cost estimates used in most appraisals.

(B) Reproduction Cost New

In this report, reproduction cost was estimated with the Comparative-Unit Method because we could not collect enough data using the two other methods. This method is defined as "A method used to derive a cost estimate in terms of Yen per unit of area or volume based on known costs of similar structures that are adjusted for time and physical differences." The method employs the known costs of similar structures adjusted for market conditions and physical differences. Total cost is estimated by comparing the subject building with similar, recently constructed buildings for which contract prices are available.

Reproduction Cost New per Unit : 000,000 Yen per □

Reproduction Cost New of the Subject Building :

?????□ x 000,000 Yen per □ □ 0,000,000,000 Yen

Note : We consider that ????? □ includes tower parking.

(C) Depreciation

As a result of our analysis of the building inspection, we estimate that remaining economic life of the subject building is 30 years. As mentioned before, the effective age is about 00 years. We decide the remaining value ratio is 00% of total reproduction cost new through depreciation methods based on economic life and through observation.

(D) Building Value

0,000,000,000 Yen x 65% = ?????,000,000Yen(000,000Yen per □)

As mentioned above, we decided that the building value is ?????,000,000 yen (000,000Yen per □).

C. Total Value of the Building and Land

Site value	?,???,000,000 Yen
Building value	?????,000,000 Yen
Total value	?????,000,000 Yen (Rounded)

As we mentioned before, due to the clause included as section 8 in the Chiyoda Ward Commercial Property Development Regulation, the developer is required to include a residential component in a commercial project with more than 3,000 square meters of total floor area.

However, since this subject property was built before this requirement, the ratio of residential components is less than the ratio defined by the requirement. We decided that this building has more productive use compared with other buildings built after the requirements. In other words, during the remaining economic life of this building, that is, until the demolition, this building does not need more residential components. Considering the building's age and the ratio of residence, etc., we judged that this advantage is 2%.

?????,000,000 Yen X 102% = ?????,000,000 Yen

As a result, the total value of the building and land through cost approach is ?????,000,000 Yen.

(2) Sales Comparison Approach

SALE DATA ID	Subject	#1	#2	#3	#4	#5
Location	O	R	K	K	G	T
Zoning	Commercial	Commercial	Commercial	Commercial	Commercial	Commercial
Site Area (sq. m.)	????.??	1900	6000	500	240	7900
Floor Area Ratio	700%	300%	700%	700%	800%	700%
Total Floor Area (round) (sq. m.)	?????	0,000	0,000	0,000	0,000	0,000
Building Use	Office/store	Office/store	Office/store	Office/store	Office/store	Office/store
Date of Sale	00/1998	00/1998	00/1998	00/1997	00/1998	00/1998
Sale Price	0,000,000,000	0,000,000,000	00,000,000,000	0,000,000,000	0,000,000,000	00,000,000,000
Potential Gross Income	000,000,000	000,000,000	0,000,000,000	000,000,000	000,000,000	0,000,000,000
Net Operating Income	000,000,000	000,000,000	0,000,000,000	000,000,000	000,000,000	0,000,000,000
Overall Rate	N/A	4.9%	4.0%	5.9%	6.0%	5.3%
Gross Rent Multiplier	N/A	10.92	17.29	10.06	11.20	12.58
	N/A	9.2%	5.8%	9.9%	8.9%	8.0%

Overall Rate	MAX	6.0%	MIN	4.0%
Gross Rent Multiplier	MAX	17.29	MIN	10.06
		9.9%		5.8%

Average GRM = 12.4

000,000,000 (Yen) x 12 = 0,000,000,000 (Yen)

(3) Income Approach

(A)General

There are two methods, direct capitalization and yield capitalization in income approach. If we can use enough available data and make no mistake, each result of two methods should be same. The purpose of this approach is to place mortgage on the subject property. Since the loan is a five –year non-recourse loan, we decided to use DCF analysis with 5 years cash flow.

DCF Analysis

Value = Present value of NOIs + Present value of the net resale proceeds

PV = CF1 / (1+Y)**1 + CF2 / (1+Y)**2 + …… + CFn / (1+Y)**n

PV : Present Value

CFn : n year's cash flow

Y : Discount Rate

(i) sum of present value of NOI (YEN)	(ii) NOI of End of holding period (YEN)	(iii) Terminal Cap. Rate (%)	(iv) Reversion (YEN)	(v) Present value of reversion (iv) x 0.7299 note * (YEN)	(vi) = (i) + (v) estimated value through DCF (YEN)
000	000	5.5	000	000	000

Note * : 6.5 % , 5 year discount rate

(B) Assumption of DCF Analysis

a. Income

The details refer to Addendum 5.

(i) Rent of office, store and warehouse

Until the expiration of the present contract: contract rent

After the expiration of the present contract:

Since the level of the present actual rents are fairly higher than that of the average rent in this neighborhood as we mention before (refer to Regional Analysis (3) Rent), we change rent to lower level.

(ii) Rent of Parking

contract rent

(iii) Fee for common services

contract amounts

b. Expense

(i) Maintenance(actual)	00,000,000 YEN
(ii) Repairs(actual)	0,000,000 YEN
(iii) Property taxes(actual)	
Land	00,000,000 YEN
Improvement	00,000,000 YEN
(iv) Insurance	0,000,000 YEN
Total operating expenses	000,000,000 YEN

c. Reversion

Reversion is the lump-sum payment received by an investor at resale of the investment.
Reversion Value = (6th year 's NOI) / (Terminal Capitalization Rate)

Terminal Capitalization Rate(TCR) = 5.5 %

TCR is based on overall rate of sales data and usually higher than initial capitalization rate since normally we have to consider about resale cost and future risk. In this case, as we mentioned before, since the present level is high, TCR is higher than that of 3rd year, that is, after adjustments.

d. Discount Rate

6.5%

We decide this after considering the performance of similar investment data. The standard rate of comparable office buildings having good location, facilities, and size is 6.5%.

□DCF CASH FLOWS□

Thousand Yen

Year	□	□	□	□	□	6
□ Gross Income Rent Parking Fee for Common Service Sub-total						
Office & Store Deposit □ Interest						
Parking Deposit □ Interest						
□ Vacancy & Collection Loss						
□ Effective Gross Income □□□□□□□						
□ Expenses Maintenance Repairs Taxes Insurance Sub-Total						
□ NOI □□□						

□PRESENT VALUE OF NOI□

Thousand Yen

YEAR	NOI	RATE	DISCOUNT RATE	PRESENT VALUE	□Assumptions□ Vacancy & Collection Loss□ X□ of Gross Income, Constant during holding period
					Maintenance □actual amount□
□		6.5	0.9524		Constant during holding period
□		6.5	0.9070		Repairs □actual amount,
□		6.5	0.8638		X% increase annually
□		6.5	0.8227		Tax □actual amount,
□		6.5	0.7835		Constant during holding period
					Insurance □actual amount,
					Constant during holding period

Note : Addendum 5 shows the details of each year's income.

3. RECONCILIATION AND FINAL VALUE ESTIMATE

The two approaches applied in this assignment resulted in the following indications of value:

The Cost Approach	0,000,000,000 Yen
The Sales Comparison Approach	0,000,000,000 Yen
The Income Approach	0,000,000,000 Yen

Before arriving at our value conclusion, we reviewed the whole valuation process with an emphasis on three aspects: first, we reexamined the characteristics of the three approaches; second, we analyzed the key rates derived or chosen in each approach; and third, we took into account the special behaviors of property investors in Japan.

In the Cost Approach, the value of a property is estimated by adding the building value of the subject property to its site value. The building value is calculated based on the construction costs. The land value, on the other hand, is determined by mainly using recent comparable land sales. Therefore, the indicated value through the Cost Approach is considered to be transaction- or historical data-oriented.

In the Sales Comparison Approach, according to the sales data, the range of GRM is from 10.06 to 17.29, the average is 12.4 and that of OAR is from 4.0 to 6.0%. We decide that in this assignment GRM is 12.0.
Omit the details

In the Income Approach, on the contrary, a value is estimated based on the present and future income-producing potential of the subject property. In this assignment, both the five-year Net Operating Income (NOI) stream counted from the effective date of the appraisal and the reversion of the subject property at the end of the five-year holding period were converted into a present value using an appropriate discount rate. The income stream was estimated based on the first year NOI and the growth rates of revenues and expenses. The reversion is an amount the investor will receive from the sale of the property.

The indicated value from the Cost Approach was derived by adding two components. In order to assure the reliability of the added value from the market participants' point of view, we compared the cap rates of recent income-producing property sales with the cap rate based on the NOI of the subject property and the indicated value from this approach. The indicated cap rates of the comparable properties which were recently sold ranged from 4% to 6%. (Please see the table on the following page for the details of each comparable. The ratio of the Gross Income against the sale price had a variation from 5.8% to 9.9%.) The cap rate of the subject property based on the first year NOI and the estimated value from the Cost Approach resulted in 6.9%. However, a 5.7% cap rate was calculated when we used the third year NOI, which reflects the market rent level after the lease rollovers. Judging from the above-mentioned cap rates, we concluded that the market data supported the overall value from the Cost Approach as a reasonable estimation.

In the DCF analysis, we used 6.5% for the discount rate and 5.5% as the terminal cap rate. We chose the discount rate after considering the following items:

-- the typical discount rate, which is around 5.0% for a prime, newly built, and large-scale down-town office building.
-- the average rate of return on regular financial investments, which is around 4.5%, and the risk premiums of commercial property investment.

On the other hand, we selected the terminal cap rate based on the cap rates of the comparable properties as well as the risk factors of real estate market recovery and interest rate increases.

In the DCF analysis of the Income Approach in this assignment, we fully incorporated the risk of office market fluctuations and employed realistic figures for the future revenues realizing both the subject property's current levels of contract rents and the forecast of office space supply within the next several years. Hence, the estimated income stream was believed to be highly probable.

It is common to place the most importance on the Income Approach for valuing income-producing properties in other countries. However, in Japan, investors still tend to rely on the concept of the Cost approach, which measures land value explicitly. In addition, the DCF analysis has not been widely accepted in the market because of the uncertain nature of future cash flows.

Omit the details

In summary, based on the foregoing review, we placed equal weight on the Cost Approach and Income Approach in order to reach the final value estimate. Therefore, we are of the opinion that the best estimate of the market value of the ownership in the property as of July x, 1998, is:

????? BILLION TWO HUNDRED MILLION YEN
(?????,000,000 Yen)

Note 1: The IRR based on the appraised value can be calculated at 6.6%. It is our opinion that this rate reflects the characterristics of the subject property and its market and is reasonable when compared with the typical rates of return on real estate and other financial investments.

Note 2: The date on which the value opinion is applicable may differ from the date of the letter of transmittal.

Note 3: The appraised value does not include the amount of consumption tax at the sale of this property.

□ ADDENDUM 3: Indicated Land Value Estimate Based on Published Land Price

Description	Standard Site Shape and Size	Published Land Price Chiyoda 0-00
a. Road Condition	27meter wide metropolitan paved road	27meter wide metropolitan paved road on the south-east side
b. Traffic Condition	400m North-east of Y Station of the JR Chuo Line, Yurakucho and Nanboku Metro Line, 160m north-east of Y Station of X Line.	230m East of Y Station of the JR Chuo Line, Yurakucho and Nanboku Metoro Line, At close range of Y Station of S Line.
c. Environmental Condition	Topography: level Utility: Water supply, Public sewage, city gas Public Nuisances etc: Nothing Characteristics: High-Rise store and office Building.	Topography: level Utility: Water supply, Public sewage, city gas Public Nuisances etc: Nothing Characteristics: High-Rise store and office Building.
d. Zoning	Commercial Fire Zone Lot Coverage Ratio 80% Floor Area Ratio 700% Class2 School Zone	Commercial Fire Zone Lot Coverage Ratio 80% Floor Area Ratio 700% Class2 School Zone
e. Site Shape and Size	0.00 □ square mid-block site	0,000 □ Rectangular Mid-block site

Effective Date		January 1 st 1998
□ Published Price		0,000,000 Yen/□
□ Time Adjustment Factor		99/100
□Adjusted Price □×□		0,000,000 Yen/□
□Physical Characteristic (Note 1)		100/100
□Neighborhood Factor Adjustment (Note 2)		100/109
□ = □X□X□ Estimate Standard Price		0,000,000 Yen/□

(Note 1) the details of Physical Characteristic

a. Road Condition	00/100
b. Traffic Condition	00/100
c. Environmental Condition	00/100
d. Zoning	00/100
e. Site Shape and Size	00/100
f. Others	00/100
Physical Characteristic	00/100

(Note 2) the details of Neighborhood Factors

a. Road Condition	00/100
b. Traffic Condition	Proximity to Nearest Station +2 100

		102
c. Environmental Condition	Retail activities	+7 00 107
d. Zoning		00 100
e. Others		00 100
Neighborhood Factor Adjustment		00 109

□ ADDENDUM 4: **Indicated Land Value Estimate Based on the Sales Comparison Approach**

	Standard Site Shape and Size	Sales Data □ 1	2	3	4
Description					
a. Road Condition	27meter wide metropolitan paved road.	36m paved metropolitan road, 11m paved municipal road and 3m paved municipal road (Under building Standard Law Article 42[3]).	36m paved metropolitan road, 6m paved municipal road and 4m paved municipal road.	27m paved metropolitan road, 8m paved municipal road.	27meter wide metropolitan paved road.
b. Traffic Condition	400m North-east of Y Station of the JR Chuo Line, Yurakucho and Nanboku Metro Line, 160m north-East of Ichigaya Station of Shinjuku Line.	200m west of Ogawamachi Station of Shinjuku Line.	300m west of Ogawamachi Station of Shinjuku Line.	450m west of Ogawamachi Station of Shinjuku Line.	680m North-east of Ichigaya Station of the JR Chuo Line, Yurakucho and Nanboku Metro Line, 420m north-east of Ichigaya Station of Shinjuku Line.
c. Environmental Condition	Topography: Flat Utility: Water Supply, public Sewage, city gas Public Nuisance etc (Note□): Nothing Characteristics: High-rise store and office	Topography: Flat Utility: Water supply, public sewage, city gas Public Nuisance etc (Note□): Nothing Characteristics: High-rise store and office	Topography: Flat Utility: Water Supply, public Sewage, city gas Public Nuisance etc (Note□): Nothing Characteristics: High-rise store and Office building.	Topography: Flat Utility: Water supply, public sewage, city gas Public Nuisance etc (Note□): Nothing Characteristics: High-rise store and Office building.	Topography: Flat Utility: Water supply, public sewage, city gas Public Nuisance etc (Note□): Nothing Characteristics: High-rise store and office building.

	building.	building.			
d. Zoning	Commercial Fire Zone Lot Coverage Ratio 80% Floor Area Ratio 700% Class2 School Zone	Commercial Fire Zone Lot Coverage Ratio 80% Floor Area Ratio 700%	Commercial Fire Zone Lot Coverage Ratio 80% Floor Area Ratio 700%	Commercial Fire Zone Lot Coverage Ratio 80% Floor Area Ratio 700%	Commercial Fire Zone Lot Coverage Ratio 80% Floor Area Ratio 700%
e. Site Shape and Size	400.00 □ rectangular mid-block site	393.34 □ rectangular double corner site	482.07 □ irregular shape double corner site	189.05 □ irregular shape double corner site	85.27 □ rectangular mid-block site
Transaction Date		March 1998	March 1998	February 1998	February 1998
□ Sale Price		5,923,628 Yen/□	6,160,931 Yen/□	2,920,000 Yen/□	2,439,310 Yen/□
□ Sales Condition Adjusted		100/100	100/100	100/100	Selling in haste 100/70
□ Time Adjustment Factor (Note 3)		100/100	100/100	99/100	99/100
□ Adjusted Price □×□×□		5,923,628 Yen/□	6,160,931 Yen/□	2,890,800 Yen/□	3,449,881 Yen/□
□ Physical Characteristic (Note 1)		100/105	100/105	100/103	100/95
□ Neighborhood Factor (Note 2)		100/133	100/137	100/70	100/88
□ Estimated Standard Price □×□×□		0,000,000 Yen/□	0,000,000 Yen/□	0,000,000 Yen/□	0,000,000 Yen/□

Note□□Natural Disaster, Public Nuisance, Dangerous or Adverse Installation

(Note 1) the details of Physical Characteristic

Sales Data □	1	2	3	4
a. Road Condition	100/100	100/100	100/100	100/100
b. Traffic Condition	100/100	100/100	100/100	100/100
c. Environmental Condition	100/100	100/100	100/100	100/100
d. Zoning	100/100	100/100	100/100	100/100
e. Site Shape and Size	Double corner site +5 100/105	Double corner site +5 100/105	mid-block site with two frontage +3 100/103	Size -5 100/95
f. Others	100/100	100/100	100/100	100/100
Physical Characteristic	100/105	100/105	100/103	100/95

(Note 2) the details of Neighborhood Factors

Sales Data □	1	2	3	4
a. Road Condition	Road width +5 100/105	Road width +5 100/105	100/100	100/100
b. Traffic Condition	Proximity to Nearest Station +1 100/101	100/100	100/100	Proximity to Nearest Station -2 100/98
c. Environmental Condition	Retail activities +25 100	Retail activities +30 100	Retail activities -30 100	Retail activities -10 100

	125	130	70	90
d. Zoning	100/100	100/100	100/100	100/100
e. Others	100/100	100/100	100/100	100/100
Neighborhood Factor Adjustment	100/133	100/137	100/70	100/88

Source: Japan Real Estate Institute. Reprinted with permission.

REFERENCES

Hines, M. A. *Investing in Japanese Real Estate*. Westport, CT: Quorum Books, 1987.

Hirota, Yuji. "New Trends in the Japanese Real Estate Appraisal Industry." *Appraisal Journal* (October 1999), pp. 405–411.

Tsukamoto, Isao. "Appraisal Practice and Japan's Bubble Economy." *Appraisal Journal*, 67:2 (April 1999), pp. 195–198.

Note: During several real estate research trips to Japan during the late 1980s and 1990s, many interviews and conversations were based on Japanese real estate appraisal methods, practices, education, and licensing.

9

Real Estate Investment Yields and Their Measurement

Domestic investors seek good real estate investment opportunities in Japan. So do foreign investors, as property prices are perceived as relatively low in terms of the history of property prices in Japan over the last 55 years. After World War II, the devastated Japanese properties were rebuilt in the recovery period from 1945 through 1950 under the guidance of the U.S. Armed Forces under the leadership of General Douglas MacArthur. As the recovery occurred, property prices again rose from low wartime levels. After property prices rose to postwar peaks in 1990 and 1991, they fell drastically during the recession of the 1990s. They were still declining as the new millennium was ushered in. Therefore, domestic and foreign investors seek good real estate investments at rock-bottom prices. The definition of "rock-bottom prices" is subject to personal appraisal of the Japanese price trend and the analyst's forecast of prices for the near term.

THE NEED FOR MEASUREMENT OF REAL ESTATE INVESTMENT YIELDS

Many property owners in Japan are considering sale of selected real property holdings as they seek more capital to bolster depressed businesses. Some are considering the sale of existing property—residential and income-producing property—and replacement with better property at the reduced prices in the marketplace. Some foreign investors want to diversify their property portfolios with good income-producing properties in Japan. Some foreign investors, for example, in venture capital funds want a fast capital gain from highly profitable, prime Japanese properties in central Tokyo or other major Japanese city; some analysts have forecast a rather rapid upswing in property prices as soon as the recession ends.

MEASUREMENT OF INCOME PROPERTY YIELDS

We need to consider the measurement of both income property investment yields and real estate security investment yields that are associated with both equity and debt-related instruments. The yield measurement methods differ between the real estate securities and the operating income properties.

Current Emphasis on Operating Net Cash Flows Rather than Capital Appreciation

Domestic investors are accustomed to the measurement of real estate investment yields by emphasis on forecast capital gains; they have become accustomed to the de-emphasis of net cash flows from the operation of income-producing properties during the spectacular "bubble era" of the late 1980s and early 1990s. The gain from the increase in property price overshadowed the gain from the increase in net cash flow from property operations. In contrast, foreign investors are accustomed to yield measurement methods that accommodate both forecast capital gains and net cash flows from operations.

The Frequency of Foreign Acquisition of Japanese Income Properties

From the reported sales of major income properties, we surmise that few major or even medium-sized and middle-price income properties are being sold by Japanese owners to foreign entities. Mitsui Fudosan has reported in its *Japan Real Estate News* magazine a few major income property sales to a few joint ventures that included foreign entities. Very few major Japanese properties have been purchased in total by foreign entities. GE Capital and American International Group, as exceptions to the general rule, reportedly have purchased one or more major income properties; then, again, even these major investors may have acquired only partial ownership of the major properties.

Among the reasons for the infrequent foreign purchase of major Japanese income properties is, first, that Japanese property owners prefer to sell to Japanese investors. They are accustomed to their "closed society" of *keiretsu* and other Japanese business arrangements. Second, foreign investors have great difficulty appraising the investment value of Japanese income properties since property operating information is kept very private by Japanese property owners. Third, foreign investors may purchase defaulted or marginally performing loans that have real estate pledged as collateral, but little information is available from the lenders about the real properties because the properties were not a part of the loan underwriting process. Fourth, the Japanese honor real property ownership so fervently that they hesitate to sell their cherished properties even in recessionary circumstances. When they sell, they attempt to sell to Japanese affiliate and subsidiary companies, to members of the same Japanese *keiretsu*, and to relatives and friends rather than to foreign individual and corporate strangers.

Since so much Japanese real estate needs to be sold in the business reform and restructuring movement that is encouraged by the government, more real properties promise to be sold to both domestic and foreign investors in the future. Personal and corporate bankruptcies may decline as the recession ends, but there continues to be a higher-than-normal level of personal and business bankruptcies that require asset liquidation in personal and business reorganization for the future.

As the real estate appraisal system changes to accommodate the greater value represented by property operating cash flows over time, the methods of income property yield measurement are changing to accommodate the current emphasis on property operating cash flows rather than capital appreciation of earlier years. Japanese real estate financial advisers may turn their attention to the measurement systems of the international real estate community that are exemplified primarily by the U.S. real estate measurement methods.

Chief Influences on Income Property Investment Yields

Property revenues, expenses, and value are affected by a number of factors. For example, property cash inflows (revenues) are impacted by lease provisions such as the rent per unit and the term of the unit lease and the non-rent lease provisions such as the net lease features, percentage of sales provisions, and renewal provisions. Operating and capital expenditures are affected by the age of the property and government fiscal policies. If the property is several years old, it may require higher operating costs that include higher repair and maintenance expenses and higher capital costs such as costs associated with the updating of the building features. The heating, air-conditioning, and ventilation system may need replacement with a more efficient and economical operating system. Government fiscal policies impact the tax expense for a building. Taxes such as ad valorem property taxes, national and local income taxes, capital gains taxes, and business premises taxes reduce the net cash flow from the property. The nature of the depreciation tax regulations and the nature of the property rehabilitation tax credit provisions also increase or decrease the net cash flow from the property. The appraised value of the income property changes with the capitalization rate used for the property and with the financial structure for the property. The capitalization rate is affected by the risk status of the property, the forecasted capital appreciation, and the forecasted net cash flows from the property. The financial structure for the investment property is determined by the relative cost and availability of borrowed money, the cost and availability of equity capital in terms of dividend yield and expected capital appreciation, and the risk-return preferences of the owner. Some of the chief influences on property investment return relate to operating costs and revenues, capital expenditures, and valuation of the property.

Measurement Methods

The measurement of investment yield in Japan has focused on forecasts of capital appreciation rather than analysis of expected net cash flows over at least a 10-year period. But computer models have been used in Japan that utilize forecasted 10-year cash inflows and 10-year cash outflows; some of the computer models have spanned 25-year periods of forecasted cash flows.

Even though some Japanese firms use discounted cash flow techniques that are associated with the calculation of the net present value and the internal rate of return of a property, these firms are in the minority of all Japanese firms. Usually, Japanese firms assess a property's profitability by looking at multiyear cash flow projections that include imputed interest charges on the property investment, or they compute simplified, one-year property rates of return. The first approach accommodates the time value of money through the imputed interest charges over the holding period.

The Imputed Interest Charge Method

The imputed interest charge method of investment yield analysis utilizes a system that leads to a break-even point in terms of time that assumes a certain required investment yield. The Japanese use this method of yield analysis for the examination of foreign and domestic properties and projects of various kinds. For instance, proposed manufacturing projects may be evaluated by using the imputed interest charge method.

The following steps are involved in the imputed interest charge method of yield analysis:

1. Calculate the initial investment.
2. Calculate the multiperiod net annual cash flows from the property operation.
3. Calculate the net reversion value of the property at the termination or sale of the property.
4. Charge the income-producing property an interest rate on the unrecouped cash flow at the beginning of the year (or the end of the previous year).
5. The residual or unrecouped investment is calculated by subtracting the adjusted cash flow from the previous residual investment. The adjusted cash flow is equal to the property's regular net cash flow minus imputed interest charges (see Appendix 9-1 at the end of this chapter).

The Payback Period. When the residual investment becomes zero, the time for the recovery of the investment from the property adjusted cash flows is

Exhibit 9-1
Property Cash Flows with Imputed Interest Charges (Millions of Yen)

Year	Property Cash Flows	Imputed Interest	Adjusted Cash Flow	Residual Investment
0	-1000			1000
1	200	100	100	900
2	200	90	110	790
3	200	79	121	669
4	200	67	133	536
5	200	54	146	390
6	200	39	161	229
7	200	23	177	52
8	200	5	195	0
9	200	0	200	0
10	200	0	200	0

Source: Adapted from James E. Hodder, "Evaluation of Manufacturing Investments: A Comparison of U.S. and Japanese Practices," *Financial Management*, 15:1 (Spring 1986), exhibit 1, p. 18.

known. At that time, the property will have produced the required rate of return for the investor. For instance, a property with an estimated ¥1 billion investment cost, ¥200 million net cash flow before interest charges per year, no expected resale value, a 10-year economic life, and a required 10 percent return would recoup its investment cost in 7.3 years (see Exhibit 9-1).

Comparison with Net Present Value and Internal Rate of Return Calculations. The property described in Exhibit 9-1 would generate an internal rate of return of 15.1 percent using standard discounted cash flow methodology. Using a 10 percent discount rate, the property would generate a positive net present value of ¥229 million.

One-Year Average Return on Investment

This major approach to property yield estimation has many variations. The basic formula entails an average property accounting income for a typical year divided by the initial investment. This method caters to the accounting background of most property managers. A "typical year" may be defined as the first year of full-time operation of the property. The typical year may vary by the company and the type of property. The income figure for the numerator of the fraction may be defined as the annual profit estimate, which includes depreciation and imputed interest charges as well as anticipated revenues and costs. The costs may include such items as maintenance and insurance expenses, property taxes, and overhead costs. The investment amount may include not only land, improvements to the land, and capital equipment but an adjustment for increased working capital. The adjustments for working capital, property taxes, and other expenses are usually calculated by specific adjustment factors that represent company or division averages.

The return on investment (ROI) calculations are often performed on a before-tax basis. Since tax rates may vary across companies, this ROI calculation is subject to comparison across property types and across companies. But not all yield measurements are calculated on a before-tax basis. A payback period may be calculated on an after-tax basis. Some inconsistency in yield calculations is evident at times.

Payback Period

To estimate the payback period for a project that may be a real property acquisition, Japanese analysts take their typical-year accounting profit projection before tax, multiply it by the factor of one minus the anticipated tax rate, and add back the depreciation charge. The before-tax accounting profit for the typical year is, thereby, converted into an after-tax cash flow for the typical operating year. This after-tax cash flow amount is then divided into the initial investment to obtain the estimated payback period. This calculation usually includes an imputed interest charge. Therefore, this payback period estimation is somewhat more conservative than the typical U.S. payback calculation that does not include such interest charges.

In today's terms, the return on investment and payback calculations is a relatively crude form of property yield measurement, but Japanese managers are increasingly using discounted cash flow methods as they become more familiar with discounted cash flow (DCF) methodology. More Japanese managers now have been trained in business schools to calculate net present value, with an appropriate discount rate, and internal rate of return for proposed property expenditures. The often-used imputed interest charge method has the time value of money features; the method closely approaches the internationally used discounted cash flow methods.

As Japanese analysts estimate property investment yields, they are still employing "consensus" methods that involve the participation of people from all company areas that have an interest in the profitability operation of the income property. By the time that each manager enters into deliberations about the acquisition and operation of the property, the estimates of revenues and expenses have been realistically formulated. The risk level of the proposed acquisition has been analyzed thoroughly, and the required yield for the risks assumed has been estimated.

The required yield may be substantially different from the interest rate utilized for the cost of capital for the investment. The long-term Japanese Treasury bonds have recently been yielding investment returns around 1.5 percent. So the cost of capital estimated for the project may be relatively low in U.S. terms.

The Adoption of International Yield Measurement Methods

As Japanese real estate financial advisers serve foreign clients who seek to acquire major or medium-sized, medium-priced properties, they will continue to hear of foreign investor requirements, particularly U.S. prospective investor requirements, that emphasize the analysis of net present value and internal rate of return for each potential property. As part of the international property analytical system, the Japanese financial adviser will hear that particular property ratios should be reported to the foreign client. Computer models and financial calculators compute the cash-on-cash yield, the net present value, and the internal rate of return for the property investment along with several financial ratios. The customary ratios include (1) the operating expense ratio, (2) the break-even occupancy ratio, (3) the debt service coverage ratio, (4) the overall rate of return, (5) the before- and after-tax cash flow to initial equity, and (6) the gross rent multiplier. The calculation of the net present value, the internal rate of return, and the ratios in general requires the computation of taxable income, income taxes payable, the projected property sale price, the capitalization rate, perhaps the net operating income multiplier, the mortgage balance at the time of expected property sale, the selling expense for the property sale, and the before- and after-tax net cash flows from operations.

Use of Benchmarks

Benchmarks are used by the management of real estate investment companies and by other investors to judge how well the yields on real property compare in the marketplace. In Japan the Mitsubishi-Ikoma real estate price index might be considered a benchmark. Mitsui Fudosan recently calculated some investment yields from a sample of major properties that might be compared with the yields calculated for other major income properties. Ten-year Japanese Treasury and investment-grade corporate bond yields might be used for the real estate yield comparisons if the typical investment holding period for the subject properties tends to be 10 years in length.

In the United States the benchmark for yields on major investment properties tends to be 10-year U.S. Treasury bond yields and the Russell National Association of Real Estate Investment Trusts (NAREIT) index, which is taken from survey data from real estate appraisers. In the United Kingdom, the Corporate Property Data Bank Index is used for property price and yield comparisons. Other benchmarks may be developed in London by participating real estate management companies, including such companies as CB Hillier Parker and Jones Lang LaSalle.

The Role of Due Diligence

Some financial service companies in Japan specialize in due diligence work that aids investors and company managers in computing investment yields. Recently, for example, many prospective real estate investors, domestic and foreign, have sought investment yields for real properties that had been pledged as collateral for many loans. Since the necessary income, expense, and cost data have not been forthcoming from the lenders who were seeking to sell the loans, the prospective investors have sought assistance from various financial advisers. In other cases, prospective investors have tried to analyze the yields associated with properties that have been placed on the Japanese market. Most property owners do not publicize the income, expense, and cost data for their individual properties. Therefore, the due diligence services of international accounting and law firms, large, well-diversified real estate companies, and real estate investment banking companies have been sought. For substantial fees these companies, which have headquarters primarily in Tokyo, assist prospective investors in the analysis of the risks and returns from various specific properties in Japan. Due to the privacy of real estate owners concerning their property operating records, the due diligence work is very difficult, as is the current real estate appraisal work involving income properties in Japan.

Sample Investment Yields Quoted in the Japanese Marketplace

Let us note some sample yields for office, retail, and apartment buildings in Tokyo.

Office Building Sample Yields

In a compilation of early 1999 estimated investment yields from seven recently sold large office buildings that rented space in central Tokyo, we note estimated yields from 4.5 to 8 percent, with the average yield a little above 6 percent. Another study by another international real estate company estimated the early 1999 Tokyo central business district office yields between 5 and 6 percent; this contrasted with their estimated yields in the mid-1990s for the same area office properties, which ranged from 3 to 5 percent. Another international real estate firm looked at Tokyo investment properties valued below 500 million yen or roughly $5 million and estimated the early 1999 yields at 5 to 5.5 percent. Another sample of Tokyo office buildings reveals estimated investment yields for both 1999 and 2000 of 2.5 percent on the low side and 3 percent on the high side. These sources of investment yield estimation are widely recognized global real estate services with experienced global real estate financial analysts. The wide range in the yield estimates reflects the difficulties of estimation when property prices are still tending to decline in Japan, including in the central Tokyo area, when vacant office space is rising, and when lease contracts are tending to change with the soft market conditions.

According to a 1999 analysis of the size of world office markets, the Tokyo metropolitan area leads the world centers with a total floor area of more than 800 million square feet or more than 23 million *tsubo* in the 23 wards of Tokyo.

Apartment Building and Project Sample Yields

Yields tend to be a little higher for apartment properties than for rented office buildings. A low estimate of both 1999 and 2000 investment yields for apartment properties is 2.5 percent, while a high estimate of these yields is a little over 4 percent.

Retail Property Sample Yields

These 1999 and estimated 2000 investment yields tend to be higher than either office building or apartment building yields. On the low side, an estimated yield is 3.5 percent; on the high side, an estimated yield is 4.5 percent. Of course, retail properties range in Japan from large suburban factory outlet malls, to high-rise shopping centers in densely populated, inner-city neighborhoods, to separate major department store buildings in the Ginza district of Tokyo. Since the new suburban malls, which attract foreign tenants, tend to have percentage leases rather than only fixed square meter leases, these malls—after their existence and merchandise and service offerings are known and well established in consumer minds in the relevant market areas—should reflect higher investment yields than the examples from the United States and the United Kingdom.

MEASUREMENT OF REAL ESTATE SECURITY YIELDS

Real estate securities of various types are available for investment by both domestic and foreign investors. The wide assortment of real estate securities has been discussed in other chapters. Their yields can be estimated from adding their dividend yields to their capital gain yields. This yield analysis is based on publicly available price and dividend information, assuming that the securities are listed or at least frequently quoted in the over-the-counter market.

Some of the Influences on Real Estate Security Yields

The rise in real estate security prices may be correlated with (1) the trend in overall national inflation, (2) the overall growth of the economy, (3) the rise or fall of the various stock exchanges in Japan, (4) the change in interest rates in general, and (5) market sentiment or preferences for real estate securities. Inflation continues to be relatively low in Japan. Economic growth remains stagnant. The stock exchanges have been rising due to the rise in most world stock exchanges and due to the activity in telecommunications and computer company shares related to mergers and acquisitions and the increasing sales of mobile phones and Internet services. For example, in mid-February 2000, the Nikkei index topped 20,000 for the first time since July 1997 due to foreign investment and activity in technology, telecoms, and Internet companies. Since interest rates are relatively low, stock prices tend to be high.

Market sentiment may have a great deal to do with the trend in prices of real estate securities. For example, real estate investment trust (REIT) shares have been selling at a 15 to 20 percent discount from book value and have shown falling values through 1999 in the United States. Often U.S. REIT shares have sold at market prices considerably less than book value. In the mid-1990s REIT share prices rose in value. Sometimes investors have preferred shares in other sectors of the economy; market sentiment has veered away from REIT shares. As stock prices have fallen, 10 percent yields are expected during 2000 with little capital appreciation.

Real estate security yields reflect the dividend payout ratio from the earnings generated after adviser fees are deducted. Company earnings are dependent on the revenue inflow from rents net of operating costs and financial costs. Accounting regulations are changing with the financial and company structural reform taking place in the financial markets. Japan is moving to market value accounting and far more disclosure of company business activities, transactions, and relationships. The marketplace is gradually becoming more transparent, but this movement has a long way to go. Companies are accustomed to privacy in their business dealings and have not been required to disclose valuable financial data.

As pension funds accumulate amounts for real estate security investment and direct real estate investment, the real estate market will become more active. Private pension funds are gradually increasing in size and will impact the whole financial market more in coming years.

CHAPTER SUMMARY

Both Japanese and foreign existing and prospective investors in Japanese real estate need to be able to measure property investment yields by methods appropriate to the investment situation. Both Japanese and foreign investors need to use investment yield measurement methods that fit the nature of the income from the Japanese properties and that fit the competitive needs of their investment portfolios. Portfolio investors from Japan are accustomed to using primarily accounting-oriented methods of yield measurement and methods that reflect the high rate of price appreciation that is linked with the "bubble era." Non-Japanese investors, primarily represented by European and U.S. investors, are accustomed to using international yield measurement methods that employ present value and income capitalization methods rather than accounting-oriented methods. Today many foreign investors seek Japanese assistance with property yield measurement and find little active Japanese use of international present value and income capitalization methods. Today property yield measurement in Japan is focused on property income represented by operating net cash flows and possible decline in property value. To adequately serve the numerous foreign investors, Japanese real estate analysts are learning to use international yield measurement methods.

Japanese real estate analysts tend to use three principal methods of property yield measurement: the payback method, the imputed interest charge method, and a one-year average return on initial investment method. International investors also utilize the payback method just as Japanese investors do. The imputed interest charge method illustrated in the chapter employs present value methodology and provides a decision-making response that is similar to the response given by international net present value methodology. The one-year average return on the initial investment method of yield determination is similar in calculation to an older, seldom used average return on the average property investment method. This method tends to be accounting-oriented; it does not employ time value of money methodology.

Benchmarks are often used in international investment circles to compare real estate yields to yields of other investments with similar effective maturities in the international marketplace. In Japan real estate today we find less use of benchmarks for yield comparisons. But we find property indexes maintained by Mitsubishi-Ikoma CB Richard Ellis. The Japan Real Estate Institute is developing additional property price indexes.

Foreign and perhaps Japanese investors are seeking due diligence services in the real estate area to ascertain more information about income-producing properties. Many non-performing loans of banks and other financial institutions have property given as collateral. As investors consider purchase of these loans, they seek more investment information about the associated real estate. At the same time, due diligence service is difficult to render by the suppliers of such services, which include the international accounting firms and the international real estate companies, because the real estate market is not transparent. Information from property owners, property managers, and real estate brokers tends not to be available.

From the investment-related information available, we note that property investment yields of 2.5 to 3 percent have been estimated for major Tokyo central business district office properties. From this low yield estimate, we can also note that higher yield estimates from other international sources for major office buildings in the same area approximate 5 to 5.5 percent. Since property prices appear to continue to fall as the recession lingers on, it is difficult to evaluate the yields. We also have noted in other chapters that the leasing practices for major office buildings are tending to change in this "post-bubble" era. It is still true that the Tokyo metropolitan area leads world centers in total floor area of office buildings. This office space includes more than 800 million square feet or more than 23 million *tsubo* in the 23 wards of Tokyo.

While Tokyo center city office building yields have been estimated at about 2 to 2.5 percent for a decade or more and range from 2.5 to 5.5 percent, apartment building yields range from 2.5 to 4 percent. Retail property investment yields may currently range from 3.5 to 4.5 percent. These yields tend to rise as property values continue to fall and as property owners focus on net cash flows from operations.

Domestic and foreign investors are studying potential yields from real estate-related securities before investing. They may view current dividend yields and estimates for future capital gains. Some securities associated with the real estate sector are currently listed on the security exchanges; others are offered in private placements by security brokers. These yields are associated with the prospects for national inflation, economic growth, interest rate change, the trend of exchange indexes, and market sentiment toward real estate and real estate security ownership. The potential investor may study the yield patterns of U.S. real estate investment trust shares as well as the yield patterns for United Kingdom and European real estate-related securities. Massive savings continue to accumulate in Japan that need good investment outlets. As the pension funds continue to accumulate employer and employee contributions for retirement use, the pension funds will increasingly demand good yielding investments with appropriate risk attributes. Real estate securitization will be encouraged by these trends.

Appendix 9-1. Example of the International Use of the Imputed Interest Charge Approach

We hypothesize that a U.S. real estate company is considering developing a commercial building in a foreign country and that it will be using the imputed interest charge approach to evaluate the investment feasibility of the project.

According to the imputed interest charge approach, the initial cash investment, CF_0, should be determined. In an international context, the CF_0 would include the initial construction costs and working capital needs net of the possibly released blocked funds by the host foreign government. Then the estimated annual net remittable cash flow to the parent company is calculated, taking into account the vacancy rate, operating expenses, management and service fees, depreciation, debt service, net tax savings, interest rate savings, reversion value, and the exchange rate of the U.S. dollar vis-à-vis the foreign currency. The next step would be to charge the proposed developed commercial building an interest on the unrecouped CF_0 at the beginning of the year (end of the previous year). The unrecouped investment in any given year is calculated by subtracting the remittable cash flow (the regular remittable cash flow minus imputed interest charges) from the previous year's unrecouped investment CF_0.

To understand the imputed interest charge method, let us consider the following case, M.E. International, Inc. (MEI-USA), a U.S. commercial real estate development company that has foreign direct investment in Beijing, the PRC, and offshore investment in Hong Kong. MEI-USA is considering expansion of its real estate investment overseas, particularly in other cities of the PRC. Specifically, MEI-USA is seriously looking into the possibility of building a multipurpose commercial building in Shanghai. Based on office space analysis, the proposed building would be leased to multinational corporations having business dealings in Shanghai. Some Japanese, German, and British companies already have expressed interest in long-term leases with MEI-USA.

In addition to the PRC's guarantee through the National Bank of China, the company would be using lease agreements as collateral to secure a U.S. $30 million, five-year eurodollar floating rate note (FRN) pegged to the Hong Kong Interbank Offer Rate (HKIBOR). The current HKIBOR on the U.S. dollar FRN is 8 percent plus 2 percent to account for default risk of MEI-USA, MEI-Beijing, and the Chinese sovereign risk. It is anticipated that with the Chinese government's guarantee of the FRN, 100 basis points would be saved in the annual coupon payment. To lower further MEI-USA's effective cost of borrowing, it is assumed that the interest on the FRN would be adjusted every year rather than every six months. The interest rate on U.S. dollars is expected to rise or decline by 25 basis points a year, leaving the average nominal interest rate on the FRN unchanged. It is assumed that the principal will be paid back in five equal annual installments.

To make the FRN appealing to potential investors, the investment banker recommended that the five-year note be in a bearer form rather than a registered form.

According to forecasts obtained from foreign exchange consulting services, it is expected that, given the purchasing power parity of the U.S. dollar vis-à-vis the Chinese yuan, the U.S. dollar would be appreciating by an average of 7 percent. NEI-USA would pay $20,000 during the first year in consulting fees to the foreign exchange consulting firm.

Given the size and the nature of the issue (fixed-income note versus equity) and the favorable climate of the Asian capital market, MEI-USA would capitalize on its Hong Kong networks by utilizing the expertise of a prominent investment banker at the Hong Kong offshore banking center to underwrite the issue for a total flotation cost of 1.1 percent of the issue. This figure includes 1 percent for the investment banker's underwriting fee and 0.1 percent for legal, accounting, and printing expenses.

There is also a strong likelihood that the Chinese government would allow MEI to recover from its existing investments in Beijing a substantial amount of funds (50 million yuan) that had previously been blocked due to a dispute over local labor policies.

According to the PRC's regulations, land cannot be owned; therefore, the land on which the proposed building would be erected would be leased from the government for 300 yuan/square meter or roughly 30 yuan/square foot per year. However, the Chinese government would waive the land use fee for the first five years. It is anticipated that the site and building sizes would be 150,000 and 500,000 square feet, respectively.

Moreover, MEI-USA estimates that the initial construction cost of the multipurpose commercial building in Shanghai would be 300 yuan per square foot. The annual building operating expenses are estimated as follows: 60 percent at 40 yuan/square foot and 40 percent at 25 yuan/square foot. The company expects the net leasable area to be 455,000 square feet. Given the office space in Shanghai and preliminary negotiations with the Japanese, German, and British companies, MEI-USA forecasts that it would lease 60 percent of the leasable area at 140 yuan/square foot and 40 percent at 90 yuan/square foot.

Based on negotiations with the principal foreign lessees and a forecast of local demand for commercial building space, as well as the past experience of its Beijing subsidiary, MEI-USA estimates a vacancy allowance at only 7 percent.

The current income tax rate in the PRC is 30 percent, plus a local surcharge of 10 percent and an additional 10 percent on income remitted out of the country by foreign enterprises. Nevertheless, MEI-USA would be able to apply for exemption from the surcharge upon application to local authorities. Furthermore, the company would be taking advantage of new laws that make the income tax rate 15 percent in special economic development zones. Therefore, the net tax rate applicable to the company's income would be only 25 percent. Of particular importance here is that, to avoid double taxation, the PRC has concluded a tax treaty with the United States.

Depreciation in China is allowable for fixed assets and is calculated on an annual straight-line basis, with a residual value generally fixed at 10 percent of the cost. The minimum depreciable life of houses and buildings is 20 years, and capital gains arising from the disposal of fixed assets are taxable at 20 percent. Given the magnitude of political and economic risks in China, MEI-USA feels that the payback period should not exceed five years. Therefore, the company expects to sell the building at the end of five years at an estimated market value of 30 million yuan.

Based on varying degrees of uncertainty associated with the materialization of different cash inflows, different discount rates will be utilized, the least risky being the recouping of the blocked funds. However, those funds will be collected at the initial stage and therefore will be deducted from the initial investment. The discount rates applicable to cash flow range from 14 percent to 16 percent; so for our purposes, the average of 15 percent will be used.

THE SOLUTION

The following six steps illustrate the application of the Japanese approach:

Step 1: Calculate the initial investment, CF_0, at the facilitation stage (107,500,000 yuan) and convert the amount to U.S. dollars at the spot rate of yuan = U.S.$0.2687 ($28,885,250). CF_0 is calculated by adding the initial construction cost of 150 million yuan (500,000 square feet @ 300 yuan/square foot) to the working capital @ 5% of cost) and subtracting the released blocked funds of 50 million yuan.

Step 2: Calculate the five-year net annual cash inflow in the operational stage (see Exhibit 9-2).

Step 3: Calculate the total remittable cash flow to MEI during the operational stage (see Exhibit 9-3).

Step 4: Calculate the net revision value of the building at the terminal stage,

Exhibit 9-2

Projected Revenue, Operating Expenses, and Net Revenue (in Yuan)

	Year 1	Year 2	Year 3	Year 4	Year 5
Annual gross revenue 455,000 square feet x 0.60 x 140 yuan 455,000 square feet x 0.40 x 90 yuan	54,600,000	54,600,000	54,600,000	54,600,000	54,600,000
Vacancy allowance @7%	3,822,000	3,822,000	3,822,000	3,822,000	3,822,000
Operating expense 455,000 x 0.60 x 40 yuan 455,000 x 0.40 x 25 yuan	15,470,000	15,470,000	15,470,000	15,470,000	15,470,000
MEI-USA's management & service fee @ 15% of the annual gross revenue	8,190,000	8,190,000	8,190,000	8,190,000	8,190,000
Foreign exchange forecasting fee	74,432	---	---	---	---
Depreciation	499,995	499,995	499,995	499,995	499,995
Debt Service Flotation cost	1,228,136				
($30 m x 1.1%)/$0.2687, interest expense @10%	11,164,868	9,603,842	7,202,881	4,801,921	2,400,960
Net revenue	14,150,569	17,014,163	19,915,124	21,816,084	217,045
Income tax @ 25%	3,537,642	4,253,541	4,853,781	5,454,021	6,054,261
Net revenue after taxes	10,612,927	12,760,622	14,561,343	16,362,063	18,162,784

Exhibit 9-3
Total Remittable Cash Flows to MEI-USA

	Year 1	Year 2	Year 3	Year 4	Year 5
Net income after taxes (from Exhibit 9-2)	10,612,927	12,760,622	14,561,343	16,362,063	18,162,784
Add-back depreciation	499,995	499,995	499,995	499,995	499,995
Operating cash flows	14,225,001	13,260,617	15,061,338	16,862,058	18,662,779
MEI-USA's management & service fee	8,190,000	8,190,000	8,190,000	8,190,000	8,190,000
Net tax savings (U.S. rate–Chinese rate)	1,273,551	1,531,275	1,747,361	1,963,448	2,179,534
Interest rate savings (100 basis points)	1,116,487	960,384	720,288	480,192	240,096
Revision value (market value – book value) less capital gains tax	---	---	---	---	22,000,020
Total remittable cash flows (yuan)	35,917,961	37,202,893	26,233,543	44,357,756	69,935,020
Yuan/U.S.$ exchange rate	$ 0.2687	$ 0.2499	$ 0.2499	$ 0.2499	$ 0.2499
Total remittable cash flows	9,651,156	9,297,003	6,555,762	11,085,003	17,476,808

given the market price and the capital gains tax. Also, recapture the working capital (see Exhibit 9-3).

Step 5: Convert cash inflow in Steps 3 and 4 into U.S. dollars at the projected exchange rate of yuan/dollar (see Exhibit 9-3).

Step 6: Charge the multipurpose commercial building in Shanghai an interest on the unrecouped CF_0 at the beginning of the year (end of the previous year). The unrecouped investment in any given year is calculated by subtracting the adjusted remittable cash flow (the regular remittable cash flow minus imputed interest charges) from the previous year's unrecouped investment CF_0 (see Exhibit 9-4).

Exhibit 9-4 indicates that at a 15 percent cost of capital, the multipurpose commercial building proposed to be built in Shanghai is economically feasible. In other words, the net adjusted remittable cash flows are sufficient to cover the imputed interest charges as well as to recoup the imputed interest charges as well as to recoup the initial investment CF_0 in 4.3 years. This is compared to 4.1 years using the discounted payback period approach. The result is consistent with the DCF-based net present value (NPV) technique, using a 15 percent discount rate. According to Hodder (1986), using the imputed interest charge approach or the NPV technique will yield a similar accept/reject decision.

Source: Musa Essayyad and G. Hayden Green, "A Japanese-Adapted Technique for Evaluating International Real Estate Investments," *Multinational Business Review*, 7:2 (Fall 1999), pp. 83–88.

REFERENCES

Essayyad, Musa, and G. Hayden Green. "A Japanese-Adapted Technique for Evaluating International Real Estate Investments." *Multinational Business Review*, 7:2 (Fall 1999), pp. 83–88.

"Foreign Investment Trends in Japan's Real Estate Market." *Japan Real Estate News*, 10 (1st Quarter 1999), p. 5.

Green, G. Hayden, and Musa Essayyad. "International Real Estate Adjusted Present Value Model." *Real Estate Issues*, 15:1 (Spring/Summer 1990), pp. 8–15.

Harney, Alexandra, and Gillian Tett. "Fear of Split Economy as Nikkei Tops 20,000 Level." *Financial Times*, February 10, 2000, p. 4.

Hodder, James. "Evaluation of Manufacturing Investments: A Comparison of U.S. and Japanese Practices." *Financial Management*, 1 (Spring 1986), pp. 17–24.

Quan, Daniel C., and Sheridan Titman. "Do Real Estate Prices and Stock Prices Move Together? An International Analysis." *Real Estate Economics*, 27:2 (Summer 1999), pp. 183–207.

Rutledge, John. "One Man's Poison." *Forbes*, 162:5 (September 7, 1998), p. 250.

Thompson, Andy. "Patricof Aiming to Break Down Barriers in Japan." *European Venture Capital Journal* (August 1, 1999), p. 17.

Exhibit 9-4

Adjusted Remittable Cash Flows with Imputed Interest Charges (in U.S. $)

	Year 0	Year 1	Year 2	Year 3	Year 4	Year 5
Total remittable cash flows (from Exhibit 9-3)	28,885,250	9,651,156	9,297,003	6,555,762	11,085,003	17,476,808
Imputed interest charges @ cost of capital of 15%	0	4,332,788	3,535,032	2,670,737	2,087,983	738,430
Adjusted remittable cash flows	0	5,318,368	5,761,971	3,885,025	8,997,020	16,738,378
Unrecouped initial investment (CF_0)	28,885,250	23,566,882	17,804,911	13,919,886	4,922,866	0

10

Financing Japanese Real Estate

The financing of real estate in Japan involves government policies and regulations, sources of real estate equity and debt funds, and methods of real estate financing. Recently, some trends have developed out of the credit liberalization and financial deregulation of Japan.

TRENDS AFFECTING JAPANESE REAL ESTATE FINANCE

Some of the major trends that affect Japanese real estate finance are (1) the need for reallocation of funds due to economic changes, (2) the need for a secondary mortgage market to give liquidity to the mortgage lenders, (3) financial needs of the growing number of retired citizens, (4) real estate securitization, (5) competition among the Asian financial centers, and (6) round-the-clock security trading and foreign intervention in Japanese markets.

Need for Reallocation of Funds

The Japanese government, business, and industry have recognized a need to refocus their productive forces toward the needs of the twenty-first century. They recognize the international competition in steelmaking, shipbuilding, auto production, electronic goods production, and textile manufacturing. The strengthening of the yen in international money and capital markets has caused a change in trade balances in addition to the new competitive changes. Japan realizes that the service industry is growing more rapidly than most industries of its economy. The government and the business community also recognize a limited market for goods and services at home due to the geographic size and population of Japan. The scarcity of natural resources and the large industrial plant of the island grouping will continue to depend on resources from outside the country. These important foreign-sourced goods are related to such sectors of the economy as nuclear power plants, fossil fuel utilization, building materials such as lumber and marble, and domestic food supplies. Housing quality needs continued improvement. The commercial sector needs more quality office and retail space. The government needs to provide better transportation and communications facilities for the expansion of the domestic economy and the rise in the nation's standard of living. As Japanese business and industry change to meet the needs of the coming decades, investable funds will be reallocated among funds users.

Need for a Secondary Mortgage Market

As financial deregulation takes place, the existing financial institutions will need more liquidity in their mortgage portfolios. Additional liquidity would provide greater facility for portfolio readjustment with the change in investment yields. Therefore, the Japanese financial community is considering the establishment of a secondary mortgage market. With the gradual increase in personal incomes, Japanese consumers are moving increasingly toward homeownership and, in particular, ownership of larger housing units. The mortgage market needs to accommodate the increased Japanese consumer needs. As the home mortgage lending institutions underwrite more mortgages, they may wish to generate fee income from the mortgage underwriting but sell the mortgages to institutional specialized investors who are a part of an established secondary mortgage market. Usually, the secondary mortgage market institutions are government-sponsored and partially government-controlled, though they are often privately owned. But, due to the high, ongoing government deficit spending, the private sector should be encouraged to fully participate in the establishment of the secondary mortgage market.

Retirement Finance

Japanese pension funds are being established, and funds are being accumulated for retirement payments to beneficiaries over extended retirement periods. The average life of the Japanese person is lengthening, and companies as well as the government are recognizing the social and economic need for inflation-protected annuity payments to retired employees. For decades elderly persons have been a financial burden on the younger members of the family. Multiple-generation households have long existed in Japan due to the family provisions for the elderly within the family household. As the more affluent elderly population wishes to live separately from its younger family generations, the increased retirement payments from the government, business, and industry will permit living in specially developed retirement community and resort areas. The retirement housing will have to be financed by private developers, the government, and the retired occupants.

Real Estate Securitization

Real estate increasingly is financed through the issuance of securities based on mortgage pools or large commercial property net receipts. The offering of such real estate securities in Japan involves the domestic and foreign brokerage and investment banking houses. Brokerage houses from the United States are already accustomed to the underwriting and marketing of real estate securities such as Government National Mortgage Association (GNMA)-guaranteed mortgage-backed securities, secondary mortgage market participation certificates, collateralized mortgage obligations, and mortgage bonds. As Japanese brokerage and investment banking houses grow accustomed to the security methods of financing real estate, the leading security houses are considering mergers with domestic and foreign partners for more competitive power.

Competition among the Asian Financial Centers

The Hong Kong and Singapore financial centers already serve the global needs of major Asian and other regional companies. Tokyo has long served as an Asian international financial center in the same league with New York and London. But Japanese banking institutions have weakened as the need for competition with Hong Kong and Singapore grows. Of course, the Asian financial crisis weakened not only Tokyo but Hong Kong and Singapore financial institutions. As the new millennium opened, mergers of weak Japanese financial institutions were being arranged by the Japanese government to avoid bankruptcy of once-global leaders in banking. At the same time, the financial institutions of Hong Kong and Singapore were recovering rapidly, and their associated stock markets were once again on the upturn. The Asian financial crisis of the late 1990s was linked with the decline in world oil prices, the decline in the shipping trade due to the recession in Europe, and the decline in tourism that coincided with overbuilt hotel markets in Asia.

Round-the-Clock Security Trading and Foreign Intervention in Japanese Markets

Foreign financial institutions have become entrenched participants in the Japanese security markets. Some foreign financial institutions such as Citigroup have developed such strong and pervasive connections in the Japanese markets that the company has established an expansive branch network for consumer banking convenience. Foreign entities have become members of the Tokyo Stock Exchange; foreign investment banking and brokerage houses have merged with major Japanese financial houses to provide wider services to more customers in Japan and across the world.

Round-the-clock security trading is possible now but will be enhanced by the establishment and operation of NASDAQ Japan, MOTHERS, and Jasdaq. Jasdaq is Japan's over-the-counter market. NASDAQ Japan is an over-the-counter market that represents a joint venture between Softbank, Japan's leading Internet investment company, and the U.S.-based National Association of Securities Dealers. MOTHERS (Market for High Growth and Emerging Stocks) is the new market set up by the Tokyo Stock Exchange aimed at providing new business ventures with crucial access to capital. These markets will have less demanding criteria for listing than the Tokyo Stock Exchange. It may take only one month to list on MOTHERS and one to two months to list on NASDAQ Japan, whereas the required years in business for listing on the Tokyo Stock Exchange is said to average 34 years.

GOVERNMENT POLICIES TOWARD REAL ESTATE FINANCE

Japan owes its phenomenal economic success since World War II to the close cooperation of business, industry, and government. Japanese government policies and regulations will no doubt continue to guide economic development and funds allocation through the twenty-first century. But this guidance needs to be tempered by market forces to a higher degree.

The financial system has been tightly controlled. Foreign investment in Japan has been tightly regulated. Japanese investment abroad has been tightly regulated. While personal and business incomes and expenditures have been controlled, the interest rates and other real estate lending terms have been regulated by the government. Of course, the government has allocated funds to public works, the military establishment, and various other economic sectors. While large-scale business has continued in the form of the *zaibatsu*, or trading companies, the government has counterbalanced the big-business activities with increased strength for small business and the consumer. As the government proceeds with financial deregulation and internationalization of the yen, the government has lost some of its control over the various sectors of the economy. Capitalistic forces are taking over more of the direction of the economy.

General Regulation of Japanese Business

As a highly industrialized, capitalistic country, Japan has a variety of laws and regulations that affect business. Some of the laws and regulations and the administrative agencies that affect real estate financing directly or indirectly are noted in Exhibit 10-1. The Ministries of Finance, Justice, and Construction share this regulation with the Fair Trade Commission. The Ministry of International Trade and Industry (MITI) has responsibilities for foreign investment by industry

Exhibit 10-1
Selected Japanese Regulations of Business

Laws and Regulations	Primary Administrative Agency
Law Concerning Control of Foreign Exchange and Foreign Trade	Ministry of Finance
Law Concerning Registration of Foreigners	Ministry of Justice
Law Concerning Prohibition of Private Monopoly and Preservation of Fair Trade	Fair Trade Commission
Securities and Exchange Law	Ministry of Finance
Commercial Code	Ministry of Justice
Various tax laws	Ministry of Finance
Civil Code	Ministry of Justice
Construction Business Law	Ministry of Construction

and business in conjunction with the other concerned ministries. This ministry is also responsible for the administration of the Law concerning Adjustments of Retail Business in the Style of Large-Scale Retail Shops.

Regulation of Japanese Financial Institutions

Banks are regulated by the Banking Law. Trust banks, savings banks, mutual banks, and credit banks are governed by laws separate from the Banking Law. Japanese insurance companies are governed mainly by the Insurance Business Law and a series of related laws and regulations.

Provisions of the Banking Law include:

1. Banking businesses require government licenses. The license requirement extends to branches of foreign banks.
2. Banks are not permitted to issue no-par value stock.
3. Outside the banking business proper, banks are allowed to operate only trust and safe-custody businesses.
4. There is a fixed format for bank financial statements.
5. The government can examine a bank's operations and properties at any time. It can also require bank submission of reports and books of account at any time.

Provisions of the Insurance Business Law and related laws and regulations include:

1. A government license is required even for foreign insurance companies.
2. Insurance companies can be operated either as joint-stock corporations (Kabushiki Kaisha) or as mutual companies.
3. An insurance company cannot operate both a life insurance business and a general insurance business.
4. Without violating the Anti-Monopoly Law, an insurance company may take joint actions with other insurance companies.
5. The insurance company must set up certain reserves; additional reserves may be permitted.
6. Insurance company investments in listed securities may be valued at the market. The amount exceeding cost must be credited to a reserve account. Capital gains on the sale of property must be credited to a reserve account.

THE FINANCIAL SYSTEM

The Japanese financial system consists of the central bank and private and public financial institutions (Exhibit 10-2). The Bank of Japan formulates and administers monetary and fiscal policy in conjunction with the Ministry of Finance. The private financial institutions consist of commercial banks, specialized financial institutions, insurance companies, and security companies. The government-owned financial institutions include two banks, nine finance corporations including Shoko Chukin Bank, over 24,000 post office savings banks, and the Trust Fund Bureau.

Banks

Japan has commercial, foreign exchange, long-term credit, trust, mutual (*sogo*), commercial and industrial cooperative, agricultural cooperative, and government-owned special purpose banks. The commercial banks are characterized as city, regional, and foreign banks. These banks finance primarily the government and large business. Mergers among city banks are taking place. For example, Sumitomo Bank, which has led the Sumitomo *keiretsu*, is merging with Sakura Bank, which has led the Mitsui *keiretsu*. The resulting bank will become the world's second largest bank in terms of assets. In the early 1980s Sumitomo Bank ranked fourth in Japan in total assets in billions of yen behind Dai-ichi Kangyo, Fuji, and Mitsubishi Banks. The Bank of Tokyo is Japan's sole foreign exchange bank.

The three long-term credit banks and the 33 trust banks specialize in long-term loans. The Long-Term Credit Bank, which was taken over by the government during the recession, has recently been sold to an investment syndicate whose chairman has experience associated with his position in Japan with Goldman Sachs investment bank. The Industrial Bank of Japan is part of the triparty-bank merger that also includes Dai-ichi Kangyo Bank and Fuji Bank. The new

Exhibit 10-2
Japan's Financial Institutions, 1997

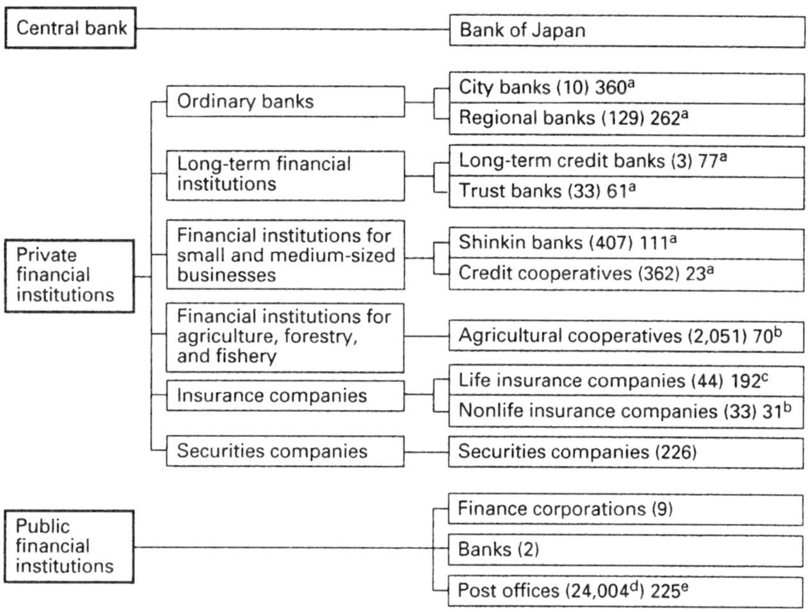

Note: Figures in parentheses show number of institutions and are followed by total assets in trillions of yen.
a. As of October 1997.
b. As of September 1997.
c. As of August 1997.
d. As of March 1997.
e. Outstanding deposits as of March 1997.
Source: Bank of Japan, *Keizai tokei geppo* (Economic Statistics Monthly), December 1997; Ministry of Posts and Telecommunications.

holding company in which each of the three banks will hold equal stakes is to be called the Mizuho Financial Group and is expected to be created by October 2000. The resulting bank will be the world's largest banking group, with expected assets valued at over $1.3 trillion. The new bank is expected to reach profitability in fiscal year 2005 with an expected 12 percent return on equity. The three banks, which had combined losses of over 1 trillion yen in fiscal year 1998, received public funds totaling 2.5 trillion yen in March 1999. The three banks have pledged to close a large number of their branch banks and to cut thousands of their employees during the first five years of the merged operation. These two actions are expected to save the new bank approximately $500 million and another $1.7 billion through synergies achieved by merging their operations. Dai-ichi Kangyo Bank has long been the largest bank of Japan in terms of yen deposits, total assets, and domestic branches; Fuji Bank has ranked second in Japan by the same measurements. The government, which stills owns the Nippon Credit Bank, is looking for an investor for this large financial institution. All three of the long-term credit banks have large holdings of non-performing real estate and other loans that have brought on their bankruptcies.

Various trust banks are merging with the approval and the financial assistance of the federal government. For example, Chuo Trust and Mitsui Trust Banks are merging so that a bank with adequate reserves for increased profitability in the future will be formed.

Other Financial Institutions

The postal savings organizations, security companies, and insurance companies are other important financial intermediaries (Exhibit 10-2). In 1997 there were approximately 24,000 postal savings banks, 226 security companies, 44 life insurance companies, and 33 non-life insurance companies. Each type of financial institution has increased in number if we make comparisons with the numbers for each type of financial institution represented 17 years earlier, in 1980. Most household savings have been placed in time and savings deposits, life insurance policies, and securities. Household savings have particularly been invested with postal savings offices. In 1997, for example, postal savings offices accounted for ¥225 trillion (roughly $2.25 trillion) in assets; their assets were essentially the same as security company assets at that time, ¥226 trillion (roughly $2.26 trillion). Stock investment has competed with investment in investment trusts in the securities markets. Some of the investment trusts provide group investment in real estate interests; other investment trusts provide potential rewards from stock and bond investment.

Financial Deregulation

Financial deregulation started in Japan in the early 1980s. The government had long regulated rigidly most parts of the financial system. Gradually, deregulation has taken place. A noteworthy listing follows:

April 1984: Financial institutions and securities companies were permitted to trade foreign commercial paper and certificates of deposit. Standards for the issuance of samurai bonds were relaxed.

June 1984: Restrictions on the conversion of foreign currency into yen were lifted.

October 1984: Foreign banks were authorized to deal in Japanese government bonds.

December 1984: Lead management of euroyen bond issues by non-Japanese underwriters was authorized. Issuance of short-term (six months or less) euroyen certificates of deposit was authorized.

March 1985: Money market certificates of deposits at market interest rates became available.

April 1985: Medium- and long-term euroyen lending to nonresidents was authorized.

June 1985: Yen banker's acceptance market was inaugurated. Decision was made to allow nine foreign banks to enter the trust banking business.

October 1985: Interest rates on large deposits were liberalized. Bond futures market was established.

February 1986: Six foreign securities companies acquired seats on the Tokyo Stock Exchange.

December 1986: Tokyo offshore market opened.

November 1987: Domestic commercial paper market was established.

May 1988: Sixteen additional foreign securities companies acquired seats on the Tokyo Stock Exchange.

October 1988: Ceiling on foreign banks and securities companies' share as underwriters of government bonds was raised.

January 1989: New prime rates that reflected the market rates for short-term loans were introduced.

June 1989: Small-unit money market certificates were introduced. Tokyo financial futures exchange was opened.

June 1992: Revision of laws regulating the financial system was approved.

June 1993: Interest rates on time deposits were fully liberalized.

October 1994: Interest rates on demand deposits were liberalized.

October 1996: Subsidiaries of life and non-life insurance companies were allowed to enter each other's business spheres.

April 1997: The Foreign Exchange Law was revised.

April 1998: The revised Foreign Exchange and Foreign Trade Control Laws came into effect.

INTEREST RATE TRENDS

Interest rates in Japan hit a peak in late 1990 and fell until the first quarter of 1999 (Exhibit 10-3). As the recession has progressed and as the demand for long-term loans has diminished, the long-term rates have declined. The average long-term prime lending rate peaked at a rate just short of 9 percent in late 1990. By the end of 1998, it reached 2.5 percent. In Japan the fixed interest rate for housing loans from city banks has tended to exceed the long-term prime lending rate for business loans in most years since 1988. In contrast, the floating interest rate for housing loans from city banks has followed the path of the long-term prime lending rate for the last 12 or 13 years. The standard interest rate for Housing Loan Corporation loans for the financing of private dwellings was substantially below the bank prime rate and the fixed and floating rates for bank-derived housing loans from 1988 until the mid-1990s. Since the mid-1990s, the standard interest rate for Housing Loan Corporation loans has approximated that of the bank prime and the bank floating rate for housing loans. In late 1998, for

Exhibit 10-3
Official Discount Rate Changes

	Japan	USA	Germany
End of 1992	**3.25**	3.00	8.25
End of 1993	**1.75**	3.00	5.75
1994	↓	3.50 (May) 4.00 (Aug.) 4.75 (Nov.)	5.25 (Feb.) 5.00 (Apr.) 4.50 (May)
1995	**1.00** (Apr.) ↓ **0.50** (Sept.)	5.25 (Feb.) ↓	4.00 (Mar.) 3.50 (Aug.) 3.00 (Dec.) ↓
1996		5.00 (Jan.)	2.50 (Apr.)
March 1998	↓	↓	↓

example, the Housing Loan Corporation rate was 2.55 percent, the bank floating rate for housing loans was 2.625 percent, and the bank prime rate was 2.5 percent. At the bottom of the interest rate hierarchy most of the years since 1988, the official bank discount rate has varied from 2.5 percent in 1988 to 6 percent at the peak in 1990 and 1991 down to 0.5 percent in the late 1990s (Exhibit 10-3).

During the 1990s, the Japanese official discount rate (3.25%) started higher than the rediscount rate of the United States (3%) and then stayed far beneath the U.S. rediscount rate for the rest of the decade. Near the end of the decade, in 1996, the U.S. rediscount rate was 5 percent, while the comparable Japanese rate was 0.5 percent, and the German official discount rate was 2.5 percent. The German discount rate at the beginning of the decade was 8.25 percent; it gradually fell to 2.5 percent by the spring of 1998. Therefore, during the 1990s, both the Japanese and the German discount rates declined, while the U.S. discount rate increased.

THE TREND OF INFLATION

The official Japanese discount rate has not followed the trend in Japanese inflation. Inflation has been low and well under control in Japan over the last two decades, as we note the trend in the wholesale and consumer price indexes. While the wholesale price index has described a somewhat erratic trend with deflationary tendencies in the mid-1980s, the consumer price index has approximated the 1 to 2 percent range for the last two decades. At the end of the decade of the 1990s, the consumer price index indicated a 1.8 percent rate of inflation for Japan, according to the Bank of Japan.

THE YEN–DOLLAR EXCHANGE RATE

Against the U.S. dollar, the Japanese yen was weak in the early 1980s. In 1985 the yen started to strengthen against the U.S. dollar. As a result of the Plaza Accord in 1985, the yen dipped for a short period and then continued to strengthen against the dollar. The Louvre Accord of 1987 accomplished the same results. On Black Monday in October 1987, the yen weakened against the dollar temporarily and then continued the upward path to reach approximately 90 to 95 yen to the U.S. dollar at the peak in 1995. At the end of the decade, the exchange rate was approximately 100 yen to the U.S. dollar; about the same exchange rate was established against the euro, also. The three currencies stabilized at this basic relationship to start the new millennium.

HOUSEHOLD PORTFOLIO COMPOSITION

Households and private, unincorporated, non-financial enterprises owned more than 60 percent of the land of Japan in 1998. Private, non-profit institutions that serve households such as hospitals, nursing homes, and other medical facilities, at the same time, own about 10 percent of the land of Japan. Non-financial incorporated enterprises, financial institutions, and the government owned less than 30 percent of Japanese land. In contrast, in the United States, the government is said to own at least one-third of all U.S. land; U.S. non-finance incorporated enterprises and financial institutions own additional amounts of U.S. land.

Household portfolio holdings of land and financial assets have grown significantly since 1970. The increase in household ownership of land reached a peak in 1990 and declined one-third in value by 1996. In comparison, household financial assets continue to grow. At the same time, liabilities of households trended upward to a peak in 1996. Household liabilities approximated 15 percent of the total value of household investment in land and financial assets at this time. About 60 percent of these liabilities were associated with loans from private financial institutions; therefore, about 40 percent of the household debt was payable to government-owned lending institutions.

METHODS OF REAL ESTATE FINANCING

The four chief methods of financing commercial real estate in Japan are business loans, key money deposits of tenants, joint ventures, and real estate security sales. Housing is financed mainly through loans from public and private financial institutions. Industrial property is financed primarily through loans from public agencies, security sales by the industrial corporations and their holding companies, and borrowings by the corporations from private sources. While the original *keiretsu* were intact, the members of a particular *keiretsu* tended to borrow from the lead bank of the *keiretsu* such as Sumitomo or Sakura Bank.

As the lead banks from various *keiretsu* merge, the original structures of the long-enduring *keiretsu* are breaking up; the old lending relationships may change with this financial deregulation.

Commercial Real Estate Financing

Construction and development financing for new buildings is often obtained wholly or in part by advance payment of key money deposits of prospective building occupants. Key money deposits are often paid on a square-meter basis by new shopping center and office building tenants in addition to regular security deposits. Quality retail and office space has been so scarce that prospective tenants are willing to finance the building developer-owner in this manner. Recently, as vacancy rates have climbed, the request for key money deposits has weakened, and tenants have tended to resist such payment.

The permanent financing of a shopping center or office building may be done through corporate issuance and sale of corporate stock and/or bonds. The security sales may finance several corporate needs at one time. The larger high-credit companies of Japan usually finance at least part of their corporate needs in this fashion. Part of their financing may come from loans from public and private financial institutions. If their credit standing is exemplary and if their corporate image reflects good business practices, the institutions have considered credit loans rather than collateralized mortgage loans for the impending real estate development or acquisition. Collateral for the real estate loans has usually been a secondary consideration; the company credit standing has been the first and most important consideration. Therefore, most loans for real estate development and acquisition have been commercial loans, not mortgage loans. Today, this lending practice is being reconsidered. In addition to credit standing or rating, corporate image, and membership of the lender's *keiretsu*, the lender may investigate the profitability of the impending loan and the underlying expected profitability of the real estate investment.

Since financial institutions often have financed their operations with primarily five-year debentures, borrowers have usually been offered five-year loans. The long-term credit banks have particularly been financed with five-year debentures. Since the three long-term credit banks are in a state of transition with an international syndicate as the new owner of the Long-Term Credit Bank, with a three-bank domestic merger including the Industrial Bank of Japan, and with a search by the government for a new, private owner for the Nippon Credit Bank, the financing of financial institutions, including the three long-term credit banks, may change in the future.

Sometimes loans for real estate purposes longer than five years have been offered the high-credit borrower—perhaps a term as long as 15 years. If the credit of the borrower is well established, the rate on the relatively short loan will approximate the Japanese prime rate.

Which institutions offer commercial loans for commercial real estate purposes? Generally, the sources consist of city banks, trust banks, long-term credit banks, life insurance companies, and pension funds. The Japan Development Bank may be a source of funds for land development by major companies.

Joint ventures are commonly used for commercial real estate financing. Several private financial institutions and well-to-do individuals may finance a major real estate project such as a regional shopping center. For example, one of the suburban regional shopping centers of Tokyo is financed by a joint venture of five or six investment partners.

Since it is difficult to acquire office space, the owner of the land and the existing office building that needs renovation may be asked to be a partner of the lender in a joint venture that would renovate or rebuild the structure. Through use of the joint venture for the financing of the needed renovation, perhaps the property owner does not incur high tax payment at the sale of the property. All or part of the additional space added to the premises may be used or owned by the outside partner as rental space. The new cash flows from the rebuilt or renovated property might be shared by the existing owner and the new joint-venture partner. The eventual sale proceeds from the property also might be shared by the joint-venture partners.

Industrial Property Financing

Industrial property is usually financed through the issuance and sale of corporate securities by the industrial company needing the industrial premises. Since extensive industrial development incentives are offered by various prefectures and local governments, subsidized or tax-exempt financing may be acquired from the involved governmental development authorities. As the industrial companies borrow from city banks, trust banks, long-term credit banks, life insurance companies, and pension funds, they may acquire money for developing and acquiring industrial facilities.

Japan's industrial development incentives include

- Tax holidays
- Loans at preferential rates
- Subsidized industrial land sales
- Government provision of infrastructure
- Industrial development grants
- Accelerated depreciation for the real assets

Equipment leasing and loans

Government policy is actively promoting industrial redevelopment. Substantial financing is required for such a redevelopment effort.

Residential Property Financing

Many leading institutions make loans for housing purposes. One-third of the funds may be provided by the Housing Loan Corporation (HLC), a special public corporation that obtains its funds directly from the postal savings system. It was established in 1950 to provide long-term capital at low rates of interest for the construction and purchase of housing. Through this agency, some government housing programs are implemented. Therefore, it is similar in this respect to the Canada Mortgage and Housing Corporation and the Credit Foncier in France. Most of the Japanese postal savings funds are deposited in the Trust Fund Bureau. The bureau uses the funds to purchase public sector securities and debentures and to make loans to government-related organizations, including the HLC. Part of the bureau's funds are usually allocated to the HLC. Most of the HLC loans are given to construct or purchase owner-occupied housing. These types of loans made up the bulk of the HLC loans. At times, such as the period 1955–1975, HLC loans were extended primarily to builders of rental housing units. At times most HLC loans are made for public housing; at other times, most of the loans are made for private housing. In terms of housing starts, recently, there have been more owner-occupied housing starts based on publicly financed housing loans than privately financed housing loans. Rental housing may be privately or publicly financed. Housing for sale may be financed either privately or publicly.

Most loans for home purchase are underwritten by the lenders on a fixed-interest basis. Some lenders offer variable-rate house loans. Mortgage rates tend to be below mortgage rates of other countries due to government influence on the HLC and due to the overall low-interest regime in Japan. Under government influence, the banks are often willing to lend at below-market rates on a limited part of their loan portfolios.

The HLC lends only on relatively modest dwellings. The smaller-sized-dwelling loans may involve under 110 square meters of space or approximately 1,100 square feet. The larger-sized-dwelling loans may involve between 135 and 150 square meters of space—approximately 1,350 to 1,500 square feet of space. The maximum housing unit size financed for any one year may be less than 130 square meters, or approximately 1,300 square feet. The loans are normally payable by the month over a typical repayment period of 25 years.

Traditionally, the government may stipulate the rate of interest at which the Trust Fund Bureau will lend to the HLC and then stipulate the interest rate at which the HLC will lend to ultimate borrowers. The government has usually established an adequate margin between the two rates of interest.

Since 1968, the interest from savings for housing has been tax-exempt. Interest on house loans has been tax-deductible since 1978.

Since 1965, the housing finance market has grown spectacularly. Part of the reason is the establishment of mortgage insurance through the Group Credit Life Insurance System and the Housing Loan Guarantee Insurance System.

Financial institutions are more willing to lend money for housing if their financial risks are reduced.

When a house lot is purchased, slightly more than half of the price may be paid from loans negotiated from lenders, 10 percent may come from the sale of real properties already owned, 30 percent may come from funds on hand from deposits and savings, and 5 percent may come from donations and other sources, according to the Japan National Land Agency. The lower the annual personal income of the house lot purchaser, the higher the portion of the lot price that may come from savings deposits accumulated. The highest-income purchasers of lots may borrow about as much money as they have saved and raise about 20 percent of the cost from the sale of other real properties.

FINANCING FOREIGN REAL ESTATE INVESTMENT IN JAPAN

Let us consider the sources of funds for Japanese real estate financing, the obstacles to foreign finance of Japanese real estate investment, the possibilities for foreign exchange and interest rate risks, and the possible means of hedging the perceived foreign exchange and interest rate risks.

Sources of Funds for Japanese Real Property Financing

Three general strategies may be used regarding sources of funds for loans for real estate investment in Japan: (1) bring funds from "home," (2) finance in Japan on the normal full-recourse basis, or (3) seek non-recourse financing in Japan from a foreign lender. Some investors, such as those from the United States, are accustomed to non-recourse mortgage financing for their real estate investment. In Japan, such investors will find that Japanese lenders are accustomed to corporate full-recourse loans for real estate investment where the lender may expect the borrower to incidentally give real estate collateral for the loan that is not included in the underwriting analysis.

Recently, the foreign venture capital funds that have been investing in partial and full ownership of major properties in Japan have been bringing their funds from "home." Many venture capital funds that have limited investment horizons for their property investments are derived from the United States. They may or may not have leveraged their equity investments with debt financing from their home countries.

The foreign investor may also seek non-recourse real estate financing from foreign lenders operating in Japan. For example, Citibank, now a major part of Citigroup, has been financing on the retail and wholesale levels in Japan for many years. Citicorp Japan is preparing to enter the real estate securitization market in Japan in a big way. The investor could explore a number of separate financing options with foreign lenders who are accustomed to non-recourse mortgage lending, mortgage-backed security sales, the sale of real estate equity instruments such as real estate investment trust shares, and other modes of property finance. Current Japanese legislation may or may not permit non-recourse real estate finance and other alternative international forms of real estate finance.

Obstacles to Foreign Finance of Japanese Real Properties in Japan

Financing in Japan as a foreign investor is subject to both foreign exchange rate risk and interest rate risk. The usual foreign real estate investor wants to repatriate funds from the real estate investment back to the headquarters country. The net cash flow from the real estate will probably be denominated in Japanese yen since the rents, the operating expenses, and the financial expenses will normally be denominated in the home country currency. The loan interest and principal payments from a Japanese-based lender will probably be payable in yen. But the amount repatriated to the home office in the headquarters foreign country will need to be in the currency of the headquarters financial statements. Foreign exchange rate risk is associated with acquisition of Japanese land and/or buildings, land development, construction, and sale of Japanese land and/or buildings.

Interest rate risk is associated with the fluctuation of Japanese interest rates, including the interest rate on the Japanese loan acquired for the financing of the property if it is a variable-rate loan. Interest rates may rise in Japan and reduce the forecast after-tax profitability of the acquired or developed Japanese property. If a fixed-rate Japanese loan is acquired, interest rates in Japan may fall—even below zero—while the loan is outstanding.

Hedging Alternatives That May Be Considered for Risk Reduction

The investor in Japanese real estate who realizes net cash flows in Japanese yen may wish to finance in Japan in Japanese yen. The yen inflows can at least partially offset the yen outflows to the mortgage or commercial loan source to reduce the foreign exchange risk.

The investor-borrower may consider hedging plans as the investment is made with the borrowed money. Currency and interest rate hedging programs may be considered. Since Japan is the second-ranked industrially developed nation of the world, the investor-borrower may find available such hedging instruments as

- Currency and interest rate option contracts
- Currency and interest rate futures contracts
- Currency and interest rate forward contracts
- Currency and interest rate swap contracts

If the investment and the associated loan are associated with a five-year or less expected investment horizon, these contracts may offer a suitable solution to the investor-borrower's foreign exchange and interest rate risk. Beyond a five-year period, the alternative contracts tend to become excessively expensive to the risk hedger. The venture fund with a two- or three-year investment horizon may be particularly well served by these contracts, whose greatest financial volume usually lies in the two- to three-year maturity categories.

Various financing methods may be available to the foreign real estate investor-financier. The land and buildings may be leased with the assistance of Japanese leasing companies that are based in Japan and abroad. Since GE Capital Corporation has an entrenched position in Japan, this source may be available for land and building leases of varying length at advantageous lease terms. The foreign investor may finance with key money deposits from Japanese and foreign retailers and office occupiers just as Japanese investors have done for years. If the real estate investment is expected to be a long-term one, the investor-financier may sell mortgage bonds based on the major property or may sell stock in the company formed for the Japanese real estate investment holding or in the foreign holding company. The sale of corporate stock may cover the financial needs of a number of domestic and foreign properties that are on the horizon.

CHAPTER SUMMARY

The system for financing Japanese real estate is changing due to a number of current forces in the economy and society. The continued restructuring of business and industry requires a reallocation of funds in general. The manner in which funds have been allocated is also changing as the long-term government–business system is changing slowly. With pressure from outside forces, funds are now being allocated more on the basis of profitability from the use of funds. Profitability of business units has long been subordinated to the goal of increased market share. As a by-product of the 1990s–2000s recession, profitability is beginning to gain in importance in the allocation of funds by government and business. As existing *keiretsu* are breaking up, the government's influence on business financing may be weakening with the economic reforms. At the same time, the government is taking the lead in bringing the economy out of recession. The heavy government expenditure on infrastructure construction and renovation to bring the economy out of recession has resulted in an exorbitant government debt level in comparison with the public debt levels of the other G8 (the Group of 8, which represent the leading industrialized countries of the world) members.

The need for an expanded secondary mortgage market and the need for an expanded real estate securitization system are recognized. Small steps are being taken in furthering the development of these financial sectors. Retirement finance is also posing a long-term financing problem for which funds must be allocated.

Retirement properties for retired persons must be financed for the increasing numbers of elderly persons.

Japan must continue to compete as a world financial center with the other Asian centers that are dominated by Hong Kong and Singapore. Japan—along with Hong Kong and Singapore—may have a continuing role in financing its neighboring countries, which are its chief trading partners. Over recent decades Japan's financial prowess dominated the Asian markets and promised support to the public and private projects and businesses of the region. Tokyo remains an important market in the round-the-clock security trading system across the world.

Government, with the active cooperation of business, has long regulated Japanese businesses, including the financial institutions. The regulated financial system comprises private and public financial institutions. Due to bankruptcies, near-bankruptcy conditions, heavy loan losses, and heavy volumes of nonperforming real estate loans, many financial institutions are being combined to form top-ranked world financial institutions that may once again prove highly profitable. The ordinary banks, which comprise both city banks and regional banks, continue to dominate the financial system under the guidance of the Bank of Japan. The three former long-term credit banks are being sold under government guidance to investment groups that include major foreign investors. Due to the many mergers and consolidations in the financial industry, the numbers of each type of financial institutions are declining. The goal of the mergers and consolidations is higher profitability for each of the surviving institutions.

Interest rates and inflation have trended downward in the past decades. At the same time, the yen–dollar exchange rate has risen, which shows the increased strength of the Japanese yen.

Household portfolios often comprise primarily real property, savings accounts at banks, including postal savings banks, certificates of deposit, and securities. Since most savings accounts and certificates of deposit offer such low interest rates, consumers seek investment trust securities and other securities that pay higher yields with only minimal extra risk. The high savings per household tend to encourage the issuance of real estate-related securities under the new wave of real estate securitization. As the interest in asset-backed securities reaches new heights in Europe, the same thing tends to be true in Japan.

The many methods of commercial, industrial, and residential property financing proliferate with the reduction in bank lending for real estate purposes. Many developers still finance part or all of their new buildings with key money and advance rent payments from prospective lessees and purchasers of the new space. This type of financing depends on the overall demand for the particular building space.

The financing of foreign real estate investment in Japan is more complex than the financing of Japan real estate investment by domestic investors. In many cases recently, foreign investors have brought their funds from foreign sources with them to the Japanese real estate market. Regardless of the domestic or foreign source of the funds for Japanese real estate investment, the foreign investor faces currency, interest rate, and other risks that should be hedged in some manner. Japanese financial markets provide some financial instruments that may be used for hedging currency and interest-rate risks.

REFERENCES

Akuzawa, Goki. *Forming a Hotel Real Estate Investment Trust: A Strategic Option for Japanese Construction Companies.* A Monograph Presented to the Faculty of the Graduate School of Cornell University in Partial Fulfillment of the Requirements for the Degree of Master of Professional Studies, May 1995.

Beattle, Alan. "Markets Report: Yen Strengthens as Nikkei Perks Up." *Financial Times*, December 23, 1999, p. 23.

Brenner, Brian. " 'This Is Going to Happen.' " *Business Week*, 3607 (December 7, 1998), pp. 106–107.

"Deal of the Month: General Growth Properties CMBS Financing in 1999 Amounted to $1.8 Billion." *Shopping Centers Today*, 21:1 (January 2000), p. 46.

Facts and Figures of Japan. Tokyo: Foreign Press Center/Japan, 1998.

"Finance and Economics: Knock, Knock." *Economist*, 352:8131 (August 7, 1999), p. 63.

"Finance and Economics: Lost in Translation." *Economist*, 352:8128 (July 17, 1999), pp. 68–69.

"Financial System." *Facts and Figures of Japan.* Tokyo: Foreign Press Center/Japan, 1998, pp. 31–34.

Financing Manual in Japan. Tokyo: Japan External Trade Organization, October 1994.

Hamlin, Kevin. "The Eclipse of Mr. ¥." *Institutional Investor*, 33:10 (October 1999), pp. 37–44.

Hayashi, Makoto. "Tokyo." *Asia Pacific Property Review*, Quarter One, 1999, MITA (P) No. 031/01/99. London: Knight Frank, March 1, 1999, pp. 16–17.

Hayashibara, Mariko. "A Risky Business." *Asian Business*, 34:2 (February 1998), pp. 32–33.

Hines, M. A. *Guide to International Real Estate.* Westport, CT: Quorum Books, 1988.

———. *International Income Property Investment.* Scottsdale, AZ: International Real Estate Institute, 1985.

———. *Investing in International Real Estate.* Westport, CT: Quorum Books, 2000.

———. *Investing in Japanese Real Estate.* Westport, CT: Quorum Books, 1987.

———. *An Overview of Global Real Estate Finance.* 3rd ed. Scottsdale, AZ: International Real Estate Institute, 1999.

Hines, M. A., with Ikunoshin Yoshida. *Japanese Shopping Centers: Financial and Investment Features.* Scottsdale, AZ: International Real Estate Institute, 1985.

"Housing Loan Rate to Be Raised 2.8%." *Japan Times*, October 26, 1999, p. 12.

Japan's Financial Markets. FAIR Fact Series II. Tokyo: Foundation for Advanced Information and Research, 1991.

Japanese Real Estate Statistics 1999. Tokyo: Mitsui Fudosan Co., Corporate Planning and Research Department, January 1999.

Kelly, Bruce. "Hitachi Will Manage Pension Money In-House." *Pensions & Investments*, 27:16 (August 9, 1999), pp. 3, 54.

Linsk, Michael, and Takahiro Tokunaga. "Bulk Sales of Japanese Troubled Loans and

Real Estate: Overview and Assessment." *Global Real Estate Now* (A publication of PricewaterhouseCoopers), 4:2 (Spring 1999), pp. 24–27.

Miyazaki, Kenji, and Makoto Saito. "On the Market Risk Involved in the Public Financial System in Japan: A Theoretical and Numerical Investigation." *Journal of Banking & Finance*, 23:8 (August 1999), pp. 1243–1259.

Murakami, Tomoeh. "Disillusioned Japanese Take Control of Their Own Finances." *Financial Times*, November 20/21, 1999, p. 4.

Nakamae, Naoko. "GE Edison Ends Toho Dispute with Takeover." *Financial Times*, December 20, 1999, p. 21.

———. "IBJ, Fuji and DKB Reveal More Details of Deal to Create World's Biggest Bank: Banks Speed Up Pace of Merger." *Financial Times*, December 23, 1999, p. 18.

———. "Interim Results Do Little to Lift the Gloom." *Financial Times*, November 26, 1999, p. 18.

———. "Japan Retailer to Apply for Bank Licence." *Financial Times*, November 27/28, 1999, p. 10.

———. "Japan Weak Economy Has Hit Demand: Recession Takes Toll on Life Insurers." *Financial Times*, June 10, 1999, p. 29.

———. "Japanese Life Groups Tread a Precarious Path." *Financial Times*, June 9, 1999, p. 16.

———. "Japan's Low Rates Revive Samurais." *Financial Times*, December 23, 1999, p. 22.

———. "Oriz Launches Convertible Equity 'Combi.' " *Financial Times*, September 22, 1999, p. 26.

Nakamae, Naoko, and Alexandra Harney. "Japanese Pension Chiefs Peer into a Bottomless Pit." *Financial Times*, July 16, 1999, p. 22.

Nakamae, Naoko, and Samer Iskandar. "Axa Strikes Deal to Take Control of Japan Life Assurer." *Financial Times*, November 30, 1999, p. 17.

Nakamoto, Michiyo. "Japan Delays Financial Reform Law." *Financial Times*, December 30/31, 1999, p. 1.

Rahman, Bayan. "Venture Capital: Tokyo Stock Exchange Launches Competitor to NASDAQ-Japan in Pre-Emptive Strike: First Listings on Japan's 'MOTHERS' Market," *Financial Times*, December 22, 1999, p. 19.

"Real Estate: An Uncertain Future." *Euroweek* (Japan in the Capital Markets Supplement) (August 1998), p. 28.

Roy, Sudip. "Deutsche Puts Japan Team Together." *Global Investor*, 125 (September 1999), p. 8.

Shibita, Yoko. "Property Scavengers Descend on Japan." *Global Finance*, 12:6 (June 1998), pp. 66–68.

Tett, Gillian. "Japanese Banks Make Good Progress Tackling Bad Loans." *Financial Times*, December 2, 1999, p. 1.

———. "Special Report: The Hidden Truth behind the Mask." *Financial Times*, June 18, 1999, p. 9.

Tett, Gillian, and Naoko Nakamae. "Japan Set to Delay New Pensions System." *Financial Times*, January 18, 2000, p. 4.

Wolf, Martin. "Private Thrift, Public Waste." *Financial Times*, February 16, 2000, p. 15.

Wolfe, Simon. "Japan: Financial Regulatory System Reform." *Financial Regulation Report* (July/August 1998), pp. 4–5.

11

Taxation Affecting Japanese Real Estate Investment

Any investor in real property needs to know the tax regulations related to the investment. National and local income taxes significantly impact the investor's rate of return. In like manner, the consumption or value-added taxes and the various taxes on real property also have a significant impact on the property's profitability. The investor should also note the transfer taxes that must be paid and the depreciation methods that may be used. The chapter also includes the nature of the tax system, the trend in corporate and individual income tax rates, and the personal income tax deductions that may be taken.

A GENERAL VIEW OF JAPANESE TAXES THAT AFFECT REAL ESTATE INVESTMENT AND MANAGEMENT

Five types of national and local taxes affect real estate management and investment: (1) taxes on income and profits, (2) taxes on inheritance and gifts, (3) taxes on property, (4) taxes on consumption, and (5) taxes on transactions (Exhibits 11-1 and 11-2). The local tax is levied by the 47 prefectures and approximately 3,400 municipalities. The taxes on income and profits include national corporate and individual income taxes and the local prefectural inhabitant taxes, prefectural enterprise taxes, and municipal inhabitant taxes. The inheritance and gift taxes are levied only on the national level. Taxes are normally levied on real property by both the national and the local governments. The taxes normally levied by the national government on land value are temporarily suspended. Municipal governments levy fixed-asset taxes, special landholding taxes, city planning taxes, and business office taxes. Consumption taxes that are value-added taxes are levied by both the national and the local governments. The consumption taxes on gasoline, local road use, aircraft fuel, petroleum,

Exhibit 11-1
National Taxes

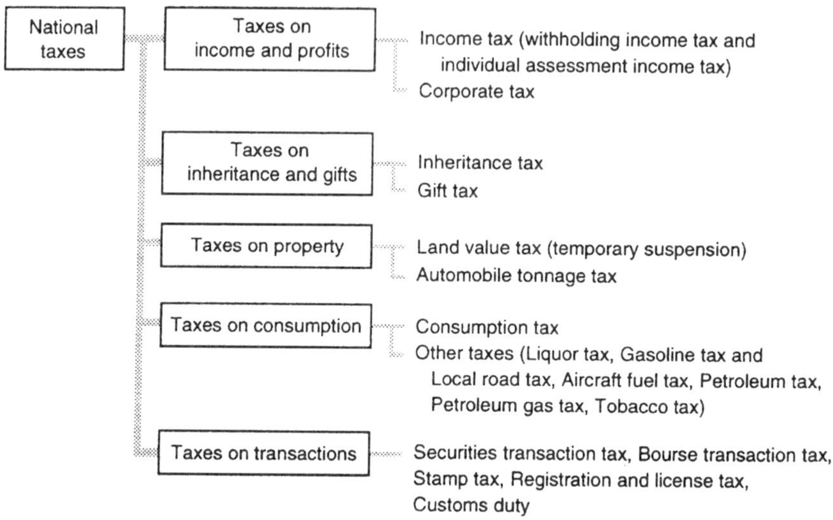

Source: Setting up Enterprises in Japan, 4th ed. (Tokyo: Japan External Trade Organization, 1999), p. 262.

golf courses, and diesel oil delivery affect the management of real properties in widespread Japanese locations. The national government taxes security transactions in general and stock exchange transactions; it also levies and collects stamp taxes and registration and license taxes. The prefectural governments levy real property acquisition taxes, as may be seen in Exhibit 11-2.

Taxation is administered on the national level by the Ministry of Finance with the implementation and enforcement by the National Tax Administration Agency and the associated Regional Tax Administration Bureaus and National Tax Offices (Exhibit 11-3). Local tax laws are administered and enforced by the 47 prefectural tax offices and approximately 3,400 municipal tax offices.

The Significance of the National and Local Income Taxes

The significance of the various national and local income taxes may be understood from a look at the tax moneys collected from each major source. About 45 percent of the national government tax revenues in 1998 came from corporate and individual income taxes—¥35.8 trillion or $358 billion, assuming a foreign exchange rate of 100 yen to the U.S. dollar. In contrast, in 1997 the national government derived about 60 percent of its revenues from individual and corporate income taxes, which amounted to about ¥35 trillion or about $353 billion (Exhibit 11-4). The Japanese government is becoming less dependent on income

Exhibit 11-2
Local Taxes: Prefectural and Municipal Taxes

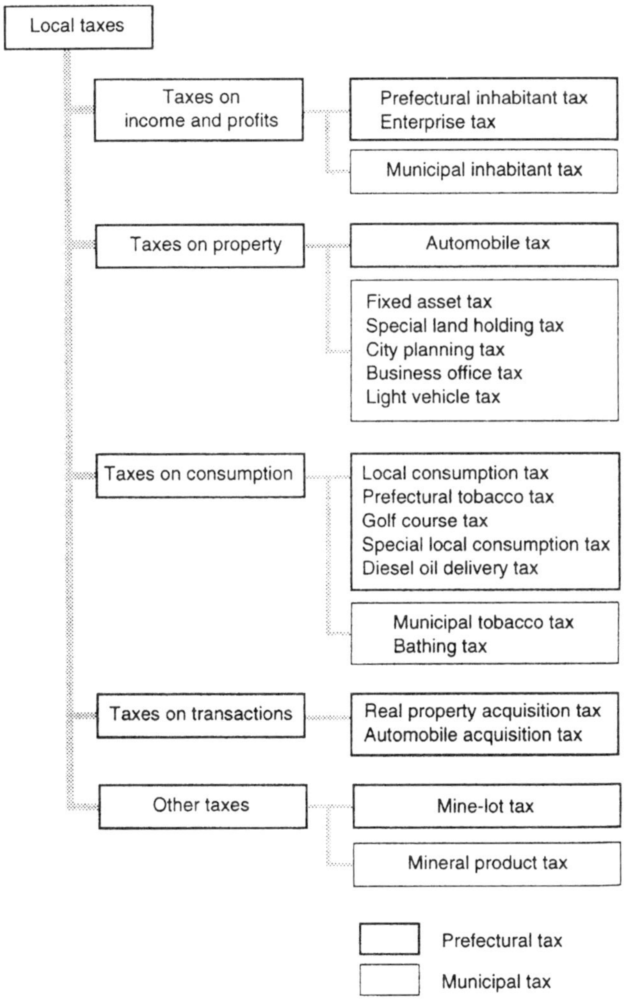

Source: Setting up Enterprises in Japan, 4th ed. (Tokyo: Japan External Trade Organization, 1999), p. 264.

taxes and is reducing the income tax rates as the years pass and as the recession persists.

The income taxes are levied on individuals and corporations on both the national and local levels. During the recession of the 1990s and early 2000s, the government sought to alleviate the tax burden of both corporations and individuals. Exhibit 11-5 shows that the effective income tax rate for corpora-

Exhibit 11-3
Japanese National and Local Tax Administration System

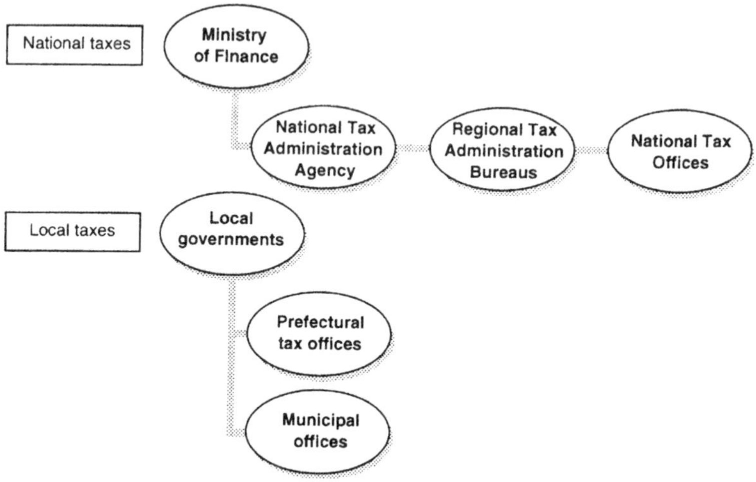

Source: Setting up Enterprises in Japan, 4th ed. (Tokyo: Japan External Trade Organization, 1999), p. 268.

Exhibit 11-4
National Taxes (Estimated Revenues), Full Year 1997

	Amount (billion yen)	Share (%)
DIRECT TAXES	37,927	63.8
Income tax	20,882	35.1
Corporate tax	14,432	24.3
Inheritance tax	2,461	4.1
Land value tax	152	0.3
INDIRECT TAXES	21,554	36.2
Consumption tax	9,813	16.5
Liquor tax	2,063	3.5
Stamp duties	2,019	3.4
Gasoline tax	1,956	3.3
Tobacco tax	1,062	1.8
Customs duties	1,093	1.8
Automobile tonnage tax	839	1.4
Others	2,709	4.5
TOTAL	59,481	100.0

Source: Ministry of Finance of Japan, *Facts and Figures of Japan* (Tokyo: Foreign Press Center, 1998), p. 30.

Exhibit 11-5
Tax Burden on Corporate Income before Tax of More Than 8 Million Yen, 1998–1999

	1998	1999
Corporate tax (A)	34.5%	30.0%
Inhabitant tax (B)		
prefectural	1.72%	N/A
municipal	4.24%	N/A
Enterprise tax (C)	11.0%	9.6%
Total tax rate	51.46%	N/A
Effective tax rate	46.36%	40.87%

Effective tax rate = ([A] + [B] + [C])/(1 + [C]). The effective tax rate is the tax rate after allowance of deduction for enterprise tax.
Source: Japan External Trade Organization.

tions with over ¥8 million in taxable income was roughly 5.5 percent lower in the 1999 tax year than it was in the 1998 tax year. The top effective tax rate in the 1999 tax year was 40.87 percent, down from 46.36 percent in the 1998 tax year. The effective tax rate for individual taxpayers in 1999 was reduced from the effective tax rate in 1998 of 53.2 percent (Exhibit 11-6). According to the Japan External Trade Organization, the highest marginal tax rate for the national individual income tax was reduced from 50 percent in 1998, to 37 percent in 1999, while the personal inhabitant tax of local governments was reduced from 15 percent to 13 percent—a total of 50 percent, down from 53.2 percent in 1998. An idea of the 1998 personal income deductions may be gleaned from study of Exhibit 11-7. Approximately ¥1 million may be deducted from otherwise taxable individual income if the taxpayer has a spouse and two children as dependents and has an annual income above ¥10 million. The deductions for a dependent spouse and two dependent children for personal inhabitant tax purposes may run ¥1,300,000 if the taxpayer earns more than ¥10 million a year.

There is a General Law of National Tax. There is also a Special Taxation Measures Law, which provides special tax concessions designed to achieve national economic goals. Generally, a property must be located in a redevelopment or industrially or economically distressed area in order to qualify for special tax concessions that fit special government incentive programs.

The Consumption, Property, and Transfer Taxes

Before briefly reviewing the federal and local income tax picture, let us briefly view the consumption, property, and transfer taxes affecting real estate investment.

Exhibit 11-6
Tax Burden on Individual Income, 1998

Annual Employment Income (A) (in yen 000s)	Income Tax (national) (in yen 000s)	Inhabitant Tax (local) (in yen 000s)	Total Tax (B) (in yen 000s)	(B)/(A)
2,300	0	0	0	0%
5,000	156	90	246	4.9%
10,000	850	515	1,365	13.7%
20,000	3,504	1,947	5,451	27.3%
50,000	16,110	6,222	22,332	44.7%
100,000	36,860	13,347	53,207	53.2%

Source: Japan External Trade Organization.

Exhibit 11-7
1998 Personal Income Deductions

	Income Tax (yen)	Inhabitants Tax (yen)
Deduction for a spouse	380,000	330,000
Special deduction for a spouse	380,000	330,000
Deduction for dependents	760,000	660,000
Basic deduction	380,000	330,000
Total	1,900,000	1,650,000

Note: Special deduction for a spouse is applicable to a taxpayer whose annual income is yen 10 million or less.
Source: Japan External Trade Organization.

Consumption Taxes

Most of the consumption tax revenue is associated with taxes on liquor, gasoline, and other commodities. These taxes affect the Japanese shopping center tenant who is buying liquor and other commodities for resale and who is buying gasoline to fuel company vehicles. Another consumption tax, the electricity and gas tax, is paid by the landlord for common area and office heating and cooling and by each of the tenants who heat and cool their own units under the lease provisions.

Property Taxes in Various Forms

The federal inheritance and gift taxes affect the landlord as a business proprietor or partner in real estate development and investment. The corporate stockholder is also affected by federal inheritance and gift taxes. Among the various property taxes, the fixed-assets tax, the city planning tax, the special landholding tax, and the business premises tax primarily concern the landlord.

Inheritance Tax on Property. An individual who receives property through an inheritance must file a tax return at the national tax office within six months. The marginal rates that the taxpayer faces range from 10 to 75 percent. This tax payment may be deferred for 5, 10, or 15 years by paying interest on a government loan. If the individual finds it impossible to pay the tax required in cash, the acquired property may be turned over to the tax authority in lieu of cash.

Municipal Fixed-Assets Tax. The annual municipal fixed-assets tax amounts to 1.4 percent of the assessed value of the land and buildings and 1.4 percent of the net book value after the declining-balance depreciation of the other assets, except automobiles. The assessed value of real property has been 60 to 70 percent of published land value. The law permits the municipality to increase the tax rate from 1.4 percent to 2.4 percent for land and buildings and from 1.4 percent to 2.1 percent for other assets. Tax payment must be made in April, July, December, and February of the following year.

City Planning Tax. A city planning tax is a surtax to the fixed-assets tax and is levied on land and buildings located in certain urban areas. This tax is levied on 0.3 percent of the value of the fixed assets.

Real Property Acquisition Tax. When land over a specified number of square meters is purchased, it is subject to a municipal tax of 4 percent of the value of the fixed asset at the time of purchase. If the acquisition of land and buildings is brought about by merger or inheritance, the event is non-taxable. The acquisition of land and buildings for residential use may be subject to reduced taxation. The real property acquisition tax applies to purchases of land comprising 2,000 square meters or more (approximately 20,000 square feet) in cities with populations of 500,000 or more residents or 5,000 square meters or more (approximately 50,000 square feet) in other urban centers or 10,000 square meters or more (approximately 100,000 square feet) in rural areas.

Business Office or Premises Tax. A taxpayer who owns business premises in designated cities must pay an annual municipal tax of ¥600 per square meter or approximately $0.60 per square foot of floor space of an existing building plus 0.25 percent of the total annual salary amount for the employees working in the space. For the asset levy, the limit to the tax exemption is approximately 10,000 square feet. The tax exemption limit for the employee salary levy is 100 employees. This business office or premises tax also specifies that a tax of ¥6,000 per square meter of floor space (or approximately $6.00 per square foot of floor space) must be paid on a newly constructed or expanded building. The tax exemption limit is approximately 20,000 square feet.

Land Value or Holding Tax. This tax has been temporarily suspended. Generally, the land value tax is payable by a taxpayer who holds land, including leasehold rights, in Japan as of January 1 of each year.

Transfer Taxes

The property owner is subject to registration and stamp taxes. The national registration tax calls for a payment of 5 percent of the assessed value of the real property at the transfer of its ownership. The registration tax for the acquisition of real property through inheritance or merger is 0.6 percent of the property's assessed value. The national inheritance tax is levied on the assessed valuation of the property at the time of acquisition. A progressive tax rate is applied to nine scales where the rate ranges from 10 percent to 70 percent of assessed valuation.

Stamp taxes are levied on agreements for the transfer of ownership of real property. The stamp tax ranges from ¥200 (approximately $2.00) for documents with lower values, to ¥600,000 (approximately $6,000) for documents involving a large amount of currency. A stamp tax must also be paid when a promissory note is registered. The rates run from ¥200 for notes of lower value, up to ¥200,000 for notes of much higher value. When a mortgage is settled, the registration tax amounts to 0.4 percent.

Housing derives preferential treatment in the area of license and registration tax. The previous upper limit for floor space—240 square meters or approximately 2,400 square feet—that is eligible for reduced license and registration taxes has been eliminated. The period for this preferential tax treatment for housing has been extended by two years. The license and registration tax base for land has been reduced to one-third of assessed value. Previously, 40 percent of the assessed value of land was the base for preferential treatment of license and registration taxes.

Depreciation Allowance

Depreciation allowances are permitted for depreciable tangible assets.

The depreciable assets whose acquisition cost per unit is less than $2,000 may be depreciated on an annual aggregate basis over a three-business-year period in place of regular depreciation, as of 1998. The acquisition cost of certain equipment and minor assets is immediately deducted as expenses in the business year of acquisition if their acquisition costs are less than $1,000 per unit. The limit on accumulated depreciation of tangible fixed assets is 95 percent of the acquisition cost; the total acquisition cost of intangible fixed assets may be depreciated. Exhibit 11-8 indicates the useful lives for income tax purposes and the depreciation methods for various tangible and intangible fixed assets. For example, reinforced concrete office buildings are allowed 50-year useful lives, and the straight-line depreciation method must be used for depreciation deductions.

Exhibit 11-8
Useful Lives and Depreciation Methods of Main Fixed Assets, 1998

Depreciable assets	Years of Useful life	Depreciation method
Tangible fixed assets		
Reinforced concrete building for:		
office	50	Straight line method
dwelling house	47	"
hotel	39	"
plant	38	
Air conditioners and heaters	15	Straight line method or declining balance method
Steel vessel	12 – 15	"
Airplane	5 – 10	"
Computer	6	"
Desks, chairs made of steel	15	"
Passenger automobile	5 – 6	"
Truck	4	"
Motion picture film	2	"
Machinery and equipment	6 – 22	"
Intangible fixed assets		
Patent right	8	Straight line method
Practical model right	5	"
Trademark right	10	"
Goodwill	5	"
Mining right	5 – 8	Straight line method or production percentage method

Source: Japan External Trade Organization.

Withholding Tax on Payments to Non-Residents and Foreign Companies

When a non-resident or a foreign company receives income from a Japanese source, the Japanese government withholds tax at the rate of 20 percent as payment is made. But a tax treaty between Japan and the national government of the non-Japanese-resident may permit reduction of the regular 20 percent withholding tax to 5 to 15 percent or no tax at all.

The following income items are subject to withholding tax of the Japanese government:

- interest on Japanese government bonds, municipal bonds, or corporate bonds issued by a Japanese company
- interest on deposits in Japanese banks
- interest on loans provided for business in Japan
- dividends received from a Japanese company
- consideration for lease of real estate located in Japan
- salary, wages, and bonuses incurred from services provided in Japan
- retirement allowance or pension payment related to services provided in Japan
- remuneration paid for services and performances rendered by artists, independent professionals, engineers, and other such people
- royalty for use of patent, know-how, copyright, motion film or consideration of their sale relating to business in Japan
- consideration for the use of machinery and equipment relating to business conducted in Japan
- redemption profit of discount bond issued in Japan
- sale of land or building in Japan by a non-resident or a foreign company.

If a non-resident or a foreign company maintains a permanent establishment such as a branch or factory in Japan, the specified income items may be exempt from the withholding tax requirement.

In 1998 Japan had concluded tax treaties with 44 countries. These tax treaties establish the withholding tax rates for the payment to non-residents or foreign companies of dividends, interest on loans, and royalties. From Exhibit 11-9 one can see that, for payment from Japan to companies or residents of the United States, the withholding tax rate for dividends paid to *related* companies or persons is 10 percent, and the withholding tax rate for dividends paid to *unrelated* companies or persons is 15 percent. A 10 percent withholding tax rate is applicable to payments of interest and royalties to U.S. companies or residents.

CHAPTER SUMMARY

Affecting Japanese real estate investment and management are five types of national and local taxes: (1) taxes on income and profits, (2) taxes on inheritance and gifts, (3) taxes on property, (4) taxes on consumption, and (5) taxes on transactions. In addition to relatively heavy national government taxes in each of these five areas are taxes levied by the 47 prefectures and approximately 3,400 municipalities. The local governments levy additional taxes on business and personal income, property, consumption, transactions, and mines and mineral products. The Japan Ministry of Finance, the National Tax Administration

Exhibit 11-9
Withholding Tax Rates for Dividends, Interest Payments on Loans, and Royalty Payments

Country	Withholding Tax Rate: Dividend – Related	Dividend – Unrelated	Interest	Royalty
U.S.A.	10%	15%	10%	10%
CANADA	10%	15%	10%	10%
BRAZIL	12.5%	12.5%	12.5%	12.5%, 15%, 20%
U.K.	10%	15%	10%	10%
FRANCE	5%	15%	10%	10%
GERMANY	10%	15%	10%	10%
ITALY	10%	15%	10%	10%
SPAIN	10%	15%	10%	10%
BELGIUM	10%	15%	10%	10%
SWITZERLAND	10%	15%	10%	10%
NETHERLANDS	5%	15%	10%	10%
AUSTRIA	10%	20%	10%	10%
NORWAY	5%	15%	10%	10%
SWEDEN	10%	15%	10%	10%
FINLAND	10%	15%	10%	10%
DENMARK	10%	15%	10%	10%
IRELAND	10%	15%	10%	10%
ROMANIA	10%	10%	10%	Cultural – 10% Industrial – 15%
CZECHO-SLOVAKIA	10%	15%	10%	Cultural – Exempt Industrial – 10%
HUNGARY	10%	10%	10%	Cultural – Exempt Industrial – 10%
POLAND	10%	10%	10%	Cultural – Exempt Industrial – 10%
BULGARIA	10%	15%	10%	10%
EGYPT	15%	15%	20%	15%
ZAMBIA	Exempt	Exempt	10%	10%
PAKISTAN	15%	20%	20%	Exempt
INDIA	15%	15%	10%,15%	20%
THAILAND	15%	20%	10%, 20%	15%
MALAYSIA	10%	15%	10%, 20%	10%

Exhibit 11-9 (continued)

SINGAPORE	5%	15%	10%	10%
PHILIPPINES	10%	20%	10%,15%	10%, 15%,20%
REPUBLIC OF KOREA	12%	12%	12%	12%
SRI LANKA	20%	20%	0%, 20%	0%, 10%
INDONESIA	10%	15%	10%	10%
BANGLADESH	10%	15%	10%	10%
PEOPLE'S REPUBLIC OF CHINA	10%	10%	10%	10%
AUSTRALIA	15%	15%	10%	10%
NEW ZEALAND	15%	15%	20%	20%
RUSSIA	15%	15%	10%	Cultural – Exempt Industrial – 10%
ISRAEL	5%	15%	10%	10%
LUXEMBOURG	5%	15%	10%	10%
TURKEY	10%	15%	10%, 15%	10%
VIETNAM	10%	10%	10%	10%
SOUTH AFRICA	5%	15%	10%	10%
MEXICO	5%	15%	10%, 15%	10%

Source: Japan External Trade Organization.

Agency, the Regional Tax Administration Bureau, the National Tax Offices, and local government tax offices implement and enforce the tax laws and regulations.

To counter the recessionary economy, the income tax rates have been reduced. The government is reducing its dependence on this source of revenue, which has represented about 60 percent of the government receipts in recent years.

To achieve national goals in specific areas, the government has special tax laws and regulations that promote redevelopment of specific areas and that promote domestic and foreign industrial investment in selected areas of business in selected geographic areas of Japan. These economic development tax incentives vary by prefecture and industry.

The consumption taxes, the inheritance and gift taxes, the property taxes, the fixed-assets taxes, the city planning taxes, and the real property acquisition taxes may inhibit personal and business investment in real properties. The business premises taxes, landholding taxes, and transfer taxes tend to discourage business investment in real estate. The license and registration taxes add to the tax burden. The depreciation regulations that offer mainly straight-line depreciation allowances over relatively long, useful building lives also discourage real estate investment. But all industrialized and many less developed countries find that, to fit their government budget commitments, these property, income, and other tax regulations in one form or another are necessary to continuing government operation.

The withholding tax on payments to non-residents and foreign companies may be reduced through bilateral tax treaties with Japanese trading partners. For example, the withholding tax rates for the United States, the United Kingdom, Germany, Italy, Canada, and Switzerland payments are reduced to 10 percent for dividend payment to related company entities and 10 percent for interest and royalty payments. Generally, the countries of the previously defined Western Europe have negotiated for these reduced rates in their individual tax treaties with Japan.

REFERENCES

Daimon, Sayuri. "Keidanren Chief Targets Recovery, Reform." *Japan Times Weekly International Edition*, 38:25 (June 22–June 28, 1998), pp. 1, 6.

Doing Business in Japan. Information Guide. New York: Price Waterhouse, 1996.

"Groundhog Day." *Far Eastern Economic Review*, 161:7 (February 12, 1998), p. 5.

"Japan: Tax Reform in Fiscal 1999 of Concern to Non-Life Association." *International Insurance Monitor*, 52:2 (Second Quarter 1999), pp. 37–38.

McDonald, James. "Structure of DC Plans in Japan Becomes Clearer." *Pensions & Investments*, 27:18 (September 6, 1999), pp. 14–16.

Setting up Enterprises in Japan. 4th ed. Tokyo: Japan External Trade Organization, January 1999.

Stuart-Smith, Jonathan, and Tomohiko Kaneko. "Japan." *International Tax Review*, 9:3 (March 1998), pp. iii–viii.

"Tax System." *Facts and Figures of Japan*. Tokyo: Foreign Press Center, 1998, pp. 28–31.

"Taxes on Real Estate: VI." *Japanese Real Estate Statistics 1999*. Mitsui Fudosan, January 1999, pp. 59–61.

12

Real Estate Securitization

After reviewing the methods of measuring real estate investment yields, the financing of real estate in general, and the taxation of Japanese real estate in the previous chapters, we approach the topic of real estate securitization, a specialized area of real estate finance that has recently been "the talk of Tokyo." This capital markets area of real estate finance has tax implications and influences and involves income property analysis and finance and the measurement of investment yields.

This chapter covers previous Japanese experience with real estate securitization and the reasons for the current emphasis on real estate securitization. The possibilities for further Japanese real estate securitization are associated with the advantages and disadvantages of securitization infrastructure. The advantages of further securitization relate to the presence of experienced financial advisers, investment bankers, and security and real estate brokers as well as the availability of computer software and credit rating services. The disadvantages of securitization relate to the relative cost of this form of real estate finance, the need for specialized legal services and additional legislation, the barriers to due diligence and income property appraisal, and government policies toward the use of offshore tax and currency havens.

Some of the real estate securities that are offered in the international marketplace and in Japan are enumerated according to three categories. Then the need for currency and interest rate risk management is established as the interests of foreign investors are considered in light of Japanese real estate securitization.

PREVIOUS JAPANESE EXPERIENCE WITH REAL ESTATE SECURITIZATION

In the current Japanese frenzy over the "coming of real estate securitization," we note that Japan is already acquainted with real estate finance and investment through the use of the capital markets. Japanese investors are already acquainted with asset-backed vehicle loan securities and equipment lease securities. In fact, in 1999 there was a substantial increase in Japanese asset-backed bond business. The new issuance of Japanese asset-backed bonds more than doubled in 1999.

A large number of Japanese real estate companies offer securities to the investing public in Japan and overseas. It has long been possible for a Japanese investor to purchase stock or Japanese depository receipts in foreign real estate companies; at least U.S. investors have long been able to invest in stock or American depository receipts in foreign real estate companies. In 1999, during the hoopla over impending real estate securitization, the Mori Building Group with Nomura Securities, an international brokerage and investment banking company with its headquarters in Tokyo, announced an offering of shares in some Japanese real properties in 2000. In the mortgage business, the Trust Fund Bureau, which manages the postal savings system of Japan, has been selling home mortgages that have been originated by the postal savings banks to the Japan HLC. Such mortgage transactions are part of a secondary mortgage market that is active in Japan. Equity investment trust shares have long been available to Japanese investors; some of the trusts represent pools of partial and total ownership of income properties. Shares of real estate investment funds, managed by Japanese and foreign entities, have also been available to Japanese investors. Investment banks such as Goldman Sachs periodically provide opportunities for investment in a diversified global real estate fund.

Therefore, Japan is already acquainted with various forms of real estate securitization and has a seemingly small secondary mortgage market in effect. Perhaps the excitement within the Japanese real estate community is associated with the impending importation of new elements of international real estate securitization methods into the Japanese financial system. Since foreign investors have shown an interest in Japanese real estate as market prices hit the bottom of a real estate cycle, the real estate community wishes to generate real estate securities that may meet domestic and foreign investor demand and improve the profitability status of the Japanese real estate establishment and the Japanese economy in general.

Japanese and Foreign Real Estate Company Securities

Many Japanese and foreign real estate companies offer securities to individuals, financial institutions, investment funds, and other investors at home and abroad. Some of the larger Japanese companies that offer stock are Mitsui Real Estate Development Company (known in Japan as Mitsui Fudosan), which was established in July 1941 and listed its securities by 1949; Mitsubishi Estate Co., which was established in 1937 and listed its securities in 1953; Sumitomo Realty & Development Co., which was established in 1949 and listed its securities in 1970; Tokyu Land Co., which was established in 1939 and listed its securities in 1956; and Tokyo Tatemono Co., which was established in 1896 and listed its securities in 1949. Other real estate companies that offer securities for sale are Diamond City, a joint venture that was set up by Jusco Co. and Mitsubishi Corp., and that was established in 1969 and listed its securities in 1989, and ANA Real Estate Co., an affiliate of the All Nippon Airways that was established in 1961 and listed its securities in 1989. Mitsui Real Estate Sales Co., a worldwide provider of real estate investment opportunities in Japan and abroad, which is an influential subsidiary of Mitsui Real Estate Development Co., was created in 1969 and listed securities in 1989. Dia Kensetsu, a high-ranking builder of residential and resort condominiums, was created in 1976 and listed its securities in 1989. This is a sample of the older and the more recently formed Japanese real estate companies whose securities have been listed on one or more stock exchanges in Japan and worldwide. Securities may also be available from Japanese real estate companies that privately offer their stock for their financing without listing the stock on any stock exchanges.

Real estate company securities from foreign sources are available to Japanese investors. The United Kingdom has many property trusts of various types that offer opportunities to invest in diversified portfolios of partial and whole ownership interests in real properties in the United Kingdom primarily; some of the property trusts originating in the United Kingdom also include real property interests from continental Europe and Scandinavia. One of the largest U.K. trusts is Land Securities, whose stock activity may be followed in financial pages of the *Financial Times* and other business-oriented newspapers. In the United States the Japanese investor may investigate and invest in various U.S.-based real estate company shares that reflect varying stock price trends, dividend trends, and exchange listing origins. Many stocks may be purchased in depository receipt form rather than in the currency of the issuer's country of domicile.

Shares in Japanese and Foreign Real Estate Investment Funds

Even though there are currently legal and tax barriers to the formation of certain kinds of real estate securities in Japan, real estate investment funds continue to offer shares of their funds to individual and institutional investors. Those shares may be in negotiable instrument form or otherwise. The fall 1999 Mori-Nomura real estate offering fits this situation as an example.

Equity investment trusts have long been managed by Japanese financial entities and offered to individual and institutional investors in Japan. Various types of assets have been pooled under the investment trust device, sold to investors, the assets managed by financial institutions, and the dividends distributed to investors. Trust banks such as Mitsui Trust and Banking Co. have pooled real property interests under an investment trust vehicle and sold shares to interested investors. The banks have managed the real properties and have distributed the cash flows from the properties in the form of dividends to the holders of shares of beneficial interest in the investment trust. Most of the Japanese equity investment trust shares have been purchased, held, and sold by primarily by Japanese investors.

International investment banks such as Goldman Sachs and Morgan Stanley have offered shares of real estate investment funds to investors from Japan and other countries. They generally market large financial participations to major investors. In recent months, shares of investment funds representing holdings of income properties only from Japan have been offered to major investors who have shown active interest in participating in ownership of major Japanese properties.

THE CURRENT EMPHASIS ON JAPANESE REAL ESTATE SECURITIZATION

The progress of real estate securitization in Japan is followed closely by the real estate establishment, the government, corporate management, consumers, and financial institutions. The legal and accounting establishments also watch the progress in the development of real estate securitization. Many know that mortgage securitization will be a normal follow-up development as financial, legal, and accounting reform takes place under the auspices of the federal government of Japan.

The current, all-consuming interest of the Japanese real estate establishment in real estate securitization is derived from a number of factors. Domestic and foreign investors may wish to purchase Japanese real estate and loans through various forms of securities as Japan's economy continues in a recession. The prices of major properties, in particular, may be attractive in this economic environment. Reasonable yields are sought by foreign investors.

Portfolio diversification is the rage. As prosperity pervades some parts of the world while recession prevails in other parts of the world, managers of large money funds seek geographic and asset-type diversification to stabilize portfolio returns and to lessen overall risk.

Financial institutions and real estate companies may avoid filing for bankruptcy or being forced into unwelcomed mergers if they could only sell partial or complete ownership of some properties and some loans with real estate collateral. The banks want to get their non-performing loans with real estate collateral off their books; they also want to sell low-yielding loans as they seek higher levels of profitability in the new business objectives. After observing Japanese and foreign success with various types of real estate and mortgage securitization, financial institutions and real estate companies realize that reducing their portfolios of real estate and loans with real estate collateral is possible on attractive terms. They may seek continued management, land development, appraisal, and financial advisory fees by marketing only partial interests in prime income-producing properties, partial interests in marginally performing properties, and partial interests in certain large loans with real estate collateral or partial interests in pools of loans with real estate collateral. The financial institutions, real estate companies, and other related businesses are adroitly studying their options before jumping into property and loan divestiture, while the Japanese government is giving support to their financial operations.

Some firms that offer accounting, legal, and investment banking services may derive more fee-driven business from an expansion of real estate securitization in numerous forms. International accounting firms are now tending to establish major legal practices also. In this expansion mode, firms such as PricewaterhouseCoopers want to attract more accounting and legal business. They think that their traditional accounting clients can be better served by the offering of related legal services in a "full-service" approach to each corporate client. International firms such as Arthur Anderson already have separate financial advisory subsidiaries and now want to expand their businesses with separate legal subsidiaries or merge legal services with their traditional accounting services. Regardless of their corporate structure and specific expansion plans in Japan, they seek more fee income from financial advising and accounting and legal services.

Investors want higher-yielding investment opportunities than what the banks and other financial institutions now are offering in the forms of certificates of deposit and savings accounts. Those who wish to finance or refinance their properties need new sources of funding since bank loan volume has dried up to a great extent. Investors seek more than 0.2 percent return from their postal savings and other savings accounts. Short- and near-term savings vehicles generally offer less than 1.5 percent as a return on savings deposits. Consumers particularly look forward to the development of real estate investment vehicles that offer investment opportunities for consumer savings that promise annual higher returns than those now available in the Japanese financial market. Japanese consumers and institutions have long looked to real property investment for exemplary returns of their money.

POSSIBILITIES FOR FURTHER REAL ESTATE SECURITIZATION

Increased use of capital markets for real estate finance will continue with the financial institution and corporate restructuring movement and the reform of the Japanese financial markets. Investor demands will be better met if the government of Japan and the business community consider the overall needs of the real estate sector and investors. The executive and legislative branches of the government will particularly be involved in the infrastructure changes needed in order to pursue greater securitization of real estate and real estate loan ownership. At this point, let us consider the current infrastructure advantages and disadvantages.

Securitization Infrastructure Advantages

The advantages of the current economic and financial system may center around the experience of financial advisers, investment bankers, and brokers who are working in the Japanese financial markets and the availability of appropriate computer software. Fully developed stock exchanges and over-the-counter security systems exist to accommodate additional security initial marketing and subsequent security trading. Both domestic and international credit rating services exist in Japan to underpin the development of a full range of rated equity, debt, and hybrid securities for the Japanese and foreign stock and bond markets.

Experienced Financial Advisers, Investment Bankers, and Brokers

The top-ranked Japanese security brokers, dealers, and investment bankers are involved in the restructuring of their companies due to mergers, acquisitions, and company policy changes. Bankruptcy, marginal business conditions, mergers, acquisitions, and company policy changes have also affected the other security brokers, dealers, and investment bankers who are based in Japan. Some of the financial companies whose businesses are related to security underwriting, marketing, and investing have been affected by the Asian financial crisis; most have been affected by the Japanese recession and its many attributes that may affect company profitability.

Joining Japanese companies—many of which represent global financial players—are foreign financial companies and their many expatriate employees. Financial executives of international financial companies that are based in continental Europe, the United Kingdom, and the United States work alongside their Japanese counterparts in serving issuers and buyers of real estate securities. Particularly important in the current Japanese financial community are Citicorp, Goldman Sachs, Morgan Stanley, and Warburg Dillon Read. The domestic- and foreign-based companies employ both Japanese and foreign expatriates in accomplishing the brokerage and investment banking work that is required. Goldman Sachs' Tokyo office was established many years ago as part of the company's globalization program. Citicorp also opened its Tokyo offices many years ago; today this company has a retail chain of widespread branches that serves numerous retail banking customers along with corporate service offices, one of which is named Cititrust. The global services of Citigroup are offered to the business and consumer communities of Japan. Another global financial institution that is also based in the United States, Morgan Stanley Dean Witter, has followed suit and operates an important Asian-oriented office in Tokyo. Warburg Dillon Read, a subsidiary of the UBS holding company for the Union

Bank of Switzerland, is particularly well entrenched in the retail area of Japanese investment banking. This financial institution is a key player in the development of Japanese real estate securitization.

As Japanese government and business adopt international accounting standards and financial disclosure practices, Japanese financial and legal advisers and accountants are working alongside foreign financial and legal advisers and accountants to further the securitization effort. Many leading international firms have established branches in Japan to offer their full range of services to Japanese and foreign clients who are working and investing in Japan. Therefore, expertise in securitization from its many angles and dimensions is represented in Japan. Foreign firms have introduced international methods and practices in joint ventures and alliances with Japanese firms as they have introduced major foreign clients to the Japanese real estate market and its existing securities.

Computer Software

The securitization of direct real estate ownership and real estate loans generally requires specialized computer software. Appropriate software aids the underwriting of security issues and the preparation of marketing materials as well as registration statements, including red herrings and final prospectuses. The analysis preceding a multiple-tranche security issue usually requires specialized software. Then the details of a multiple-tranche issue must be analyzed and approved by the investment banking team of experts using appropriate software. The yield of each of the tranches of a multiple-tranche security must be evaluated; laborious computations can be facilitated with appropriate investment yield software. When the Japanese alliance or joint-venture partner requires specialized computer software, the foreign partner may provide the necessary models from previous development and use in foreign markets. The foreign financial experts are stationed in the important Japanese security markets and have immediate access to the necessary software that may be adjusted to fit the Japanese security market and regulatory circumstances.

Credit Rating Services

Japan currently has at least three domestic credit rating agencies that serve the needs of domestic security issuers who target Japanese customers. When a large real estate security issue that is associated with a major Japanese income-producing property is targeted toward major foreign investors—as well as major Japanese investors—the prospective foreign investors usually require that the issue be rated by a recognized international credit rating service. Therefore, Moody's Investors Service and Standard & Poor's Corporation have located in Japan and have affiliated with various Japanese companies to serve this important marketplace. Major foreign investors prefer the credit ratings of these international services to the local Japanese credit ratings due to their familiarity with their decision rules and their insistence upon restatement of Japanese financial statements into those dictated by international accounting standards.

Securitization Infrastructure Disadvantages

Some the factors that may be considered as disadvantages include the relative costs of real estate securitization, the need for specialized legal and accounting assistance, the need for additional legislation, the barriers to due diligence and real estate appraisal work, and government approval of the use of offshore conduits for tax and currency purposes associated with securitization.

The Relative Cost of Real Estate Securitization

If bank loans—syndicated through a number of banks or from only one bank—were available on reasonable terms in the needed volume and currency from the viewpoint of the borrower, the borrower would usually pay a far lower total cost than if capital markets financing were selected instead. The real estate money could be raised in the capital market by privately placing the shares or the debt or by listing the shares and perhaps the debt in the form of mortgage bonds. Or the issuer might utilize the over-the-counter market in the marketing of appropriate stock and bonds. Generally, total costs are lower if the issuance of securities does not include security exchange listing. But securitization costs generally far exceed the costs of bank loans in the same general marketplace.

The costs of securitization may include the compensation of specialized attorneys and accountants, the compensation of investment bankers who initially create the securities that are designed to fit the specific needs of the client at that time, the compensation of investment bankers for work with the securities regulators in drafting securities that meet the Securities and Exchange Commission registration requirements, the compensation of the investment bankers for surveying the market demand for securities such as those of the issuer and for underwriting, pricing, and distributing the issue, the compensation of the credit rating agency for its services, and the printing of the prospectus. If the issue is privately placed to prospective domestic purchasers, the costs of Securities and Exchange Commission (SEC) security registration and credit rating agency service may possibly be avoided. If the security must be listed to fill the needs of the issuer, listing requirements must be met, and the investment bankers will need to be compensated for supplying the appropriate services in getting the company and its security issue listed on the selected Japanese exchange.

Specialized Legal Services

Japan is known for its consensus society, where few attorneys have been needed for the high volume of business transactions executed. Today Japan may have only 4,000 to 5,000 attorneys for the legal work of the second-ranked industrial economy of the world. Real estate securitization usually requires teams of specialized attorneys who represent high salaries for their specialized legal training and experience. Japanese attorneys can be supplemented by attorneys from foreign firms who work in Japan in getting the necessary legal work done for the flotation of securities in the international marketplace. International legal firms based in the United Kingdom and the United States are currently attempting to acquire Japanese law firms so that appropriate Japanese contacts are made for future service and so that the international law firms will be represented by a full complement of legal talents and experience. The Clifford Chance law firm from England is particularly attempting to expand and compete with international law firms such as Baker & McKinsey from the United States; the firm is attempting to expand the number of attorneys whom it has in Japan to better serve the Japanese market. As Japanese law firms work worldwide for their Japanese corporate clients, they may wish to merge with leading foreign law firms for similar reasons.

The Need for Additional Legislation

Most analysts involved in real estate securitization in Japan point to the need for additional legislation. Some areas for legislative amendment may be mentioned. Generally, a fire wall needs to be erected between the borrower/issuer and the special-purpose vehicle that is used to hold the assets whose ownership interests are marketed to various investors. The investors do not wish to be involved in borrower bankruptcy or loan default by mortgagors. The special-purpose vehicles need non-recourse liability status. When loans or real estate interests are sold to a special-purpose vehicle, the transactions need to be tax-free, or there will be little incentive for the financing method. The Home Loan Mortgage Corporation needs greater authority, greater loan guarantee ability, and greater government financing to underpin a large and active residential mortgage-backed security market.

Barriers to Due Diligence

In creating real estate securities that satisfy investor needs, sources and amounts of property revenues, operating costs, and financial and other expenses must be revealed in preliminary registration statements, approved prospectuses, and marketing material. Japanese real estate owners and borrowers are accustomed to financial privacy. Due diligence work in real estate finance requires financial data that are normally not provided by real property owners, property managers, and lenders. In fact, Japanese lenders usually do not underwrite loans based on the real estate collateral given; the loans are underwritten on the credit status and *keiretsu* standing of the borrower. The giving of real estate collateral is merely incidental and usually expected but not scrutinized in the loan decision-making process. Therefore, lenders usually do not ask for real property operating information and do not receive it. As a result, when foreign investors seek basic operating information about a major property in which they are interested, their financial advisers who are charged with the due diligence process have a difficult time finding any information about the current and recent operating status of a major building.

Barriers to Real Estate Appraising When the Income Approach Is Employed

The barriers to the due diligence process are also barriers to the real estate appraisal process when the appraiser seeks to use the income approach to value for a property valuation. Japanese real estate appraisers generally used the market approach to value and annually published government standard values from 1,000 locations in Japan to arrive at appraised values of properties during the "bubble era." Now that property values have significantly declined and may be stabilizing, the use of the income approach to property valuation is more apropos. But real estate appraisers are stymied by the absence of property operating revenues and expenses from property managers and property owners who are unaccustomed to divulging such private information.

Offshore Tax and Currency Havens

Foreign investors often seek to use offshore havens for tax and currency purposes in foreign investment. In the case of Japan, the government has jealously guarded the privilege and its approval of use of offshore locations for tax reduction and currency management. Most governments do not wish to lose tax revenues to offshore financing vehicles that involve onshore income-producing properties and the distribution of property operating cash flows to domestic and foreign investors. Often foreign investors seek to avoid currency conversion from the currency of the country of the property domicile to the currency of the investor's home country. This is a substantial expense and risk that foreign investors attempt to avoid in every way that their attorneys can devise. Foreign exchange risk can be substantial.

REAL ESTATE SECURITIES OFFERED IN THE INTERNATIONAL MARKETPLACE

Japan can look to the various kinds of real estate securities offered across the world to match their characteristics against the securities needed in today's Japanese security markets. The characteristics of some of the real estate equity and debt securities in non-Japanese countries are reviewed briefly at this point. The discussion is organized around the three categories of securities: (1) securities based on a single loan or a loan pool, (2) securities based on the ownership of one or more properties, and (3) securities based on real estate ownership and debt.

Securities Based on a Single Loan or a Loan Pool

In this category may be found syndicated real estate loans, mortgage-backed securities, and mortgage real estate investment trust securities. Let us briefly review some characteristics of each type.

Syndicated Real Estate Loans

The shares of a syndicated loan may be drawn up as negotiable or non-negotiable instruments. These mortgage instruments are normally non-negotiable in nature. The primary lender who underwrites the real estate loan sees that the required loan exceeds the maximum loan permitted by regulations and sells part of the loan to other lenders, who are usually other banks. The loan underwriter who is the lead underwriter usually takes a higher portion of the fee from the loan than the other loan syndicate members due to the extra responsibilities and liabilities that may be incurred as the lead underwriter. The share of the large loan has limited marketability, good liquidity, and limited transferability in the investment community. The relative cost for the issuer is related to the opportunity costs of financing real estate through other means such as the capital markets. The share of the syndicated real estate loan is traded in the over-the-counter market among various commercial banks usually.

Mortgage-Backed Securities

The largest volume of mortgage-backed securities is collateralized by residential mortgages, but a growing volume of mortgage-backed securities is collateralized by income-producing property mortgages. At the present time, the real estate establishment of Japan is primarily focused on commercial property ownership and loan securitization. Few of the loans on income-producing properties may be labeled mortgage loans because, traditionally, loans for the financing of real estate are underwritten without consideration of the real estate collateral that normally accompanies the loan.

Mortgage-backed securities that are normally created as negotiable instruments range in form from pass-through grantor trust vehicles, to collateralized mortgage obligations (CMOs), to real estate mortgage investment conduits (REMICs), to financial asset securitization investment trusts (FASITs). Since the development of mortgage-backed securities has changed over time, FASITs are the latest development in mortgage-backed securities in the United States.

These mortgage-backed securities range in credit risk from the extremely low credit risk of paper that has government-guaranteed principal and interest to extremely high credit risk of non-government-guaranteed principal and interest of pools of mortgages on commercial properties that reflect high tenant vacancy rates and relatively high operating costs in comparison to the scheduled rents and mortgagors with marginal credit standings. High-credit-rated residential mortgage-backed securities are traded in high financial volume in the over-the-counter market; commercial mortgage-backed securities have not yet attained the high financial volume that the residential mortgage-backed securities (MBS) have.

MBS generally have high marketability, particularly among institutional investors, a high degree of liquidity, and a high degree of transferability among many types of institutional and non-institutional investors and exhibit relatively high investment yields in comparison with benchmark one-year Treasury bonds.

Mortgage Real Estate Investment Trusts

REITs have been offered investors since the creation of the REIT in the United States through changes in the Tax Code in 1960. According to the U.S. Tax Code, the earned income of the REIT is tax-exempt as long as certain requirements are met. Among these tax requirements are that (1) at least 75 percent of the value of the REIT's assets must consist of investment primarily in real estate mortgages, shares of other REITs, and short-term, low-risk U.S. Treasury and other highly marketable securities for REIT liquidity, (2) 95 percent or more of the taxable income is distributed to the holders of shares of beneficial interest, (3) at least 75 percent of REIT gross income must come from rents, interest on obligations secured by mortgages, gains from the sale of certain assets, or income attributable to investments in other REITs, and (4) not more than 5 percent of the value of the assets may consist of the securities of any one issuer if the securities are not includable under the 75 percent test.

Share prices of REITs tend to be low enough for a consumer to conveniently purchase 100 shares or a round lot for an investment. But REIT shares have traditionally been an institutional investment category for bank trust departments and other institutions that wish to diversify their portfolios and receive ample dividends from the REIT securities. Dividends received by corporations are normally tax-exempt. The marketability of shares of listed REITs is high; liquidity of the shares is high; these negotiable instruments are highly transferable to many types of investors, including financial institutions and individuals. The REIT yields may be compared to preferred stock investment yields, while these investment instruments provide exposure to income-producing properties that is a separate investment category from non-real estate stocks and bonds.

Securities Based on Real Estate Portfolio Ownership

In this category may be found equity real estate investment trust shares, shares of real estate investment funds, hybrid real estate investment trust shares, and property unit trusts of the United Kingdom.

Equity Real Estate Investment Trust Shares

Unlike mortgage real estate investment trust shares, equity REIT shares are associated primarily with investment in income-producing properties with limited investment in other REIT shares and highly marketable and liquid securities for the liquidity of the equity REIT. The listed equity REITs reflect highly marketable shares, highly liquid investment, high transferability to many categories of investors from large institutional to small individual investors, and relatively high investment yields. The non-listed equity REITs also tend to have the same characteristics, even though they are traded in the over-the-counter market. These tax-exempt real estate equity mutual funds benefit from favorable tax regulations. The Japanese government may wish to study the favorable tax regulations for REITs in general and may find this type of real estate security suitable for a wide investor market in Japan and overseas.

Shares of a Real Estate Investment Fund

Even though the shares of a real estate investment fund are usually not negotiable instruments, these representations of ownership of real estate interests may fall under the topic of real estate securitization. The shares are not marketable, but the redemption of part or all of the funds invested may be followed by the marketing of the investment fund share to another major investor. The investment fund shares are not transferable directly to other individual or institutional investors. The investment yields may exceed yields from security investment since investment costs may be spread over a larger investment in major properties. The marketing costs for the originator of the investment fund may be less than the marketing costs for other fund originators that must market to a much wider investor clientele, whose contributions may be much smaller on average.

Hybrid Real Estate Investment Trust Shares

The shares represent investment in both real estate ownership and mortgages on income-producing properties. A balance between real property ownership and ownership of mortgages and construction loans is usually established by the real estate investment trust's board of trustees. The operating management must carry out the policy directives of the board of trustees and manage the hybrid REIT in such a way that the tax-exempt status of the financial institution is maintained.

Shares of listed hybrid REITs are highly marketable and highly liquid with a high degree of transferability of the shares among many types of individual, corporate, and institutional investors. The investment yield may attract investors seeking an unusually high payout ratio in the form of dividends.

Property Unit Trusts of the United Kingdom

The listed property unit trusts face a large investor market for their shares. The trust managers must meet the tax, other regulatory, and listing requirements in order to maintain the high degree of marketability, liquidity, and transferability of these shares that reflect property ownership.

Securities of Real Estate Companies Including Construction Companies

Shares of Diversified Real Estate Companies with Leveraged Property Ownership

The company shares may be listed or not on security exchanges. If the diversified real estate company shares are not listed, their shares may lack some marketability, liquidity, and transferability. The investment yield from these company securities depends on the decisions of the management related to dividend payment and expansion of real estate ownership. If the company finances its property holdings with borrowed funds, the owner of the company shares participates in income from mortgage-financed real estate ownership. The equity funds of the real estate company may spread further to partial and complete holdings of additional income-producing properties. Mitsubishi Estate Co., Sumitomo Realty and Development, Mitsui Real Estate Development, and other Japanese real estate company shares that represent multinational real estate holdings may be purchased from security brokers.

Construction Company Securities

The investor may participate in the success of the construction company and its income-producing property holdings by purchase of company shares. If the company shares are listed on one or more security exchanges, the shares may be highly marketable, may be highly liquid, and may be highly transferable to many types of individual, corporate, and institutional investors. Japan houses large multinational construction companies that operate worldwide. There is active trading in Ohbayashi, Shimizu, Kajima, Kumagai Gumi, and Komatsu construction company securities.

CURRENCY AND INTEREST RATE RISK MANAGEMENT

Real estate securitization involves currency and interest rate risk management. Foreign investors who anticipate receipt of a foreign currency cash flow from an investment wish to protect their returns from possible erosion from foreign exchange conditions. Domestic and foreign investors who anticipate the change in value of the real estate investment from changes in interest rates of the host country wish to protect their values from possible reduction from rising interest rates. Foreign investors may wish to manage both currency and interest rate risks.

Investors need to talk with their financial advisers about the availability of currency and interest rate futures contracts, currency and interest rate options contracts, currency and interest rate forward contracts, and currency and interest rate swaps. Many currency swaps actually are a combination of currency and interest rate swaps.

The issuer of real estate securities that may interest foreign investors should consider currency problems of the typical individual and institutional purchaser. Offshore conduits that may alleviate tax and currency problems of foreign investors may be considered as government Treasury officials are consulted about offshore organizational regulations.

CHAPTER SUMMARY

The chapter initially reviews the existing Japanese real estate-related securities. The recent real estate security offerings are based on a long history of real estate investment trust offerings. Since the existing real estate securities, other than the exchange-listed real estate company securities, tend to lack liquidity for the investor and may require larger amounts of funds for investment than some potential investors wish to commit, the financial industry is attempting to meet the demand for new forms of real estate securities. The tax needs of the various types of potential real estate investors are also being considered in the development of new securities. At the same time, the potential sellers of real estate loans and income-producing and residential real estate have needs that must be met by the newly created securities.

Real estate investment funds are being accumulated mainly from large institutional sources for investment in Japanese loans and real estate ownership. Some of the offerings of banks, real estate owners, and other financial institutions are designed to appeal to the various domestic and foreign real estate investment funds. Some of these large funds have been called "venture capital" funds by Japanese real estate people who are observing and taking part in the market activity.

The movement toward new forms of real estate-related securities is based on (1) the need for portfolio diversification, (2) the demand for higher-yielding investment opportunities in a market where the government federal funds rate approximates zero, and (3) the presence of large holdings of non-performing real estate loans at Japanese banks that are trying to increase their profitability. There is a recognized business need for more fee income from increased services of international and domestic accounting firms, international and domestic investment and commercial banks, international and domestic stock brokerage houses, international and domestic law firms, international and domestic real estate marketing companies, and other companies actively involved in real estate. The recession has resulted in lower fee income from services that could be enhanced by greater real estate securitization that would be associated with a higher level of private real estate activity, including land development, construction, appraisal, finance, marketing, consulting, and property management. The savings level is high among consumers, and consumers feel that profitability is associated with real estate ownership. Major institutional and other investors need profitable investment outlets for their large accumulations of funds, so further real estate securitization is encouraged in Japan.

There are advantages and disadvantages associated with further development of real estate securities in Japan. The advantages of real estate securitization are associated with the presence of experienced domestic and international financial advisers, real estate investment bankers, and brokers in the Japanese financial markets. The basic computer hardware and software are available that can be adapted to the expanded Japanese market needs. The Japanese credit rating services are being supplemented by international credit rating services that are developing in Japan. The disadvantages are associated with the relatively high cost of marketing small- and medium-sized issues of real estate securities; the economies of scale operate to lower the marketing costs of large security issues. The Japanese government needs to pass legislation that will enable securities with the appropriate tax, liability, and management characteristics to be created to meet the needs of prospective investors. A larger number of attorneys who are skilled and knowledgeable in real estate securities and international business must be available to handle the large and continuous flow of legal business. As prospectuses and other legal security offering material must be developed that meets the government and stock exchange regulatory requirements, the business culture needs to change toward more transparency in order for the needed due diligence and income-producing property appraisal to take place. The current business privacy of the Japanese market and culture does not lend itself to due diligence and appraisal analysis. The government policies toward non-use of offshore tax and currency havens for financial purposes may need liberalization in order for real estate and other securities to attract large sums of investable capital that is averse to taking foreign currency and foreign interest rate risks.

Three categories of real estate securities are described in terms of the international real estate marketplace: (1) securities based on a single real estate loan or a loan pool, (2) securities based on real estate ownership, and (3) securities of real estate companies. Some of these security types already exist in Japan; other types might be appropriate in the future for this marketplace. The first category includes syndicated real estate loans, mortgage-backed securities, and mortgage real estate investment trusts. The second category includes equity real estate investment trust shares, shares of real estate investment funds, hybrid real estate investment trust shares, and property unit trusts such as those of the United Kingdom. The third category includes the shares of diversified real estate companies with leveraged property ownership and construction company securities.

Foreign investors need to consider the use of hedging instruments such as currency and interest rate forward contracts, futures contracts, options contracts, and swaps contracts to reduce their currency and interest rate risk in loan and property investment in Japan. A variety of such contracts exists in this sophisticated financial market that is associated with the second-ranked industrialized country in the world.

REFERENCES

Baytas, Ahmet, and Nusret Cakici. "Do Stocks Really Provide the Highest Return in the Long Run?" *Journal of Investing*, 8:3 (Fall 1999), pp. 89–96.

Brueggeman, William B., and Jeffrey D. Fisher. *Real Estate Finance and Investments.* 10th ed. Chicago: Irwin, 1997.

Cohen, Norma. "Time to Buy in Sickly Shares (As Shares in Property Companies Trade at Big Discounts to Asset Value, Managers Must Grasp the Opportunity for Arbitrage)." *Financial Times*, February 4, 2000, p. 22.

Cullen, Lisa Reilly. "How Nomura Drowns Its Sorrows." *Money*, 28:1 (January 1999), p. 30.

Drummond, Sara. "Think Globally, Sell Locally." *Commercial Investment Real Estate Journal*, 18:4 (July/August 1999), pp. 46–47.

Fabozzi, Frank J., ed. *Issuer Perspectives on Securitization*. New Hope, PA: Frank J. Fabozzi Associates, 1998.

Fabozzi, Frank J., and David P. Jacob, eds. *The Handbook of Commercial Mortgage-Backed Securities*. 2nd ed. New Hope, PA: Frank J. Fabozzi Associates in conjunction with Nomura Securities International, 1999.

Gjertsen, Lee Ann. "Japan Typhoon Risk Securitized." *National Underwriter*, 102:26 (June 29, 1998), p. 3.

Green, George. "Life Insurance Companies Reposition to Increase Market Share." *Commercial Investment Real Estate Journal*, 18:4 (July/August 1999), pp. 10–11.

Hines, M. A. *Financing Real Estate with Securities*. New York: John Wiley & Sons, 1988.

———. *Guide to International Real Estate Investment*. Westport, CT: Quorum Books, 1988.

———. *International Income Property Investment*. Scottsdale, AZ: International Real Estate Institute, 1985.

———. *Investing in International Real Estate*. Westport, CT: Quorum Books, 2000.

———. *Investing in Japanese Real Estate*. Westport, CT: Quorum Books, 1987.

Hudson-Wilson, Susan, and George J. Pappadopoulos. "CMBS and the Real Estate Cycle." *Journal of Portfolio Management*, 25:2 (Winter 1999), pp. 105–111.

Japan Company Handbook. First Section. Tokyo: Toyo Keizai, Summer 1990, Real Estate Section.

Japan Company Handbook. Second Section. Tokyo: Toyo Keizai, Summer 1990, Real Estate Section.

Japan's Real Estate Sector. Tokyo: Warburg Dillon Read, Research Department, October 1999.

Jennings, John. "Capital, Re Market Link Urged." *National Underwriter*, 102:44 (November 2, 1998), pp. 3, 22.

Levy, John B. "CMBS Market Slows, but Secondary Markets Active." *National Real Estate Investor*, 41:7 (June 1999), p. 40.

———. "The Ground Floor: Loan Securities' Pricing Yo-Yos." *Barron's*, 79:22 (May 31, 1999), p. 39.

———. "Rate Bump Sends Property Borrowers to the Sidelines." *Barron's*, 79:27 (July 5, 1999), p. 34.

Lindsey, Lawrence B. "Japan: What's the Hurry?" *Forbes*, 164:4 (August 23, 1999), p. 203.

Londevich, Dan. "Tokyo Disney Securitizes $200m Cat Risk." *National Underwriter*, 103:21 (May 24, 1999), p. 3.

Mackintosh, James. "N Rock Aims to Sell Public Mortgage-Backed Bonds." *Financial Times*, January 27, 2000, p. 29.

McDonald, James. "Kampo Increase Indirect Equity Exposure." *Pensions & Investments*, 27:16 (August 9, 1999), p. 22.

Nakamae, Naoko. "Japanese Financial Institutions Eye the Post Office's $700bn Savings Honeypot." *Financial Times*, January 12, 2000, p. 4.

O'Leary, Christopher. "Chase/First Union Venture Scores Big on Its First CMBS." *Investment Dealers Digest*, May 17, 1999, pp. 5–6.

———. "CMBS Market Is Transformed by Info and Indexes." *Investment Dealers Digest*, June 28, 1999, pp. 4–5.

———. "Europe, Japan: Battlefields of the 2000s." *Investment Dealers Digest*, August 2, 1999, p. 18.

Ostrovsky, Arkady. "European Asset-Backed Volumes Jump." *Financial Times*, February 8, 2000, p. 30.

PaineWebber. *Annual Summary of Investment Recommendations: Real Estate Investment Trusts*. New York: PaineWebber Equity Research, January 2000.

———. *REIT 1999 Review and 2000 Outlook*. New York: PaineWebber Equity Research, January 2000.

Real Estate in Japan 1999. Tokyo: Warburg Dillon Read, February 1999.

Schut, Jan H. "Shake, Rattle and Roll." *Institutional Investor*, 32:3 (March 1998), p. 35.

Slatin, Peter. "The Ground Floor: American Investors Set Up Camp in Tokyo Seeking Bargains in Japanese Property Loans." *Barron's*, 78:32 (August 10, 1998), p. 46.

"Sumitomo Launches Real Estate ABS First." *Euroweek*, 608 (June 25, 1999), p. 16.

Weston, Gregory M. "The CMBS Market: A 1998 Review and the Top Ten Trends for 1999." *Real Estate Finance Journal*, 15:1 (Summer 1999), pp. 14–17.

"Wharf Surmounts Difficulties to Reopen HK Asset Backed Market, Set Asian ABS Record." *Euroweek*, 591 (February 26, 1999), p. 17.

Yeskey, Dennis P. "The Ground Floor: Steady as She Goes: After a Rocky 1998, Realty Investment Makes a Comeback." *Barron's*, 79:25 (June 21, 1999), p. 48.

13

Prospects for the Future

Japanese real estate investment is alive and well. Investors—whether from Japan or from worldwide origins—must merely recognize that protracted economic changes in Japan mean changes in real estate investment along with the associated investment yields. This is an established real estate phenomenon that has been and continues to be true the world over. Admittedly, the real estate "bubble period" of Japan that lasted from about 1987 to 1991 was spectacular, but there have been many stock market and other financial "bubble periods" around the world at various times in history that have been spectacular. Adjustments are made, and the world moves on. Investment may decline for a short period and then move upward to greater heights.

THE JAPANESE ECONOMY AS IT AFFECTS REAL ESTATE INVESTMENT

The recessionary forces in Japan appear to be weakening as the new millennium opens. The Japanese people, the government, and the institutions are ready for a change in the economic environment. Investors tend to remain optimistic, even though they experience causes for pessimism as unemployment climbs, opportunities for employment promotion decline in lower-growth industries, and taxes are forecast to increase after the recent declines. Investors see investment opportunities in growth industries such as telecommunications and other high-technology areas. Employment opportunities have been disappearing as major companies are downsizing and restructuring in order to move ahead in global business with a profit-making foundation. The continuing mergers and acquisitions offer opportunities for profit for the financial services industry. Real estate financial services are a part of the growth environment.

The exploding public debt will cause problems for several years. Public spending is forming a basis for economic expansion, but the government projections note the possibility of the national debt's reaching 130 percent of the GDP. At present, the government debt approximates 115 percent of the GDP. The OECD, a Paris-based think tank, is worried about the relatively high level of Japan's debt and the repercussions in the future of the reduction of this debt to stable and manageable levels. The OECD forecasts rises in taxes in Japan in the near future to reduce this formidable debt burden. Recently, the Japanese government has been reducing tax rates to stimulate the economy, as the reader noted in Chapter 11. The government hopes to pull the economy out of the recession and get it on a stabilized economic basis before the coming elections for the lower and upper houses of the Diet. After the elections, tax increases may have to be considered. Other fiscal and monetary measures may have to be considered at that time.

FINANCING REAL ESTATE

As the second-ranked industrial nation of the world, Japan has immense financial resources. As the recession of the 1990s and early 2000s took its toll among the rankings of Japanese banks among the largest banks of the world, recently announced mergers have recaptured some of the slots for the top 10 banks again for Japanese banks. The leading Japanese banks are said to have sought larger shares of the banking market rather than pursue profitability for the banks' stockholders.

A better-financed public and private pension system is needed by Japan retirees, the government, companies, and the financial system and, indirectly, by the real estate market of Japan. Government legislation for the enhanced pension system has been delayed due to the lower tax receipts that are being experienced in the recession from lower total income flows and lower tax rates. But the development of the pension system with greater reserves of companies for their ongoing pension obligations should benefit real estate investment; funds should be available for all types of real estate financing of all types of properties from single-family homes and apartment projects, to large commercial and industrial projects and new towns with high-technology centers.

THE CAPITAL MARKETS

The Japanese brokerage community has been reporting unusually high profits as the new millennium opens. The 87 percent rise in the security markets in 1999 propelled their profits to high levels. The Japanese are hopeful that this prosperity will continue as companies merge and acquire new companies, as companies reorganize and restructure for future profitability, and as the world market environment is favorable. Europe's economy is prosperous. The long-term U.S. period of prosperity may continue. Asia's economy is rising to higher levels; these markets are the primary markets for many Japanese products and are key locations for investment for future manufacturing and service businesses. The Japanese capital markets may reflect the world capital markets.

Japanese investors seek higher yields from the investment of their funds. As investment trusts based on real property investment are offered to the public along with newer investment instruments, Japanese investors may be ready for opportunities that may offer higher yields from the real estate market. They are favorably attuned to the risks and returns of real estate investment.

TAXATION OF REAL ESTATE

Due to the growth in the national debt to approximately 130 percent of Japan's GDP, the real estate industry will probably experience higher taxation overall in the coming years in order for the government to bring the total debt down to reasonable levels. The reform and restructuring of business may allow the tax rates to peak short of the last peak in tax rates in the late 1990s. The government will not seek to raise income tax rates except marginally until consumer expenditures and business profitability pick up with momentum upward from the long recession.

The impending higher taxation of real estate will reduce the after-tax cash flows from property. Both the net cash flows from property operations and net cash flows from property sales will be reduced due to the higher tax rates that are possible on annual income and on capital gains. But the property investment yields may rise over the yields experienced in the mid-1990s because property values and property purchase prices may remain relatively low. As tax rates increase and as interest rates rise from increased government debt refunding and new fund-raising, the government should not encourage the elevation of property prices due to very favorable loan terms for real estate finance. Property prices will probably remain relatively high in world terms, but the return of the "bubble era" of extraordinary property values should not be encouraged.

LAND DEVELOPMENT AND CONSTRUCTION

As basic industry continues to change toward the service sector and the creation of high-value-added products for such growth sectors as telecommunications and computer software, property once devoted to heavy manufacturing and now slow-growth industries will be renovated and rebuilt to suit current and future space requirements. Growth companies may continue to seek larger sites along existing rail lines in suburban or at least outlying city areas rather than seek larger sites in the city centers. Headquarters offices may still seek sites and computer-supportive buildings in center cities. Their professional service suppliers such as international accountants, international law firms, and international advertising firms may seek office space nearby.

The trend toward larger residential spaces for households likely will continue whether the residential space is located in the center city or at the outskirts. As economic prosperity returns with greater consumer affluence, larger homes will be desired that will accommodate the greater volume of electronic equipment, including the home computer.

The increasing proportion of the elderly population of Japan will motivate land developers to design full-service retirement communities where medical facilities and assisted-living provisions are integrated into the developments. These retirement communities will need to be advantageously located so that the service providers and the extended family members and friends of the retired residents may reach the locations easily.

The infrastructure for the new land development will have to take into account the need for replacement of much of the urban infrastructure in coming years. During the extended recession of the 1990s and early 2000s, some of the infrastructure was rebuilt and maintained as a government effort toward stimulation of the economy and creation of jobs. The high level of local and national government indebtedness will slow down any massive rebuilding of the infrastructure of cities such as Tokyo. But the overutilization of the rail systems, particularly during employee rush hours, must be faced by the private and public rail companies and the local, prefectural, and national governments. The continuing problems of water treatment and energy systems of the major cities must be addressed as land development moves to meet the residential, commercial, and institutional needs of the citizens.

THE APPRAISAL OF JAPANESE REAL ESTATE

Appraisal systems for Japanese property may continue to be based on sales comparisons and systems that involve interest imputation on the declining capital investment. As more foreign entities invest in property in Japan, some elements of Western-style appraisal methods may enter the appraisal service sector. If property values remain relatively low and relatively stable in amount, the income capitalization approach to appraised value will become more important. The sales comparison method will continue to be applied to land and improvements to land. Discounted cash flow methods of value estimation may become more important as foreign clients demand the use of such valuation methods.

PROPERTY INVESTMENT YIELD CALCULATIONS

As older company managers are replaced with younger managers who are university- and professionally trained and less bound to accounting conventions, the newer managers may use more often computer or hand-calculator methods for determining net present value and internal rate of return. These internationally used methods of investment yield calculation may be found in use more often in Japan. As more major Japanese income properties are acquired by foreign investors, these entities will require investment yield examination with use of these internationally adopted methods.

As the national government accounts are opened to the public, the company accounts, including those of major real estate companies, may become more available to the public. The increased transparency of real estate data will facilitate property investment comparisons and the better estimation of property values. The adoption of international accounting conventions along with greater property account transparency will facilitate a more capitalistic property system in Japan and more international comparisons of investment properties.

REFERENCES

Abraham, Paul, and Gillian Tett. "The Circle Is Broken." *Financial Times*, November 9, 1999, p. 18.

Nakamae, Naoko. "Japan's Big Brokers See Sharp Profits Rebound." *Financial Times*, January 29/30, 2000, p. 1.

Nakamoto, Michiyo. "Opposition Boycotts Diet as Consensual Approach Ditched." *Financial Times*, January 29/30, 2000, p. 4.

Rahman, Bayan. "East Japan Railway Privatisation Delayed." *Financial Times*, January 26, 2000, p. 22.

———. "NEC to Sell Tokyo HQm." *Financial Times*, January 19, 2000, p. 18.

Tett, Gillian. "Japanese PM Holds Back from Tackling Debt Burden." *Financial Times*, January 29/30, 2000, p. 4.

———. "Out of the Ice Age (Japan's Economy Is Divided between Fast-Growing Technology Companies and Depressed Traditional Industries: Which Will Dominate the Country's Future?" *Financial Times*, February 24, 2000, p. 12.

Tett, Gillian, and Naoko Nakamae. "Japan Set to Delay New Pensions System." *Financial Times*, January 18, 2000, p. 4.

———. "Japan Set for Rate Rise as Economy Recovers." *Financial Times*, February 2, 2000, p. 4.

Index

About the Author

M. A. HINES has held the Clarence W. King Endowed Professorship of Real Estate and Finance at Washburn University, Topeka, Kansas, since 1982. She is the author of four major real estate textbooks and more than 37 international- and U.S.-oriented books and monographs, six published by Quorum: *Investing in Japanese Real Estate* (1987), *Guide to International Real Estate Investment* and *Marketing Real Estate Internationally* (both 1988), *Global Corporate Real Estate Management* (1990), *The Development and Finance of Global Private Power* (1997), and *Investing in International Real Estate* (2000). Her most recent book is *Investing in Japanese Real Estate: Links to International Trade* (2000).